Contents

Conservation of Resources

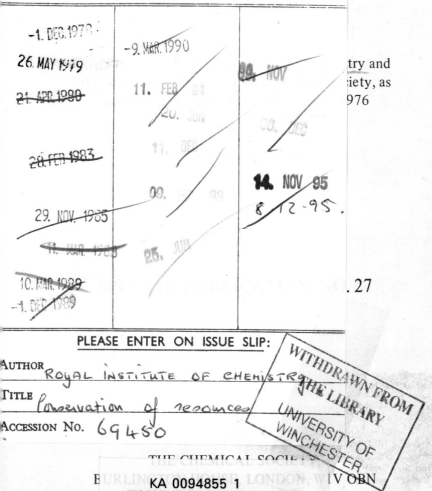

...try and ...iety, as ...976

...27

THE CHEMICAL SOCIETY
BURLINGTON HOUSE, LONDON, W1V OBN

The opinions expressed in this book are those of the authors
concerned, and do not necessarily coincide with the views of
the Society or the Institute.

ISBN 0 85186 208 X

Typeset in IBM Press Roman by
Preface Limited, Salisbury, Wilts.
Printed in Great Britain by
Fletcher & Son Ltd, Norwich

Contributors

F. A. Robinson, LLB, DSc, CChem, FRIC, President of The Chemical Society, 1975/6.

Sir Samuel Curran, DL, DSc, LLD, FRS, Principal and Vice-Chancellor, University of Strathclyde, Glasgow.

J. K. Hambling, BSc, PhD, British Petroleum Co. Ltd.

Ian Fells, MA, PhD, CEng, FInstF, CChem, FRIC, Professor of Energy Conversion, Department of Chemical Engineering, University of Newcastle upon Tyne.

H. L. Roberts, MA DPhil, General Manager, Research and Development Department, Imperial Chemical Industries Limited, Mond Division.

J. S. Broadley, FRSE, PhD, BSc, CChem, MRIC, AIM, Head of Health & Safety Division, United Kingdom Atomic Energy Authority Reactor Group, Dounreay Experimental Reactor Establishment.

L. E. Reece, BE, MSc, Department of Mechanical Engineering, New South Wales Institute of Technology, Sydney, NSW, Australia.

R. M. Kenedi, BSc, PhD, ARCST, CEng, FIMechE, MRAcS, FRSE, Professor of Bioengineering, University of Strathclyde, Glasgow.

C. R. W. Spedding, MSc, PhD, DSc, FIBiol, Professor of Agricultural Systems, University of Reading.

J. S. Sawyer, MA, FRS.

J. A. Tatchell, BSc(Eng), ACGI, FIEE, Energy Adviser, Imperial Chemical Industries Limited, Agricultural Division.

R. J. P. Williams, MA, DPhil, CChem, MRIC, FRS, Napier Research Professor of The Royal Society, Inorganic Chemistry Laboratory, Oxford, and Fellow of Wadham College, Oxford.

Charles Kemball, MA, ScD, CChem, FRIC, MRIA, FRSE, FRS, Professor of Chemistry, University of Edinburgh; President of the Royal Institute of Chemistry 1974–76.

P. F. Corbett, LLB, BSc, BSc(Eng), CChem, FRIC, CEng, SFInstF, FIGasE, Managing Director, Corbett Industrial Consultancy Limited, 63 Neal Street, London, WC2.

J. E. Lovelock, DSc, PhD, BSc, FRS, Visiting Professor, University of Reading.

A. K. Barbour, BSc, PhD, CChem, FRIC, Environmental Scientist, RTZ Services Ltd., Bristol; Immediate Past President, CS Industrial Division.

G. R. Bainbridge, BSc, PhD, CEng, FIEE, FInstP, JP, Director and Professor of Energy Studies, The Energy Centre, The University of Newcastle upon Tyne.

R. S. Silver, CBE, MA, BSc, PhD, DSc, FInstP, FIMechE, FRSE, James Watt Professor of Mechanical Engineering, University of Glasgow.

Preface

THE need to conserve material resources is now widely accepted because of the rapid expansion of the world's population, but a contributory factor not always recognised is the desire of every nation to improve its standard of living by demanding an ever-increasing share of the resources that have hitherto been available only to the industrialised nations. Although the population of the United Kingdom is virtually static, the population of the world as a whole is still increasing exponentially; it is now approximately 4 billions and is doubling itself every 33 years. If this rate continues and there are no other factors influencing the production and consumption of resources, then by the year 2009 twice as much food, twice as much water, twice as much energy and twice as much mineral ore will have to be produced simply to maintain the standard of comfort (or discomfort) to which each nation has become accustomed. Moreover, twice as much domestic and industrial waste will have to be disposed of in a way that does not interfere too much with that standard of comfort. It is most unlikely that the countries of the Third World will accept the status quo without making some attempt to use the resources they possess to improve their position, as indeed the OPEC countries already have.

Attention was first called to the implications of exponential population growth in the Club of Rome's report, "The Limits to Growth", but it was only in 1973 when the Arabs more than quadrupled the price of their crude oil that people in the United Kingdom and other West European countries and the USA began to recognise that the high standard of living they have hitherto enjoyed was largely the result of having had access to cheap energy and that this would not be available in the future. It also became increasingly clear that many of the material resources that the industrialised nations had used with such prodigality were legacies from the geological past that would never be renewed. More and more attention has since been paid to the conservation of these resources, and this book is a contribution to the debate that is going on and will go on for some time about conservation, and what policies should be pursued in order to find replacements for natural resources as these begin to dwindle and pressures for "fair shares" continue to build up.

The book is a collection of papers presented at the Annual Chemical Congress in Glasgow in April 1976 and they give a very broad picture of the problems of conservation both in this country and in the world as a whole. It is important that chemists should be aware of these problems because in the past it was they who were largely instrumental in finding substitutes for natural products — synthetic fibres to replace cotton and wool, synthetic medicinal substances to replace galenicals, and synthetic polymers to replace natural matter. They may soon be called upon to find substitutes for some of these substitutes, unless steps are taken to conserve supplies of petroleum for chemical feedstock and reduce the amount being used as fuel.

Many of the contributions in this book relate to energy. Consideration is given for example to the energy requirements of different communities and the wide disparity between the demands of the industrialised countries and those of the Third World; to the need for economy and the importance in due course of finding renewable forms of energy; to the very substantial losses of energy that take place when oil and coal are converted into electricity or when sources of energy have to be transported. The problems of nuclear power are discussed and in a consideration of the involvement of the chemical industry in energy, proposals are made for reducing the input of energy in the manufacture of chemicals.

These papers provide a useful background to the National Energy Conference that was held two months later by the Secretary of State. Admittedly the Conference was largely concerned with the political and social consequences of the abundancies of North Sea oil during the 1980s and the declining levels during the 1990s, and not much attention was given to Dr. Walter Marshall's report on "Energy R & D in the United Kingdom". Indeed the debate on the feasibility of some of the proposals put forward for conserving energy or replacing one source by another have only just begun, and chemists are likely to become increasingly involved in this debate. Much of the essential data necessary for an understanding of the problems are to be found in this book in the papers relating to energy.

Energy is not, of course, the only resource to which conservation measures need to be applied. The human body requires energy for every activity, even inactivity, and the requirements for different purposes are discussed in one chapter and the way in which food is utilised and produced in other chapters, including a discussion of the vexed question of whether it is wasteful to feed crops to animals intended for use as food instead of feeding them direct to human beings. Consideration is also given to the amount of energy used in agriculture to produce food, the effect of human activity on climate, and the role of photosynthesis and oxidative phosphorylation in biological energy conservation; one day perhaps simulation of these mechanisms may be used to supplement other sources of energy. The conservation of two substances normally taken for granted — fresh air and water — also receives attention and Professor Charles Kemball in his Presidential Address to the RIC has many pungent comments to make about the conservation of manpower resources.

For many years, the Society and the Institute have been greatly exercised over the declining numbers of students turning to chemistry as a career and over the reluctance to enter industry of many of those who do. Consideration of the problems surrounding the supply of resources in the future — energy, minerals, food and water — suggests that satisfactory answers will only be found by having available greater numbers of scientists and engineers, including chemists, who to quote Professor Kemball "are self-propelled, who show initiative, who are alert and interested in applying their knowledge to the kind of problems industry faces". No one believes that technology alone can provide the answers to problems that include political, economic, social and even psychological elements, but without technology in the hands of first-class men it is doubtful if the answers will provide that quality of life that men and women have come to expect and indeed, until a few years ago, took for granted.

F. A. Robinson

Society's Future Energy Needs

by Sir Samuel Curran; Principal and Vice-Chancellor, University of
Strathclyde, Glasgow

I was pleased to receive an invitation to provide an opening paper to
the Joint Industrial Division/R.I.C. Symposium on "Conservation of
Resources". As a former member of staff on the U.K. Atomic Energy
Authority, I hope that my review of the future energy needs of
society will in no sense be prejudiced, and that it can be taken as an
impartial view from someone who is extremely interested in the
question of our energy resources and sufficiently long divorced from
a particular approach to be impartial. There have been many recent
publications[1] on the subject and occasionally one feels that there is a
grave danger that discussions become repetitive. For myself I have
contributed several such papers and articles but even so the subject is
so very wide that new and fresh aspects constantly appear. I hope
that what I have to say about some of these will be of interest.

What is Energy?

All of us are well aware today of the great importance of energy so
far as meeting human needs and aspirations is concerned. Recent
upheavals in the price of petroleum have upset many of our ideas
about the way to meet human needs, but in the longer term, and
from the scientific point of view, there may be many advantages in
the recent shock to our ways of thinking about energy.

Historically, man has always had to be much concerned about
energy, and primitive man realised instinctively the need to increase
his effectiveness as a worker. The primitive tools that he fashioned
illustrated vividly this anxiety which was ever present in his mind.
Even today there are in existence primitive agricultural systems
which clearly illustrate the ingenuity that man has exercised since
very many centuries ago in providing himself with the necessities of
life. Rappaport[2] has published a very interesting study concerned

1

with the flow of energy in an agricultural society. He establishes in the most vivid way evidence that raising crops and husbanding animals have often been man's most important means of exploiting the energy that is continuously stored in primary plant production. In the practice of agriculture this energy store, which in turn supports various food chains, enabled him to rise above the mere subsistence level of hunting and gathering and allowed him to develop a culture which has resulted in the complex social systems of today. His study of the flow of energy in an agricultural society, and in particular of that in New Guinea, highlights a mode of gardening which has been known for thousands of years and practised in relatively unpopulated parts of the world. Not only did man accomplish this but he devised a relatively stable ecosystem.

Similar methods of agriculture have been employed outside the Tropics and indeed were used in medieval England. It consisted essentially in the clearing of a small part of a forest, followed by the burning of the cuttings, the planting of the garden, the harvesting, and then the abandonment of the clearing so that it returned again to the forest state. At the most a very few plantings were done in the same area.

I mention this fact because without doubt the needs of society, so far as energy is concerned, depend almost entirely on the kind of society man wishes to provide. Energy is extremely abundant. Modern man has been much concerned with stored energy especially in the form of fossil fuels which are themselves stores of solar energy, but it is only in the last few centuries that man has depended so much on these stores. The abundant flow of energy from the sun means that energy itself need never be in short supply and it is only our present methods of availing ourselves of energy that cause considerable concern, not least today when we have evolved a social system so closely dependent on the supply of conveniently stored energy in the fossil fuels. These stores took million of years to form and they could easily be exhausted. All the advanced countries use stored energy in their effort to increase the industry-based prosperity.

It is useful to remind ourselves of the scale on which solar energy constantly reaches our Earth. Kaplan[3] in his study of various energy systems reminds us that the solar energy falling on horizontal surfaces greatly exceeds our requirements. To illustrate this it is pointed out that if we had a practical system of photovoltaic energy production even in the case of the U.S.A. roughly 65% of the electric energy generated in the U.S.A. in 1970 would be provided by the system if it covered only 0.1% of the U.S.A. land area. This estimate is based on an assumed 10% efficiency of the solar rays and a moderate value for the average daily insolation of 4 kWh/m². We must remember at the same time that the consumption of energy in the U.S.A. is the highest per capita of all the advanced industrial countries, exceeding that of any other country by a factor of about 2. Indeed the energy consumption per capita in the U.S.A. means that each citizen has the equivalent of 100 to 200 human slaves. Obviously the U.S.A. is a very different kind of country from that inhabited by the people of Tsembagaland in northern New Guinea. In fact, in the case of Tsembaga the energy of the sun reaching the clearing and converted through gardening and animal husbandry exceeds by a factor of about 16 the energy expended by the people themselves. Their method of agriculture provides them, in an entirely different fashion and in a modified sense, with the equivalent of some 16 human slaves. The energy flow diagram for the U.S.A. shows a great dependence on "artificial" resources and without including plant storage it is seen to be very high indeed.

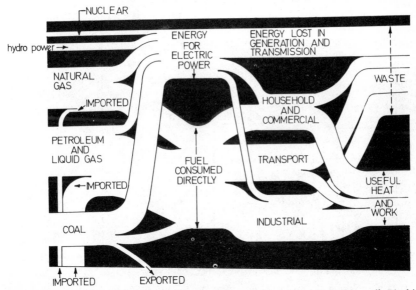

FIGURE 1 Based on E. Cook in "Energy Resources and the Environment" Blackie, Glasgow, 1975, p. 30. Reproduced by kind permission.

We see then that much depends on the kind of society that we want when we turn to the problems of meeting energy needs. I would guess however that most of us wish to have social systems like those that have been developed during the last few hundred years, particularly from the time of the first industrial revolution. That revolution was relatively sudden. Fossil fuels, especially coal, were recognised to be the key to improvement in the standard of living and such discoveries as those of Watt with his steam condenser made it much more practicable to apply the energy stored in coal. Machine tools arrived quickly on the scene and transformed our capacity to provide for many new needs. Our concern with energy is therefore largely concerned with the means of exploiting the energy from the sun stored in fossil fuels, or our means of converting to useful form the energy continuously reaching the Earth's surface from the sun. Most of the less developed nations have ambitions to develop in ways not dissimilar to those of the U.S.A. and the more advanced

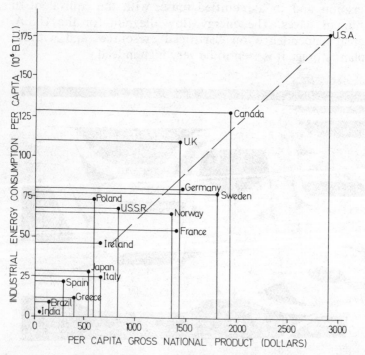

FIGURE 2   Derived from E. Cook, "Scientific American", September 1971, p. 142.

countries. As has been shown in Fig. 2, the energy consumption per capita is fairly closely in direct relationship with the standard of living and as the standard of living rises the energy consumption per capita must necessarily increase. Cook has pointed out that this does not mean man should be profligate − the use of wasteful large "cars" is an example of unwise consumption.

Nature of Energy

We have rather assumed that we understand what is meant by the term "energy" and in practical terms even primitive man readily appreciated some aspects of the concept. He was aware of the need to sustain his body temperature and this need was so great at times that sun-worship was practised. But from the scientific point of view our understanding of energy came rather late. It is only 100 years ago that Carnot, Kelvin, Clausius, and others were much engaged in theories about heat, and it is just over seventy years ago that Einstein began to establish the fact that energy and mass were different forms of the same "thing". He expressed this in his simple equation $E = mc^2$. Here mass m and energy E are stated to be equal, the constant connecting them being the velocity of light, c.

Einstein's law opened the way to new speculations about the tremendous abundance of energy in all materials. We have already established the important fact that the energy reaching us from the sun is of massive amount but the attraction of stored forms of energy, concentrated forms, is ever present; we are surrounded by mass or material and Einstein's relationship showed that with sufficient scientific ingenuity we might convert such mass into energy.

Implicit in the experiments of nuclear physicists, and perhaps more especially in those of Rutherford and his school, was the experimental verification of the Einstein equation. In 1917 Rutherford effected the artificial transmutation of an atom for the first time and in the transmutation it was clear that a large amount of energy had been released and that this arose from the disappearance of a small fraction of the matter involved in the nuclear reactions. In all chemical reactions that are exothermic, that is energy-releasing, extremely minute amounts of matter disappear and energy is made available, but when nuclear reactions occur the amounts of matter transformed into energy rise by a factor of between 10^5 and 10^6.

In the 1930's references were often made to the mighty atom, but

Table 1: Fuel reserves

	World	
Coal	10^{12}	TCE approx
Petroleum	10^{11}	TCE approx
Gas	10^{10}	TCE approx

British fossil fuels			
	Total MTCE	Predicted annual use	Duration (years)
Coal	6,000	120	50
Coal (lower grade)	50,000	250	200
Colliery spoil	750	15	50
North Sea oil	7,500	150	50
North Sea gas	1,000	50	20

Source: M. W. Thring, Sylvanus P. Thomson Lecture, 1976.
Reproduced by kind permission of Professor Thring.

more accurately they should have been made to the mighty nucleus. It was not until 1939 that the possibility of a nuclear chain reaction, in the particular form of fission, could be envisaged as a practical energy-releasing system.

If we turn today to the examination of our energy resources we find therefore that they are plentiful and diversified. When we are internationally anxious about the present energy scene it is good to remind ourselves that there is in fact no shortage. The difficult problems are essentially political, economic and social. From the point of view of basic science the problems are almost non-existent. This statement can be supported by looking at the table of world fuel reserves. The table which I show has been taken from Thring's Sylvanus P. Thomson Lecture and slightly modified. We see that coal reserves amount to about one million million tons equivalent, petroleum reserves are roughly one-tenth of that great quantity, and gas about one-tenth of the petroleum. Broadly speaking, if we do increase per capita energy consumption at only a modest rate we know that we have in these reserves sufficient to meet our energy needs for at least one hundred years. If we then introduce the fissile materials, uranium and thorium, depending on our means of constructing nuclear reactors we can supply our total needs for at least another one hundred years without any dubiety. Scientists are not encouraged much to think beyond one or two hundred years and the political time-scale is all too often one or two years!

In spite of this there is much concern everywhere about providing sufficient energy to meet our human needs. We might pause for a moment to consider why this should be so. Clearly we must recognise the fact that the decisions of politicians and economists can greatly influence the mode and scale of provision. This can be said with assurance because people want energy at as cheap a price as possible. Also, the reserves are not uniformly distributed throughout the world. The price of the fossil fuels can therefore, almost overnight, affect the total economy of any country. In this situation it becomes important that we consider the availability of energy on a *national* basis, the flexibility of our method of meeting the various requirements and, thirdly, the much more challenging problem of meeting our needs into the long-term future, say for a period of one thousand years.

From the strictly scientific point of view the third problem is the easiest. We can assert that the world has extremely large amounts of uranium and thorium and both can be turned to account in reactor systems. In our oceans there are virtually unlimited amounts of uranium and only the long-term problems have to be solved to enable us to avail ourselves economically of this store. There would appear to the scientist to be no insurmountable difficulty here but obviously the cost factor is a substantial complication in satisfying all others. We can also assert that the abundant and continuous flow of solar energy is real long-term insurance against our failure to find adequate resources. It seems very unlikely indeed, considering that research on conversion of solar energy through photovoltaic and semiconductor devices has been pursued seriously for at most a few decades, that we cannot raise by a large factor the efficiency of conversion of existing devices. At the same time we have to solve the problem of manufacture of such conversion devices, but here again there is little doubt that future work should bring about considerable success. The rate of advance of modern solid-state studies is reassuring and offers promise for the future. Personally, I would back this resource as the final long-term solution.

Other Energy Resources

Till now I have refrained from speaking about the more speculative energy resources; I have mentioned the continuous flow of solar energy to the Earth's surface and the possiblity of efficient conversion of such solar energy. The solar energy is however converted by Nature into a variety of forms. Notable among these is the energy in the atmosphere and in the oceans. The most obvious manifestation on land is in wind power and, in the case of oceans, in wave power. In wind power the energy flux is at low density and while wind power might provide us with a useful component of our total needs it is certainly not likely to prove adequate in amount. Wave energy is more concentrated and calculations and early experiments indicate that here we have a reserve which could prove very valuable indeed. We have already, in fairly large measure, turned hydro-electric power to good account; this is of course derived from the potential energy stored in the water evaporated from the oceans by the sun and which is returned to us in some degree as rain on higher ground. Damming this water and controlling the release we have hydro-electric energy made available. At the present rate of consumption it would only be sufficient to meet a relatively small percentage of world needs (ca. 1%).

Without being exhaustive in considering these resources, reference must be made to the resources which we have within the Earth. The Earth's interior is at a much higher temperature than the surface. Unfortunately the energy trapped in the Earth (and which is maintained almost entirely from the energy of radioactive decay of certain naturally unstable elements, especially potassium) is of low density and the thermal conductivity of the Earth's crust is also low in value. While the source of heat therefore is very great indeed, the research needed to make it available in practical ways presents major problems. None of these problems appears insuperable and once again we are justified in concluding that there are, among the more speculative forms of energy resources, very abundant amounts. If we can assume successes in the scientific approaches to the problem presented, and there are good reasons so to assume, we need have no fears of meeting long-term energy requirements.

As a physicist who has been engaged in fusion research I find myself unwilling to include fusion energy among the available though more intractable resources. As our knowledge stands at the minute it should not be included in this category. We are still a factor of one hundred or more short of achieving a self-sustaining release of energy from the light nuclei. It would be unwise to assume that practical release of hydrogen energy can definitely be achieved; it has been released by man in the hydrogen bomb but there is much yet to be done to release it in the process of controlled fusion. On the other hand, it is right to stress that if we do achieve the controlled release of hydrogen energy we are making available to ourselves one of the most abundant energy resources known to us. The sun with its enormous density continuously consumes hydrogen, converting it into helium with the destruction of some of the mass and the release of immense amounts of solar energy. We have great quantities of heavy hydrogen in our oceans and if fusion is achieved in a controlled fashion then man would have available almost unlimited amounts of energy and there would be few problems for many thousands of years.

The Form of Energy

The actual form in which energy is provided or required is of real importance. One of the features of the scene that troubles both scientists and economists is the substantial average rate of growth of energy needs. In our own country this can be roughly estimated as around 3%, and a compound rate of increase of 3% implies a doubling in some twenty or so years. It is true that there are discontinuities in the rate of growth especially when large price increases occur but inevitably one must assume that there will be no sustained diminution lasting over many years but rather a steady, if somewhat reduced, rate of increase in demand. This observed average increase in consumption leads us to examine rather closely the range of needs and from Fig. 3 we can see that the most substantial demand arises in the industrial/commercial sector. The next most substantial is for domestic purposes, and the third large sector is in transport. In both of the two largest elements we see roughly half of the need is for heat as such. For many heating purposes, notably space-heating, a relatively low-grade energy is adequate. Conversely

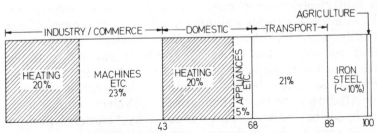

FIGURE 3   Percentage breakdown of U.K. energy consumption. Based upon data from "Observer", 6th October 1974.

for transport the form of energy is usually closely specified and, for example, in personal transport by automobile we depend heavily at present on the availability of petroleum. Most public transport requirements can be met with electrical energy derived from a variety of fuels. The use of coal as such for public transport has become insignificant.

It is when we turn to the question of efficiency with which we convert energy resources that we realise the importance of the form in which the energy is required. For space-heating purposes the low-grade form is usually adequate, yet in electricity generating stations such low-grade heat is almost completely dissipated as "waste". In a few countries a large part of this "waste" heat, which amounts to about 60% of the total energy in modern generating stations, is used for space-heating especially in the homes built in the reasonably near vicinity of the power station. If this were done extensively, in effect the efficiency of the station would be increased almost two-fold. In modern societies electrical energy accounts for between 30 and 40% of the total consumed so that by using the "waste" some 30 to 40% additional energy is provided to the community. This illustrates the size of the dividend that can be secured by overall planning of an energy programme. Such a programme runs across the fields of responsibility of two or more Ministries and again indicates the importance of a combined scientific, political, and economic approach to the question of energy needs. From the efficiency angle, electrical energy is a comparatively unattractive form except for its flexibility. Even so its flexibility does not yet extend to cover personal transport and we have mentioned the dependence in that matter on petroleum supplies. If electrical energy could be still more efficiently generated, if we used the "waste" heat of the power stations well, and if success followed research into electrically-propelled cars and transport vehicles we would be in a much happier position regarding the "burning" of our primary fuels to provide other useful forms of energy.

Another answer to the conversion problem can be found in providing an efficient means of conversion of other fuels to a more versatile single fuel; this idea is at the heart of the so-called hydrogen economy. Hydrogen, or other chemicals of equivalent nature, can be obtained by using the heat energy released by "burning" primary material to break the hydrogen bond constituting the water molecule. On the other hand if we use a primary fuel such as coal or

1. $CaBr_2 + 2H_2O \xrightarrow{730°} Ca(OH)_2 + 2HBr$ (water splitting)

2. $Hg + 2HBr \xrightarrow{250°} HgBr_2 + H_2$ (hydrogen switch)

3. $HgBr_2 + Ca(OH)_2 \xrightarrow{200°} CaBr_2 + HgO + H_2O$ (oxygen shift)

4. $HgO \xrightarrow{600°} Hg + \frac{1}{2}O_2$ (oxygen switch)

Sum: $H_2O \longrightarrow H_2 + \frac{1}{2}O_2$

Source: C. Marchetti, "Chemical Economy and Engineering Review", 1973, 5, (no. 1), 7.

FIGURE 4: Mark-1 cycle

petroleum to generate electrical power and use this in turn to provide us through electrolysis with hydrogen we have in the hydrogen at best one-third of the initial energy. This poor return has stimulated considerable interest in research into use of, for example, the heat in high temperature reactors to effect chemical chain reactions where the final product is free hydrogen. An example of such a chain is shown in Fig. 4. It is still very early days in these researches but the theoretical and somewhat tentative examination of some of the chains shows that the overall efficiency might well be around 70%. Those starting with a fuel such as uranium would in a sense have it in a versatile form as hydrogen, and hydrogen would then in turn be used as a fuel in generating stations when electricity was essential to our application or it could, as hydrogen or a derivative of hydrogen, be the fuel for cars and other forms of transport. It would obviously lend itself very readily to space-heating of industrial or commercial buildings or homes.

We have said enough to show that energy conversion should always be borne in mind in any programme involving substantial investment in the use of our primary energy resources.

The Question of Price

This brings me naturally to the question of price of a unit of energy. In some senses it is accurate to say that energy, as such, is cheap; we have it flowing continuously without charge on to the surface of the Earth. In some of the fossil fuels, for instance in the case of petroleum as found in the Middle East or in Russia or in the U.S.A., it can readily be "tapped". The market price therefore is largely artificial and bears little relationship to the cost of "winning" the fuel. In a way this artificiality in the situation presents a major handicap to a scientist or engineer exploring new means of meeting the energy needs of society. If the new method is comparatively costly in terms of human effort and resources, a sudden change in pricing policy can nullify the value of the investment. It would appear that international co-operation is vital. Energy resources are distributed without regard to national frontiers and in consequence the price of energy can be used extremely readily to the advantage or disadvantage of different nations. Even within one nation the same problem arises. Thus North Sea gas can be imported even now at relatively low cost as compared with the cost of providing the equivalent energy as coal or oil from the more northerly waters of the North Sea. In consequence of such facts there can be much reduced incentive to invest heavily in any of the more costly methods of making energy available. The scientist, however, has little to offer here in the way of answer and he must simply strive as best he can with the help of the engineer to discover more and more economical methods. If he succeeds in this then the energy price, whatever its source, is of less moment. Work in energy analysis has led some scientists[4] and economists to the point of suggesting that energy is more fundamental than money in regulating our human affairs. It seems to me too early to adopt such an extreme view – while the cost of energy has risen comparatively rapidly it is still far from being the major element of cost in the manufacture of most goods. Scientists have always found ingenious answers to problems of this kind and they represent the kind of challenge to which young scientists may well provide the answers. It is unfortunate but true that challenge is stimulating and we need only look at the achievements in science and technology in war-time to realise that the sharper the need the more rapid and ingenious the response.

The Image of Science

It is appropriate at this point to say a little about the attraction, or lack of attraction, of science today. In many universities, and not least in the subject of chemistry, there has been clear indication that the interest of many of our most able young people has drifted away from the scientific disciplines. There are many reasons for such a change but among them is the criticism of technology that is all too frequently expressed and which is undeserved. Increased interest in the environment (in matters of resources, pollution, human health and well-being) has given rise to some of these expressions of criticism. At the same time the great achievements of technology, especially in the 20th century, have been conveniently ignored or at least largely discounted. No amount of concern for the environment on the part of the uninformed will lead to appreciable improvements. For one thing they are generally not prepared to pay the substantial price of such in terms of reduced standard of living; for another, our society is so complex in its industrial and commercial achievement that only insighted scientific and technological study can bring about great improvements in the present situation. Nuclear energy is frequently regarded with anxiety for the future and we hear much talk of the danger of contamination, the hazard of plutonium and other radioactive materials, particularly waste. However, to date, the atomic energy industry is one of the very safest in the world. Admittedly the first industrial revolution, primarily based on coal, brought about much undesirable deterioration in our environment but modern coal-burning electrical generating stations are vastly improved compared with the small and dirty installations of former times; indeed recent advances in matters such as fluidised-bed combustion show that extremely low-grade coal can be burned efficiently and cleanly and few pollution problems are introduced. Research and full-scale plant construction should both be tackled in this important area.

This is not to say that rather more subtle environment problems do not exist and will not emerge in the future. While the atmosphere may be kept healthy the combustion of coal and petroleum leads to the production of huge amounts of carbon dioxide. The study of the interchange of carbon dioxide with the Earth, the atmosphere, and the oceans as well as the biosphere should be pursued more vigorously. Changes in the weather which might be induced by altering the percentage of carbon dioxide in our atmosphere (around 330 parts per million) could be quite marked. It is along these more general and still speculative avenues that our research should be pursued more vigorously. We pay a lot of attention to the rather obvious, and are able to claim with some confidence that the far more apparent and clearly deleterious effects on the atmosphere of the recent past have been virtually entirely eliminated. For instance Glasgow has halved fog frequency by imposing clean-air zones. In saying this one is aware that from time to time there will still be problems to resolve such as that which was serious in the particular case of Los Angeles; smog was produced by the high concentration of the exhaust gases from automobiles and exposure to sunlight. We must concentrate now on efficiency in using energy resources and clearly the higher the efficiency of utilisation the less the pollution and contamination. As science and technology enable us to achieve higher efficiency, pollution and contamination problems will be substantially reduced in scale. Much of the trouble will be eliminated at the source.

The most serious feature in the expressions of concern regarding nuclear fuel and radioactive waste lies in the areas of theft, vandalism, and terrorism. Deliberate acts of sabotage of nuclear installations were certainly not in the minds of the scientists and engineers who launched the nuclear age. Here again we realise that the real problem is neither scientific nor technological but rather that we are confronted with a basic fact of the way of life, both national and international. It is indeed difficult to know how to move in some areas of modern science if new technologies can be turned to unforeseen purposes in a world where law and order may be overturned.

The Longer-term Future

The conclusion that we reach is that the resources available to man are entirely adequate and with any reasonable assumptions about the scientific and technological capability of man to use them there is no cause for concern. Where deep concern does arise however is in the social, political, and legal spheres. In the well-ordered society few problems emerge that seem daunting to the technologist. Perhaps the help that the scientist of this age must try to provide is to shift the traditional emphasis and do his utmost to foresee abuses of the end-product of his work. For example, if extremely effective means can be found to convert solar radiation and if the electrical power thus made available is, when necessary, conveniently transformed to still more versatile forms such as hydrogen, we would have a comparatively safe energy resource, one which was able to meet the diverse types of human need. Such a goal is certainly not beyond the ingenuity of our scientists and technologists and they have at least one hundred years to crack the problem. It is perhaps notable that I have not chosen fusion as the most attractive long-term answer. My justification for this lies in the lack of certainty that it will work and also in its vulnerability to the terrorist. In any event I look upon the sun as a marvellous fusion reactor placed at a very comfortable distance from our Earth.

The needs of man as man may be stated very simply, though in some nations they appear to be extremely diversified. The prime needs are nevertheless heat, especially in our homes, food to sustain the body and of course the materials to build our homes. I have already mentioned the clever answer primitive man sometimes found so far as the provision of food was concerned. In contrast modern man, when we look at his agricultural effort with energy foremost in our minds, seems to be comparatively ill-informed and wasteful of resources. We now know that in the manufacture of chemical fertilisers very large amounts of energy are required almost exceeding the equivalent amount of energy of the food produced, and this in spite of the fact that the plant itself is efficient at storing solar energy which is, as it were, provided free. Again in the manufacture of pesticides we have the use of energy in very substantial amounts. So modern agriculture is wasteful of energy and even the method of preparing the ground and transporting the food is also wasteful, involving us in the consumption of a lot of fuel. On this basis some would advocate that modern agricultural methods are very seriously in error. It is difficult, however, to be entirely convinced of such an argument. As we have maintained, energy basically is available free and its value can all too easily be overestimated. So far as food production in the very long term is concerned there might be problems about the continuous fertility of the ground, but meanwhile the fixation of nitrogen though it is expensive would seem to be justified as a method of producing desirable chemical fertilisers. The food problem increases rather than diminishes essentially because the world population increases. The world population mainly increases to some extent because of the beneficial effects of modern medical treatments and the increase in life expectation even in the less developed countries. Perhaps we can, with a fair measure of certainty, expect that education will prevent gross over-population of the Earth.

As regards homes and buildings in general, it does appear that we have certainly not reached a critical stage in the provision of adequate energy for the important space-heating requirement. (I leave aside of course all questions of price as such.) In an advanced industrial society, such as that in the U.S.A., immense amounts of energy are used in air-conditioning. This process is not, in general, efficient and much more thought should be given to energy economy in making homes and offices more habitable. So far as we can see, construction materials become more and more diversified in spite of the fact that some modern construction materials involve the use of the application of energy but no-one could suggest seriously that construction materials represent a truly serious problem. Many of them can be recycled and used over and over again and if energy is available there is no need to be pessimistic about recycling as such.

Summing-up

We have reviewed a wide range of needs and considered the many ways in which these needs involve the provision of energy. The form in which the energy is actually applied has been shown to affect our judgment on the value of resources as such. All of the study is reassuring in that we conclude that energy as a commodity is in plentiful supply. The more economical use of resources is an attractive field of work for scientists and engineers. At the same time new resources present extremely interesting challenges and undoubtedly merit much increased effort in both research and development. The extremely awkward problems really arise in respect of such matters as pricing policy, national and international, and the elimination or reduction of deleterious environmental, ecological, and climatological effects. These two aspects of energy study are themselves connected. Lastly we have observed that science must be fully conscious of the possibility that the state of society, not least the regard for law and order on an international scale, will possibly be in the future a determing influence on the research goals that are chosen. From this point of view really massive investment in fission or fusion, for example, must be seriously questioned. On the other hand it is this kind of consideration that reinforces the attractive features of programmes on such resources as solar energy, especially if real success with solar cells is forthcoming.

References

[1] *Scientific American*, Energy and Power issue, Vol. 224, No. 3, September 1971; Energy Resources and the Environment", Eds J. Lenehan and W. W. Fletcher, Blackie, Glasgow, 1975.
[2] R. A. Rappaport, *Scientific American*, September 1971, p. 117.
[3] G. Kaplan, *IEEE Spectrum*, December 1975, p. 47
[4] C. G. M. Slesser, *Nature*, 1975, **254**, 170.

Energy Resources: Problems and Opportunities

by J. K. Hambling; British Petroleum Co. Ltd., London

THE scope presented by this title is enormous, and clearly I can only give what must be a highly personal view of the situation.

Few would question the statement that we will pay an increasing price of the energy we consume. The nature of the problem is that of describing a plausible situation wherein supplies are forthcoming at a conceived possible lowest cost. Energy and economics are inseparable twins. "Energy at any cost" is a maxim which would apply to a very limited number of demand sectors.

But before discussing the future the scene should be set by a quick review of the recent past.

World economy grew at an unparalleled rate between 1950 and 1972. Economic growth rates averaged 5% per annum uninterrupted by major recessions. Such a sustained period of growth would have been impossible if energy supplies had been unable to meet the resulting 5% annual growth in energy demand.

Figure 1 shows how this increasing energy demand was satisfied. The overall growth rate concealed a major change in the demand on individual resources. During the period shown there was virtually no increase in the demand for coal, the fuel which had been the major energy source for the first half of the century. Natural gas demand increased, but costs and problems of transportation restricted its use mainly to producing regions and by 1972 it only satisfied 18% of demand. Hydro and nuclear electricity together only contributed a small proportion of energy consumption throughout the period.

The bulk of the increased energy demand was supplied by oil made possible by the development of giant oil fields in the Middle East. The low cost of producing the oil and the economies of scale achieved in transportation, refining, and distribution allowed the real price of oil to fall, encouraging consumption and providing little or

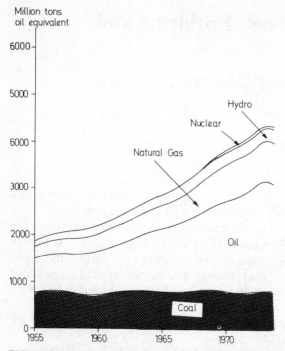

FIGURE 1. Historic view of resource supply meeting demands for the non-Communist world (1955–1972).

no incentive to the efficient use of energy. As a result, oil increased its share of World energy from about 28% in 1950 to over 45% by 1972. In the World outside Comecon and China the dependence on oil was 53% by 1973; Fig. 2 shows that this dependence varied from 99% in the transport sector to 39% in the industry sector, oil being the most important fuel in all sectors. In volume terms the use of oil increased more than four-fold between 1950 and 1972.

With oil demand doubling every decade, the dangers of supply coming under pressure began to become apparent in the early '70s. However, oil could still be imported at a lower price than the cost of producing substitute fuels such as coal or nuclear power in the demand centres of the World. Energy-consuming countries were more influenced by the short-term economic benefits of low-price oil than the longer-term dangers inherent in increasing dependence on imported oil. The result was that the dependence of the main

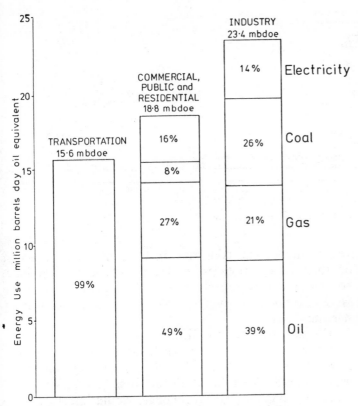

FIGURE 2. Historic resource utilisation by demand sector for the non-Communist world, 1972, not including processing losses.

oil-consuming countries in Europe and Japan on imported oil continued to increase; and the U.S. became for the first time a major competitor with the prospect that, by 1980, 50% of its supplies would come from abroad.

The two basic premises underlying the energy policy of most oil-importing countries namely that oil supplies would continue to be cheap, and that dependence on imported oil offered minimal security risks, were shattered by the so-called oil crisis at the end of 1973. A five-fold increase in price made the cost of imports a major burden on the balance of payments. The accompanying political embargo or threat of an embargo, on shipments of oil to some countries initiated the general view that oil was a less than secure

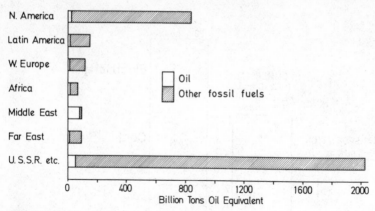

FIGURE 3. World Hydrocarbon reserves by area.

energy source. Oil-importing countries had to make an urgent reappraisal of their energy policies. Reduced dependence on imported oil became the new objective, and all possible means of achieving it were examined and analysed. The results of these efforts are slowly emerging.

So much for the past. Now for the future.

Our traditional resource bases, the fossil fuels, are still extremely large. Proved world reserves of oil and gas, tar sands, oil shale and coal, are shown in Fig. 3. The total of all the fossil-based reserves — some 3,400 billion tons of oil equivalent — would meet World energy demand at today's consumption levels for just over 500 years. Coal, of course, is much the most significant of all these sources. Looked at another way, so far we have used up some 16% of total possible recoverable oil reserves, and only about 4% in the case of coal. Hence, for a long time to come, there should be no shortage caused solely by *inadequate reserves*, although there are many important and difficult problems to be overcome in technical, political, environmental, and financial spheres before these sources become available for general and adequate use.

The importance of Russia and North America is quite apparent. It can also be seen that Western Europe and Japan (which is included in the Far East bloc), are relatively lacking in indigenous resources. As far as oil is concerned many of the reserves are located away from centres of consumption, and transportation is an important factor.

The breakdown of proven oil reserves by geographical area is

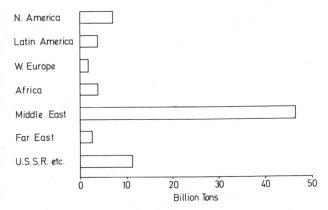

FIGURE 4. World proven reserves of oil.

shown more clearly in Fig. 4. The strength of the Middle East as the world's major oil source is clear, at least until alternative fuels to oil can be found which will reduce the dependence of World consuming areas on oil. At present, Middle East production accounts for one-third of total world requirements, and on the basis of the above reserves, of which it holds some 60%, its relative importance is unlikely to decline.

It is also relevant to note that as we move into more difficult areas of oil exploration and production, costs escalate tremendously. The cost of developing a barrel per day of oil in the North Sea or the North Slope of Alaska is over 10 times that in the Middle East and Africa during the past decade.

The resources available in the non-Communist World – proved and possible – are presented in Fig. 5.

Oil is a non-renewable source of energy whose reserves are limited, and hence production cannot continue to grow indefinitely. At some date in the future the production of oil will peak and then begin to decline, although this does not mean that it will run out. The point at which the decline will occur depends on the interaction between supply and demand. As the remaining undiscovered reserves fall, the difficulty in finding them will increase along with the cost of developing them. At the historic growth rates of oil demand, a new oil province such as the North Sea or Alaska would need to be discovered every one or two years to maintain such growth into the 80's and 90's. This is not likely.

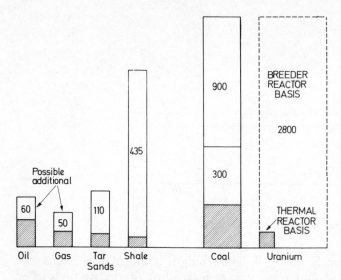

FIGURE 5. Non-Communist world energy resources: billion (10^9) tons oil equivalent.

A projection of possible oil production is given in Fig. 6; a similar curve, Fig. 7, indicates a view on gas supplies. The added implication from my preceeding remarks is that the unit price of these resources is likely to increase relatively rapidly as one progresses from left to right. Thus, oil and gas supplies are seen to be limited, and are seen to be increasingly expensive to produce.

On nuclear energy I have but little to say; it is a subject which has been and will be debated at very great length elsewhere.

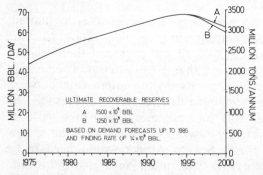

FIGURE 6. Future oil production potential: non-Communist world, 1975–2000.

Million Tons
Oil Equivalent

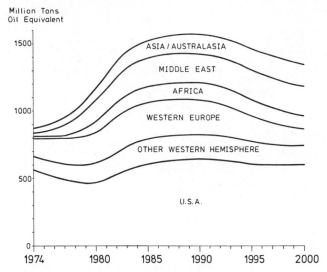

FIGURE 7. Future natural gas production potential: non-Communist world, 1974–2000.

I have assumed a nuclear contribution of 0.5 billion tons o.e. in 1985, as compared with 0.2 billion in 1980. After 1985 the greatest imaginable rate of nuclear ordering would be to capture the entire order book for new thermal power stations. With the electricity market presumed to grow at 3–6% p.a. to the year 2000, and after allowing for the hydroelectric contribution, the nuclear contribution is then limited to between 1.5 and 3.2 billion tons o.e. in the year 2000.

We now come down to the two final contributing sectors of resources namely coal and the "catch-all" labelled "others".

The level of production of coal from the large resource base shown earlier depends on many factors including level of recovery, investment, and the development of infrastructure to transport and consume coal. Therefore the forecasts of the amount of coal which will actually be produced vary over a wide range. However, when we remember the numerous fears regarding nuclear power – from uranium shortage or normal industrial accidents to the novel risks of plutonium or active wastes, of proliferation, sabotage or blackmail, and the financial vulnerability of high technology to inflation, then I think that a more optimistic view should be used for the probability

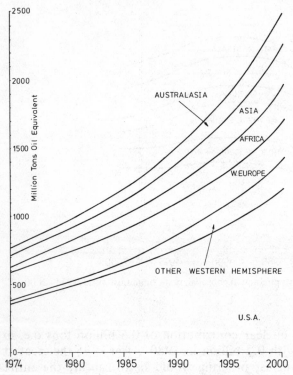

FIGURE 8. Future solid fuels production potential: non-Communist world, 1974–2000.

of relatively high levels of coal production for the period post-1985. This is shown in Fig. 8.

The "others" which comprise for example tar sands, oil shales, geothermal, solar, wind, waves, tides, and biomass, I will refer to later.

The implications of the foregoing are summarised in the table of production ranges below in Table 1.

These are, in my opinion, plausible ranges of production levels of the various components of our energy resources. Opportunities are only illustrated when this resource scenario of supply is compared with the possible demands. The resource base of historic world energy demand has already been indicated. The following table (Table 2) is relevant further background to any assumption regarding future trends.

Table 1

Non-Communist world resource	Billion tons of oil equivalent	
	1974	2000
Oil	2.25	3.1
Gas	0.85	1.3
Coal	0.85	1.7–3.2
Nuclear	0.06	1.5–3.2
Hydro	0.30	0.80
Others	–	0–1.0
Total	4.3	8.4–12.6

Table 2: Total energy demand, 1970

	Total energy (MTOE p.a.)	Population (10^9)	Energy per capita (TOE p.a.)
Free market economy	2833	0.76	3.74*
Centrally planned economy	1381	1.13	1.21
Developing nations	524	1.74	0.31
Total	4738	3.6	1.31

*7.14 in US; 2.74 in Western Europe.

Against this backdrop it will be clear that even if the high consumers temper their hunger for energy and slow their growth via extreme conservation directed by Governments, the World as a whole will show a continued increase in demand for primary energy.

The manner in which some developed nations used energy is illustrated in Table 3.

Table 3: Net energy used by major sectors 1972 (%)

	U.S.	Japan	U.K.	Sweden
Transport	25.0	16.1	13.5	14.8
Agric/mining	2.6	3.8	2.4	4.7
Commercial	5.0	6.9	1.9	3.1
Public	–	–	4.0	5.5
Industry	25.0	46.8	32.7	39.3
Residential	18.4	6.8	16.3	24.5
Total demand (MTOE)	1800	340	221	40

The demand requirement of each country is of course quite different. Each thus offers a varying energy conservation potential, and each faces a differing problem with respect to increasing the flexibility of its resource base.

However, for the purpose of this review a consolidated view of energy demand in the non-Communist World for the period 1975–2000 has been based on a series of plausible projections which are covered by an average rate of GNP growth within the range of 3–4.5% p.a., representing energy growth rate ranges of 2.6–3.8%. Wherein Western Europe has an energy growth rate of 1.9–2.6%, and OPEC countries the highest energy growth rate projection of 6.4–10.1%.

The maximum GNP growth rate of 4.5% over the period is itself a composite resulting from an expected somewhat higher rate during the first few years due to some potential for catching up on capacity following the severe current recession. Reduced rate of growth of the population of working age in the developed countries, restructuring of economies in response to higher-cost energy, and energy supply

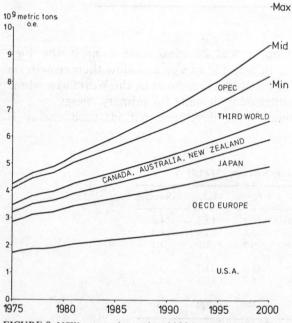

FIGURE 9. NCW energy demand to 2000 by geographic sector.

constraints, are likely to limit this maximum forecast of economic growth to a level lower than rates achieved pre-1973. However, a factor tending to increase the average rate of growth is the increasing weight of OPEC and Third World countries with much faster economic growth rates than the developed countries.

A mid-point estimate of GNP growth is a rate of 3¾% over the period 1975–2000.

A speculative view of this energy demand is broken down into geographic areas in Fig. 9. This midpoint demand is illustrated with regard to the resource potential discussed earlier in Fig. 10. These figures offer a restatement of the problems and uncertainties that are envisaged in providing for energy demands.

Conservation and an increasing efficiency in use are the more obvious ways of influencing technically the absolute magnitude of demand. Basically there are two broad categories of problems associated with supply:

1. Provision of new energy resources (the "Others" in the above Table), and smooth continuation of traditional resource exploitation.

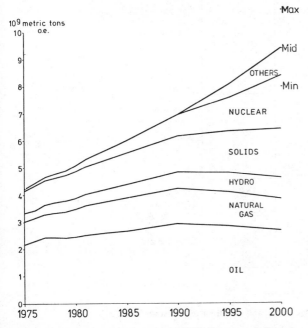

FIGURE 10. NCW energy demand to 2000. Resource indicated.

2. Provision of technology allowing flexibility of resource utilisation.

The opportunities afforded by solving parts of these problems are best determined by an appreciation of the specific demand sectors in specific geographic areas. However as a broad first indicative generalisation, one can conceive of having to satisfy the demands in terms of supply of hydrocarbons, heating requirements, and electricity generation.

Clearly, not all the resources considered can contribute to all the demand sectors. There is a preferred listing of resources associated

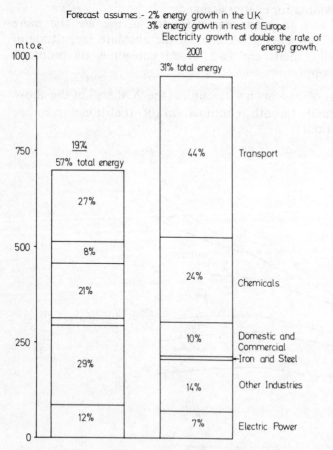

FIGURE 11. Relative change in demand on oil barrel: Western Europe.

with every demand sector. Using simply the three broad sectors quoted, oil, gas, and coal have a unique role in satisfying the demands for liquid hydrocarbons, whilst nuclear and hydroelectric power serve the power demand sector. All resources interact, for example, in satisfying the basic demand for heat — be it industrial or domestic.

The medium-term opportunity is thus to evolve the technology which would allow gas, oil, and coal to be utilised in a manner which reflected this trend, based on the underlying knowledge that natural gas and oil supplies cannot continue to supply all traditional markets or outlets. The types of fuels used for basic heating requirements are those that will undergo most drastic change at the earliest time.

By way of example, the nature of the changes of demand on the oil "barrel" which anticipates the above philosophy is given in Fig. 11. Here it can be seen that demand for the lower-boiling oil fractions used for transportation and the production of chemicals will increase compared with the decreasing demand for the heavier fractions used by the domestic and industrial sectors.

The technology for this increased "lightening of the oil barrel" is well known — although undoubtedly with the longer-term trend referred to earlier involving deeper, more intensive processing of ultimately every crude oil barrel to a narrow band of relatively light products, coupled with the increased cost of fuel oil, there is scope for improvement. In addition, as selection of low sulphur-containing crude oils becomes a costly luxury so the problem of sulphur content of crude oils will tend to be more acute. Catalyst systems capable of performing effectively with higher sulphur content feedstocks will have to be developed. Further, the deeper processing of sulphur-containing crude oils might well result in larger volumes of sulphur-containing gases being generated. Cost-effective control of such emissions, probably via stack gas desulphurisation, is a problem common to the projected increase in coal utilisation.

A second conclusion, namely that coal will be used initially as a direct substitute for oil in heat generation applications, can also be made. This substitution will release heating oils, which in turn can be processed to low-boiling products required for the transport sector of demand and the fast growing petrochemical feedstock requirements.

Further, as oil and gas supplies decrease, coal will have to be converted via processing into gas and liquids. The requirements for additional gas supply will probably significantly predate the general need for liquids from coal – the timing of this latter requirement being particularly obscure. The essential prerequisite is to improve the probability of coal being economically available in the energy demanding centres of the World. The rebirth of an international coal industry must be viewed as a major opportunity. By way of example Fig. 12 indicates a view of international movements of coal, based on the production potential. The problems of transporting these large volumes of solids at low cost across lands and oceans are real and have yet to be faced. For example, seaborne international trade in coal in 1973 was only 105 million tons.

Having spent a great deal of time on global generalisations, I think a more parochial view should be taken when thinking of the development of the other or alternative resources such as solar, wind, tides, etc. From the cumulative demands presented it can be seen that in the light of the degree of uncertainty regarding the defined conventional resources, the timing of the requirement for these alternative resources is impossible to predict.

Resources should be developed only when there is seen to be an economic or social need – actions and views of governments apart.

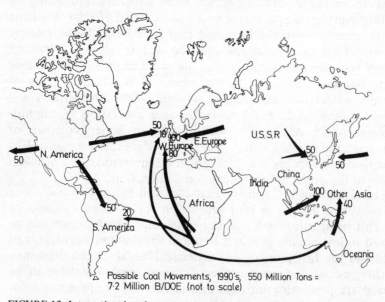

Possible Coal Movements, 1990's, 550 Million Tons = 7·2 Million B/DOE (not to scale)

FIGURE 12. International coal movement.

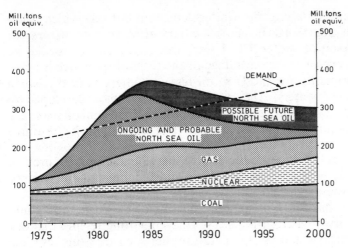

FIGURE 13. U.K. energy supply projection.

New resource development requires not only capital but also the commitment of a significant proportion of a country's technological skills over a long period of time. No one country can hope to cover all possibilities. Each country must be selective and its judgements carefully valued.

A view of the energy supply/demand situation of the U.K. is given in Fig. 13. The curves will be familiar; the energy demand curve is a presumed 2% p.a. growth rate. The value we ascribe to alternative (indigenous) resources is governed by several factors:

1. The cost of developing existing resources relative to these alternatives.
2. The value others put on our existing resources.
3. The cost of importing resources from others with due regard for security of supply.
4. The degree of imbalance between supply and presumed demand.

The interplay of these factors will differ from country to country — and hence the concept of opportunity will vary.

The United Kingdom, with a strong basis in conventional resources, and with a significant stake and growing importance in nuclear energy programmes, should question the wisdom in competing with other nations in say, solar energy — a resource which is in relatively short supply in the United Kingdom but one which other nations with high solar insolation would tend to rate of greater economic resource potential. Using this argument it would be sensible, however, to take advantage of the technology which is being developed primarily for the U.K. oil resource interests in the North Sea and deeper waters. The strong engineering base developed to exploit this oil resource could be evolved to encompass the technology required to harness the power of waves. This is a resource which to us is relatively plentiful.

The concept of the production of harvested crops to provide organic fuel is well documented. The land requirements in Western Europe for the production of foodstuffs would indicate a relative preference for this form of energy resource growth. Fuel crops would have to be harvested from the sea − I have a strong feeling that our climatic conditions and sea temperatures are such that this resource potential, whilst of interest, must be treated as extremely speculative.

I have indicated the belief that our technological efforts should be directed primarily at the more traditional resources. The deeper processing of the oil barrel, coupled with cost effective control of sulphur problems, illustrates the future problems of the oil industry. An increased, and increasing, application of high technology to the mining, transportation, and ultimately processing, of coal offers both domestic and global opportunities.

Finally, we should apply selection criteria to projected work on the development of any alternative resources. These criteria should be firmly based on views of the relative economic potential and benefit to us of each alternative contributor to our energy portfolio − relative, that is, when compared with the situation and potential of that alternative resource to other energy-deficient nations of the World.

Energy — Transmission, Storage and Management

by Ian Fells; Professor of Energy Conversion, University of Newcastle upon Tyne

THE storage of energy has not previously presented any real problem; its transmission and management have! Up to now the primary fuels, coal, oil, and natural gas, have been stored in stockpiles, tanks, gas holders, or more sophisticated cryogenic stores. Otherwise they have been stored in their natural place of formation and exploited as need arose. This arrangement has worked surprisingly well, accommodating fluctuations in demand and only recently showing signs of strain as industrial disputes and politico-economic action have distorted the ebb and flow of supply with market demand. Now a strategic supply of oil sufficient for 90 days is mooted in E.E.C. countries, and with it the attendant financial implication which means a 17% price increase to pay for the "frozen" ninety-day supply. The storage of derived fuels presents more difficulty. Plutonium formed during the fission process of natural or enriched uranium which is central to the operation of the present generation of nuclear power stations is a strategic military material as well as the fuel for a future generation of nuclear reactors. Fortunately the specific energy release capacity per unit volume is very high [for ^{235}U, energy release $= 4.2 \times 10^{13}$ Btu/ft^3] and the radiation hazard — and perhaps more importantly the danger of politically inspired theft — are problems which overshadow the physical storage problem. Electricity provides the biggest difficulty and the greatest challenge. It is undoubtedly the most convenient and versatile form of energy, and perhaps it is worth remarking that the laws of theromodynamics tell us nothing about relative merits of energy in its different forms or for that matter about the time taken for energy conversion processes to take place. Unfortunately the storage of electricity as electricity presents formidable difficulties.

Storage of Electrical Energy

The impetus to develop electrical energy storage derives from the varying demand for electrical energy during each 24 hours. Fig. 1 shows the daily variation in demand at different times during the year. Clearly some means for storing energy at times of minimum or low demand, so that it can be released at peak demand periods, reduces the size of the overall generating capacity that is necessary. This is particularly important as more and more nuclear electricity generation is brought into the network. Such plant currently supplies part of the base load (about 10% of total generating capacity at the moment) but with an additional 8000 MW of capacity coming on line in the next few years and more planned, it is essential to run this plant almost continuously to capitalise on its low running cost. As the base-load demand is met and exceeded by nuclear generating capacity, means must be developed for storing night-generated

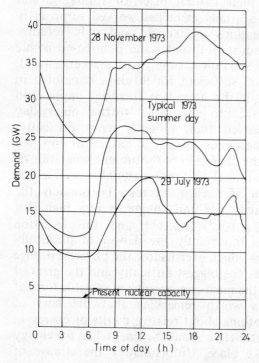

FIGURE 1. Reproduced by courtesy of "CEGB Research".

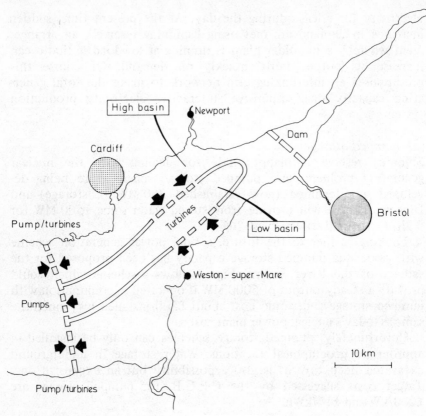

FIGURE 2. Reproduced by courtesy of "CEGB Research".

back to the air for the generation period; under these circumstances it would be unnecessary to burn fuel in the turbine. It has been estimated that an 8 GW scheme storing for 8 hours and generating 390 MW for 16 hours with a cycle efficiency of about 75 per cent would have a capital cost between £125 and £160 per kW.

(c) Magnetic Storage

It is now much easier, thanks to the development of superconductors, to produce high magnetic fields over large volumes. Such schemes are small, however, and only suitable for specialist application where high costs can be accepted. The CERN superconducting magnet for the bubble chamber stores 220 kWh in its 3.5T field at a capital cost

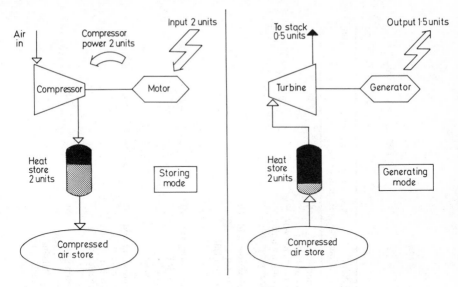

FIGURE 3. Reproduced by courtesy of "CEGB Research".

of £8000/kWh. Although some improvements in magnet design and costs are anticipated, magnetic storage will be too expensive for large-scale application.

(d) Electrochemical Storage

Small-scale storage of electricity in batteries is a well tried and proved technology. Battery storage units are unlikely to be larger than 0.5 MW and would therefore be sited at "substation sites" close to the consumer. There are two basic battery types, the straight-forward rechargeable system where current is reversed through the battery to recharge at off-peak periods; the other system is the fuel cell in which off-peak electricity is used to electrolyse water to H_2 and O_2 which is recombined electrochemically in a fuel cell for peak-load operation. Table 1 gives some current "state of the art" figures. It is taken from Hart and Webb's analysis[3] for the C.E.G.B. and includes an estimated cost based on a 0.5 MW power output and 6 MWh storage capacity. Hart and Webb set a cost target of £22/kW sent out per annum and conclude that only lithium–sulphur and lithium–chlorine show clear promise, although further work on redox systems, sodium molten salt cells, and aluminium–chlorine cells could be attractive. A major problem is the scaling-up of cells to

Table 1: Features of electrochemical storage batteries

Battery	Open-circuit Voltage, V	Approx. operating temp., K	Electrolyte	State of development	Approx. power/power efficiency (%)	Est. costs £/kWh output p.a.*
1. H_2/O_2	1.2	300–1250	Various: aqueous KOH to solid ZrO_2/CaO	Commercial electrolysers; fuel cells proven in military and space projects	46	38
2. Fe/air	1.3	340	aqueous 25% KOH	Laboratory and prototype traction cell units	40	25
3. Zn/air	1.6	340	aqueous 30% KOH	Laboratory and prototype traction batteries	40	28
4. Zn/Cl_2	2.1	300	aqueous 30% $ZnCl_2$	Laboratory and prototype traction batteries	50	24
5. Pb/acid	2.0	300	aqueous 30% H_2SO_4	Commercial large 1–2 MW installations and s.l.i. car batteries	80	44

6a. Ni/Fe	1.4	300	aqueous 25% KOH	Commercial traction batteries	60	50
6b. Ni/Zn	1.7	300	aqueous 25% KOH	Laboratory	60	60
6c. Ni/Cd	1.3	300	aqueous 25% KOH	Range of commercial batteries	65	80
7. Na/S	2.1	600	Solid β-alumina	Laboratory and prototype traction batteries	60	26
8. Li/S	2.2	630	molten lithium halide eutectic	Laboratory	> 80	15–26
9. Li/Cl$_2$	3.6	830	molten alkali halide eutectic	Laboratory	> 80	17

*Including cooler and electrical gear, excluding site and buildings. Aug. 1974 prices.

large modular systems with the associated chemical and control engineering required.

(e) Mechanical Storage — Flywheels

Flywheels have been used for centuries to iron out fluctuations in shaft speed in machines of various kinds. More recently they have been used as the energy source for vehicles such as buses, over short distances between "boosts" for the flywheel. Post and Post have suggested[4] that with new materials flywheels storing energy of 10 MWh for recovery over a few hours are now possible. Ideally materials with low density and high strength are required; carbon fibre reinforced plastic (CFRP) and glass reinforced plastic (GRP) look attractive. C.E.G.B. costing for 10 MWh flywheel suggests that CFRP would be best, but even then the cost would be £200/kWh which is an order of magnitude too high. The costing depends strongly on the cost of CFRP. With GRP the working stress must be increased by an order of magnitude for it to look attractive. Absolute integrity of a flywheel structure storing 10 MWh of rotational energy would be essential as disintegration of the structure would be accompanied by an explosion of considerable magnitude.

(f) Heat Storage

Heat is transported by various media such as water and steam in thermal power stations or, in the case of nuclear stations, carbon dioxide, helium and molten sodium. By storing heat preferably in the medium of hot water — at a pressure of 18 MN/m^2 the stored energy per unit volume for steam is 320 MJ/m^3 compared with 890 MJ/m^3 for water — or as liquid sodium in a fast breeder reactor, the plant up to and including the heat transfer section can be run at constant speed and any fluctuation in electricity demand taken care of by passing more or less heat to a store. As demand for electricity increases heat is drawn from the store. In this way the plant can be run more economically and the performance optimised although at the expense of providing additional heat storage vessels. A cost assessment based on Margen's figures[5] updated by Gardner *et al.* gives, for a 500 MW(e) output, storage costs of £110/kW or £9/kWh, which are within the expected guide-line costs.

The various methods for "storing" electrical energy have been itemised; each has its place depending on circumstances, but all are expensive, although judicious use of storage can very much improve the overall performance of power stations operating with fluctuating load, giving economic advantages. Although electrical energy is the most convenient form of energy it is the most expensive. With today's high prices for all fuels energy conservation is essential and the storage of heat or thermal energy for use as heat can be very attractive.

Thermal Energy Storage

Thermal energy storage can be of value in various ways. For example if solar energy can be stored as heat when available in excess and the heat transferred and perhaps upgraded by a heat pump when needed later, the economics of solar collectors are much improved. Or, in a metal works where large quantities of heat are released intermittently, if the heat can be stored and used for process or district heating there is an obvious advantage. The technology of thermal energy storage must of course go hand in hand with efficient techniques for heat transfer and heat transmission.

(a) Low-temperature Thermal Energy Storage: below 120°C

The properties of materials for heat storage are particularly important. Specific heat is obviously a key parameter, with water a very useful fluid. Storage of heat in rocks raises problems of fluid flow and heat transfer.

Phase-transition storage, particularly involving heat of fusion, is well understood, although problems arise with supercooling. A large number of salt hydrates and their eutectics has been explored and salts such as sodium thiosulphate pentahydrate investigated experimentally for solar heat storage.

An ingenious storage technique involves the use of metal hydrides which decompose to metal and hydrogen reversibly at modest temperatures. By connecting two reactors together containing, say, lanthanum nickel hydride and "mischmetall" nickel hydride, and maintaining the reactors at different temperatures, hydrogen can be made to flow from one reactor to the other. The system can store heat or cold, or the hydrogen can be made to do mechanical work. Unfortunately the material costs are high.

On a large scale, reservoirs can be used to store thermal energy for district heating and industry. Reservoirs containing hot or cold water, ice or rock and gravel beds are all appropriate for large-scale storage. A number of problems remain to be solved, particularly those of heat recovery from the reservoir and the chemistry associated with large volumes of warm water.

(b) High-temperaure Thermal Energy Storage: 120 – 1250°C

Storage of thermal energy as sensible heat in refractories is a well established process in the steel and metallurgical industries, with installations containing as much as 20,000 tonnes of refractory and cycle times of 45 minutes. Top refractory temperatures in above-ground installations are as high as 1500°C. Underground packed-bed systems are also attractive, provided problems of water inleakage and so on are contained by proper pressure control. Packed-bed units associated with underground steam accumulators for load-following in electricity generation can add "super heat" storage and consequently improve overall efficiency. Heat for industrial application can also be stored in large rotary generators fitted with a metal or ceramic matrix which can operate up to 1000°C. A novel technique using fluidised solids can provide storage up to 1500°C with very rapid transfer of heat in and out of store made possible by effective heat transfer coefficients as high as those for water.

Storage using liquids, particularly pressurised hot water, is accomplished above ground in units as large as 500 m^3 and pressure of 20 bar. Containment costs are high, and large-scale operation is best carried out underground. Liquids other than water can be used; organic materials are available up to 350°C, inorganic liquids, liquid metals and mixtures of molten salts can be used up to 800°C and above. Liquids can be used in association with packed beds. As a large part of the cost of such storage systems is the containment, various attempts are being made to store hot and cold fluid in the same vessel by controlling stratification.

The latent heat of fusion of various solids is an attractive method of storing high-grade heat at constant temperature, although heat transfer and containment problems arising from contraction and expansion and corrosion must be overcome.

Chemical energy storage has been neglected hitherto, but a number of possible reactions now appear attractive. Catalytic endothermic reactions and thermal dissociation reactions are useful for storage. A good example of a catalytic reaction is the steam reforming reaction.

$$CH_4 + H_2O \rightleftharpoons CO + 3H_2 \quad H^0 = 59.8 \text{ kcal/g.mole; temp.}$$
range 700–1200°C

This is operated in a closed-loop system for storage and is known as the "Adam–Eva Process" (EVA comes from the description of test rig *E*inzelspaltrohr *V*ersuchs *A*nlage). It has applications in energy transmission and is referred to as the "Chemical Heat Pipe". A number of similar reactions are being investigated. High-temperature storage of this kind is particularly appropriate for industrial processes, but presupposes a high-temperature heat source such as a High Temperature Nuclear Reactor or possibly a solar heat source. As development of an HTR reactor with an operational temperature of $1200°C$ is still some way off it, is important to develop closed reaction systems which will operate at lower temperatures. Decomposition of sulphur trioxide at $725°C$ has been suggested as a

$$SO_3 \rightleftharpoons SO_2 + \tfrac{1}{2}O_2 \text{ operational temp. } 600°C$$

storage technique with the SO_2 stored as liquid and the O_2 as compressed gas. Hydration–dehydration reactions can also be used for storage. For example:

$$Ca(OH_2) \rightleftharpoons CaO + H_2O$$

takes place at $520°C$ giving an energy density of 411 kWh$_t$/m^3.

It should be clear from this short eclectic survey of thermal energy storage techniques that there are a number of useful possibilities for storing energy on a large or a small scale. Such storage facilities make possible the smoothing of demand cycles, the sensible use of waste heat rejected intermittently, and the use of solar energy without alternative techniques for use when the sun is not shining.

An interesting use of a high-intensity thermal store is the insertion of a hot block heat source into an automobile equipped with a closed-cycle gas engine such as a Stirling Engine. This arrangement could provide pollution-free in-town motoring with "refuelling" by exchanging thermal store blocks at a central depot.

Energy Transport

Energy is transported in various ways; as oil by sea and pipeline it represents much the largest single transported commodity world wide. Coal is transported by train, road, or occasionally by slurry pipe line. Gas is usually carried by pipe line, but is occasionally transported in liquid form by both ship and road tanker. Electricity is, of course, carried by the high-voltage grid. Recently the economics of different methods of transporting energy has been analysed. The ratio of costs for conveying unit quantity of energy a unit distance by oil pipeline, gas pipeline, coal train and 500 kV electrical transmission line has been quoted by the Institute of Fuel as 1:2.5:5:17 ("Energy for the Future", 1973). The logistics of energy transport are frightening: with a large coal-fired power station consuming up to 100 tons of coal per hour, this means a continual "milk round" of coal trains from pit to power station and back. Energy transportation is costly, and with growth in energy demand still relatively uncurbed, alternative techniques are being examined. As natural gas imports become necessary in the U.S.A., for example, a comparison of shipping liquid natural gas in specially constructed gas ships with conversion of natual gas into methanol at source followed by transportation in conventional large tankers costing only one-fifth of the cost of equivalent "gas ships" shows that for distances of over 9000 miles methanol transport is cheaper than LNG transport. As inflation hits shipping costs and chemical plant construction the "break even" point changes.

The very high cost of transporting electricity compared with other fuel transport and the losses of between 7 and 10% sustained during transmission have led to the examination of alternative schemes for the future.

One interesting possibility is the so-called "hydrogen economy". For its success, a thriving nuclear industry is postulated with the capability of producing cheap hydrogen during off-peak operation. The routes to hydrogen are either via electrolysis (which anticipates considerable improvement above the current 60% in electrolyser efficiency) or via a thermal route such as:

$$CaBr_2 + 2H_2O \longrightarrow Ca(OH)_2 + 2HBr \qquad 730°C$$

$$2HBr + Hg \longrightarrow HgBr_2 + H_2 \qquad 250°C$$

$$HgBr_2 + Ca(OH)_2 \longrightarrow CaBr_2 + H_2O + HgO \qquad 100°C$$

$$HgO \longrightarrow Hg + \tfrac{1}{2}O_2 \qquad 600°C$$

$$H_2O \longrightarrow H_2 + \tfrac{1}{2}O_2$$

A variety of such routes has been postulated, but all require the development of a High Temperature Nuclear heat source and all are still at the bench stage of development. Nevertheless, the prospect of piping hydrogen from a central nuclear source giving both an important storage capability to smooth the power station operation and providing a fuel to consumers via an environmentally acceptable underground pipeline has much to commend it. Comparison of energy flow with a 36-inch natural gas pipeline shows a drop from 4×10^5 therms/h for natural gas to 2.4×10^5 therms/h for hydrogen, a drop in energy flow capacity of about 40% as a result of the lower calorific value of hydrogen. By increased compression this can be reduced to a 20% reduction in capacity. In certain circumstances, rather than pump hydrogen it would be better to convert it into methane using a plentiful carbon source such as coal. Another possibility is to form methanol which, as a liquid, has even more attractive pipeline economics for energy transport.

At the user end, the hydrogen could be used to generate electricity either via a fuel cell or gas turbine with waste heat recovery giving decentralisation of power generation to areas where waste heat could be used easily. Other possibilities are the direct use of hydrogen as a fuel or feedstock in industry and possibly as a fuel for aircraft or cars.

C.E.G.B. researchers[6] have carried out a cost analysis for hydrogen production by electrolysis and distribution. They give a cost of 258p/GJ but this figure could be reduced to 205p/GJ by using off-peak nuclear power. These figures can be compared (1975) with oil at 80p/GJ and Frigg natural gas at 25p/GJ. Hydrogen could be converted into methanol using CO_2 from limestone for a further 140p/GJ. Transmission costs are 0.8p/GJ per 100 km for natural gas and 1.4p for hydrogen. The average distribution costs for all electricity in the U.K. is 80p/GJ, for natural gas 40p/GJ, and for hydrogen would be 60p/GJ. These figures give some indication of comparative costs and show that the hydrogen economy is some way off in economic terms; dramatic increases in oil and gas prices could materially affect the position, however. Improvements in grid transmission costs with high-voltage DC transmission and super-cooled underground cables show that there is scope for improvement in straightforward electricity transmission.

There is growing interest in heat transmission over long distances and economies that can be effected by, for example, piping "waste" heat from large remotely sited nuclear or fossil-fuel power stations or even large solar collectors into urban areas for district heating. A heat grid is being built up in West Germany with attractive operating costs. Where higher temperatures are required in industrial complexes, heat can be transmitted using fluidised solids or chemical heat pipes. In

Table 2

Technology	Delivered temp. range	Max. transmission range
1. Hot & cold water in pipelines	5–70°C	100 km (some authorities quote 1000 km)
2. Steam pipelines	100–250°C	50 km
3. Physical transport of sensible or latent heat e.g., coke, ice, etc.	0–800°C	5 km
4. Chemical heat pipe	60–600°C	500 km
5. Fluidised solids	250–1000°C	100 m

the chemical heat pipe, storage as well as heat transmission is effected by packing and unpacking the pipeline. A 120 km pipeline could supply 8 hours' storage. The following table (Table 2) gives some indication of the methods available for thermal energy transport.

Thermal energy transport makes possible a variety of energy-saving applications. Heating and cooling can be provided centrally for residential and commercial property. Industrial process steam and high-grade heat can be provided from central power station sources, high-temperature nuclear reactors, or as waste heat from steelworks and so on. Combined electricity and thermal generation from even remotely located power stations can be provided in urban areas and low-grade heat provided for agricultural purposes.

The combination of new techniques for energy storage and transmission adds a whole new battery of interlocking systems for energy networks which will make appreciable energy savings as they are gradually developed.

Energy Management

The growing awareness of the central role played by energy in industrial economies has led to increased attempts at energy planning. The long lead times, usually ten years for power station construction or new coal mining developments, provide restraints in any energy plan as do shortages of capital, lack of materials, and a diminishing pool of trained manpower. Taking just the nuclear industry, a recent OECD report (19 March 1976) shows a requirement of $356 billion for nuclear plant construction by the 24 member countries during the next ten years. This will require a tenfold increase in engineers to implement the plan.

It is difficult to formulate a flexible plan with these restraints built into the system, but flexibility is necessary as forward demand predicitions for energy are difficult and unreliable. Flexibility of supply and increased efficiency in energy usage can be effected by using the new energy storage and transmission technologies outlined in this paper. Some further R & D is required but the basic principles are firmly established. The stumbling block to provision of an integrated energy grid in Europe or the U.K. is the tendency to leave individual fuel suppliers to pursue their own individual plans without any sensible firm co-ordination. The separate fuel industries of the U.K. – coal, gas, electricity, and oil – cannot provide an efficient basis operating as they do in competition and with little co-ordination even of R & D, never mind capital investment. The situation within the E.E.C. is no more satisfactory, with no real signs of inter-industry collaboration; it is hardly surprising that the achievement of a common energy policy presents apparently insuperable difficulties. The provision of an Energy Board with a strong co-ordinating role would certainly do much to improve energy planning in the U.K. and hasten the implementation of an integrated U.K. energy grid calling upon each individual fuel where appropriate to fulfil a particular demand whilst encouraging flexibility in supply and energy conservation.

I would like to acknowledge the many useful discussions I had at the NATO Science Committee meeting on "Thermal Energy Storage" held at Turnberry in March 1976.

References

[1] "Electrical Energy Storage", by G. C. Gardner, A. B. Hart, R. Moffit, and J. K. Wright, C.E.R.L. RL/L/R 1906.
[2] "Storing the Energy of Compressed Air", by I. Glendenning, C.E.G.B. "Research", May 1975, No. 2, p. 21.
[3] "Electrochemical Batteries for Bulk Energy Storage", by A. B. Hart and A. H. Webb, C.E.G.B. Report RD/L/R1902.
[4] R. F. Post and S. F. Post, *Scientific American*, 1973, **229**, (6), p. 17.
[5] P. H. Margen, "Thermal Storage in Rock Chambers", 4th International Conference on Peaceful Uses of Atomic Energy, 1972, **4**, p. 177.
[6] "Will Hydrogen Transmission replace Electricity?", by P. J. Hampson, A. B. Hart, B. Jones, D. T. Swift-Hook, J. J. Syrett, and J. K. Wright, C.E.G.B. Report RD/L/R1901.

electricity for release during the day. At the present time, sudden increases in demand are met using "spinning reserve", an arrangement whereby some older plant is running at low load so that it can increase its output fairly quickly on demand. Of course this presupposes an interlinking grid network to make the total generating capacity one responsive, interactive electricity production system.

(a) Pumped Storage
Spinning reserve is inappropriate for dealing with the nuclear generating problem, and pumped storage schemes are being developed at Ffestiniog (now established 360 MW of storage) and Dinorwic which will provide from stored water some 1500 MW for 5.2h at an overall efficiency of 26%.[1]

Looking further to the future, a tidal power generation scheme with associated pumped storage capacity has been proposed for the estuary of the River Severn. Fig. 2 shows a scheme which could provide a steady output of 5000 MW if operated in conjunction with pumped storage and would cost about £500/installed kW, much the same as today's nuclear power plant cost.

Unfortunately, pumped storage schemes can only be installed in appropriate geographical locations. Water storage in underground excavated deep caverns is also a possibility but an expensive one. Target costs suggested by the C.E.G.B. for pumped storage are £200/kW and £17/kWh.

(b) Compressed Air Storage
The storage of energy in the form of compressed air in huge underground chambers has been mooted for 25 years, but without practical demonstration, although a German company NWK is building a 290 MW installation due to be completed in 1977. The principle is straightforward and the object to improve on the efficiency of the peak-load gas turbine. Air is compressed and cooled using an electrically driven compressor during off-peak periods. At peak demand, the air is released and burnt in the gas turbine with distillate fuel oil. This uprates the gas turbine efficiency by a factor of 3. A serious energy loss in this system is the heat lost in cooling the compressed air before storage. The C.E.G.B. has proposed[2] a scheme for storing this energy in a regenerative system between the compressor and the cavern (Fig. 3) so that the heat can be returned

Energy-efficient Processes for the Chemical Industry

By H. L.Roberts: Imperial Chemical Industries Limited, Mond Division

THE manufacture of chemical products involves the extraction of basic raw materials, their conversion into intermediates, and a succession of steps by which these chemical intermediates are converted into products for the eventual use of the end consumer. Each one of thesesteps has an energy associated with it, and in considering energy-efficient processes it is necessary to consider the overall energy usage, as economies at any one stage can cause diseconomies in the others. Indeed, perhaps it is desirable to go even further and look at the use to which the final consumer makes of the product, as it is here that the greatest economies may be possible. (Fig. 1).

I shall, here, concentrate on the intermediates which go into a chemical process and the subsequent steps rather than involve myself with the extractive industry, about which I know too little to make any useful comment. Further, I intend to use a small number of processes to illustrate the principles by which one may appoach a more energy-efficient chemical industry rather than try to give any global picture of how things may change. I shall start by considering the steps which need to be carried out in the conversion of salt and crude oil into poly(vinyl chloride), as this illustrates a number of important principles. (Fig. 2).

The first point to note here is the constraints imposed by co-production of other materials. In the case of salt to chlorine and caustic soda, there is a fundamental constraint of Nature that for every atom of chlorine there is an associated metal ion. This must either be used or disposed of in some way. In the case of crude oil, it is conceivable in theory at least that all of it could be made into ethylene; this does not yet seem an objective at which we could usefully target a programme of work. Therefore we are dealing with a

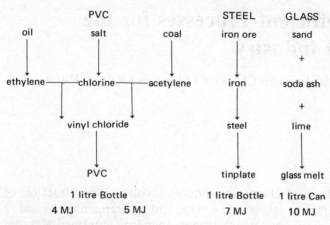

FIGURE 1   Energy input to non-returnable containers.

complex energy and economic balance. The second point, which is at once obvious, is the substantial number of steps involved and the potential that exists for telescoping these. This, however, is probably more significant for savings in manpower and capital than in energy. It is worth noting how little the energy content of the manufacturing plant itself contributes to the overall energy usage (see Table 1). This is not to belittle process integration savings, as in terms of production costs they could easily outweigh energy savings.

Let us now turn to the individual steps in a little more detail. (Fig. 2).

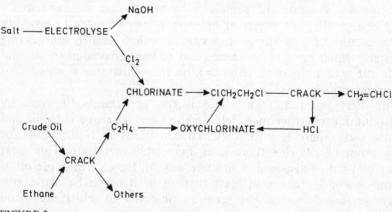

FIGURE 2

Table 1: Capital energy content of 100,000 tonnes/year plant

	GJ	Percent of cost
Vessels and machinery	5430 ⎫	20.1
Column packing and internals	1150 ⎭	
Pipework	4040	9.1
Civil engineering	1030	1.2
Structural steelwork	1550	1.2
	13200	

Manufacture of chlorine and caustic soda is now carried out exclusively by electrolysis. This at once imposes an energy penalty. The generation of electricity by thermal power, whether the source of heat is fossil, nuclear, or thermo-nuclear, involves the operation of a Carnot cycle which limits energy usage to about 45%; the current C.E.G.B. average for power purchased from the grid system is about 30%. This can be increased up to an upper limit of 80% if the power station is sited on the chemical plant itself, enabling the pass-out steam to be used in other factory operations such as distillation or drying, although a figure of 50—60% would be more usual. This shows that there is a considerable incentive to find a non-electrolytic route to chlorine. One possible system is shown in Fig. 3.

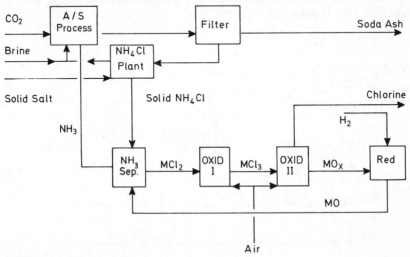

FIGURE 3

Table 2

Chlorine from NH_4Cl	GJ/t Cl_2
Production of solid NH_4Cl	1.6
Production of Cl_2 from NH_4Cl	
Fuel oil	8.9
Hydrogen	5.2
Electricity	3.6
Steam	0.7
Credit to A/S process	−4.0
Total Energy Content	16.0
Chlorine by Electrolysis	
Electricity	21.6

An energy analysis of this process is itself very instructive. It is necessary to use energy in three main ways (Table 2):

(1) Subliming NH_4Cl
(2) Heating and cooling the reaction mass
(3) Pumping gases

When all these energy steps are added up, it is found that the overall energy usage is not greatly different from that for the direct production of chlorine even at 30% generation efficiency, and is greater if 50% is achieved.

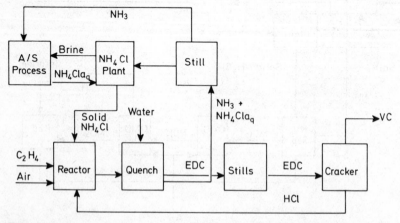

FIGURE 4

Table 3

| | Energy content | GJ/t VC |
	Conventional route	NH_4Cl route
Ethylene	40.3	40.3
Chlorine	14.4	
Ammonium chloride		−1.6
Processing	15.0	19.8
	69.7	58.5

It can be seen from Fig. 2 that the first thing to be done with chlorine is to treat it with ethylene. This reaction is an exothermic process where heat is available only for low-grade use at the best and may well be wasted.

If the ethylene can be introduced into a chemical route for chlorine, could this be an energy saving step? The answer to this is both encouraging and a problem.

Figure 4 shows a system for the reaction of C_2H_4 with NH_4Cl to give EDC directly.

This makes a major energy saving by (in effect) using the heat of chlorination of ethylene to sublime ammonium chloride. The problem is to find a catalyst which will catalyse the oxidation of HCl

Table 4

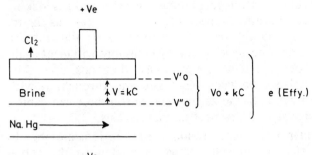

$$Energy = \frac{0.756(Vo + kC)}{e}$$

= 3.68 MWh D.C./t electrochemical unit.

≡ 1.8 MWhac/t Cl_2

Vo = 3.3 V

K = 0.18 VM^2/kA

c = 7 kA/M^2

e = 0.93

while not catalysing that of NH_3. While not impossible in principle this is difficult in practice. The problem is essentially that conditions which do not burn ammonia give an inadequate conversion of C_2H_4 and NH_4Cl and vice versa. Given success, however, the energy savings are substantial.

If, however, for the present, electrolytic routes to chlorine are the only ones available then what can be done to conserve energy? Let us first of all set out an energy budget for electrolysis using a conventional mercury cell.

The first term is the reversible EMF of the cell. The other factors we can, in principle, alter. Clearly the closer the gap between the electrodes the less the energy used, and improvements have been made continuously in this direction from 4 mm in 1950 to 2.5 mm in 1975. The other interesting factor is current density. The equation for cell energy consumption can be written:

$$E = \frac{0.756 \, (\text{Vo} + kc)}{e}$$

Where Vo = reversible EMF

C = current density in amps m^{-2}

e = current efficiency

k = constant

This term kc is mainly a function of Ohm's law up to the point at which over-voltage due to atom recombination rates and gas locking at electrode surfaces become important. Therefore for maximum energy economy one should pass no current! This illustrates a general point which anyone seeking energy economy will meet again and again. The most efficient energy usage demands very slow kinetics, and the balance between plant size and throughput with energy usage will always change as the relationship between capital and manpower costs vary with respect to energy costs.

Which other, and perhaps more fundamental, options are open to us here? Clearly the overall cell voltage is related to the actual process taking place at the electrodes. In electrolysis with the mercury cell we have two reactions:

(1) Formation of Na/Hg
(2) Cl_2 production

$$(\text{Glucose})_n \xrightarrow{\text{cellulase}} (\text{Glucose})_{n-3} + 3\,\text{Glucose}$$
$$\text{polysaccharide}$$

$$3\,\text{Glucose} + 3O_2 + 3H_2O \xrightarrow{\text{glucose oxidase}} 3\,\text{gluconic acid} + 3H_2O_2$$

$$RH + Cl^- + H_2O_2 \xrightarrow{\text{chloroperoxidase}} RCl + OH^- + H_2O$$

FIGURE 5

In principle the subsequent reaction of Na/Hg with water could be done as a fuel-cell reaction to give H_2 + NaOH + electrical energy. This would give a saving of 1V and at once give an energy saving of 30%.

The practical problems of doing this have never been solved. The economic rewards are immense from saving 30% of the electrical energy or at least 0.6 MWh per ton of chlorine, with a world production of 22 M tons.

The second approach would be to make C_2H_4 or other reagent available at the chlorine-evolving electrode. This again could lead to a cell voltage reduction of the order of 0.5 V. This also has been tried but no successful procedure has emerged.

Another approach to industrial chemical synthesis is to look at the way Nature produces compounds of the equivalent type, as natural processes involve only low temperatures and are often specific and efficient. It may be possible to use the natural production system directly, or by understanding it mechanistically, adapt the principle to chemical synthesis. However, natural synthetic routes are not always very efficient energetically. A well known example of this is the 10% energy conversion by beef cattle of feedstock to meat, and although the soya bean balances its energy budget rather better, people still prefer roast beef. Another example is a brewery where the capital and operating cost per ton of alcohol produced is still vastly in excess of the corresponding petrochemical plant.

It is not widely known that Nature does produce very significant quantities of chlorinated hydrocarbons. The best established example is methyl chloride for which Lovelock [2] has estimated a production of 28×10^6 tonnes per annum from seaweed, although slash-and-burn agriculture also contributes. Lovelock has also proposed on the basis of its geographical distribution that carbon tetrachloride is also produced by Nature. Certainly plant species also contain C–Cl bonds in addition to chloride salts of organic bases.

One synthetic pathway by which C–Cl bonds are formed is via the enzyme chloroperoxidase.[3] The available evidence suggests that the active chlorinating agent is a form of Cl^+ or OCl^- rather than Cl. Although, in principle, ethylene could be oxidised to vinyl chloride in the presence of Cl^-:

$$C_2H_4 + Cl^- + \tfrac{1}{2}O_2 \longrightarrow C_2H_3Cl + OH^- \quad \Delta G^0_{298} = -46.4 \text{ kJ Mol}^{-1}$$
$$\Delta H^0_{298} = -83.7 \text{ kJ Mol}^{-1}$$

the initial step of the chloroperoxidase route can not be achieved by molecular oxygen.

$$Cl^- + \tfrac{1}{2}O_2 \longrightarrow OCl^- \quad \Delta G^0_{298} = 93 \text{ kJ Mol}^{-1}$$
$$\Delta H^0_{298} = 73 \text{ kJ Mol}^{-1}$$

Hydrogen peroxide is the key intermediate

$$Cl^- + H_2O_2 \longrightarrow OCl^- + H_2O \quad \Delta G^0_{298} = -11 \text{ kJ Mol}^{-1}$$
$$\Delta H^0_{298} = -34 \text{ kJ Mol}^{-1}$$

This treatment totally ignores the problem of how to deal with the co-produced alkali, which in Nature is taken up by the buffer capacity of the organism. The mechanism for the production of methyl chloride by seaweed is less well known, but may be via CH_3I or CH_3Br and halogen exchange to give CH_3Cl. Once again the OH^- co-produced is taken up by the pH buffer provided by the ocean, a resource not available to an industrial process.

So far we have been concerned with energy-efficient ways of producing a single product, poly (vinyl chloride). The type of analysis carried out could be applied to any other chemical product, and no doubt similar thinking has been done for these products by their producers. Let us now take a look in a different direction.

Table 5 shows the energy content of two familiar articles, a 1 litre bottle and a fertiliser sack. This Table shows that it is important to consider not only the energy content of the material used but the

Table 5

Energy content	Glass	P.P.	PVC	Paper
Material GJ/t	19	107	82	59
End product MJ/unit				
1 litre bottle	9.7	2.1	4.1	
Fertiliser sack		8.8	16.8	29.4

Table 6: Energy used in various cultivation systems

	Fuel l/ha	GJ/ha
Traditional cultivation	46.7	1.56
Reduced cultivation	32.7	1.09
Paraquat (0.56 kg/ha)		0.26
		1.35
Direct drilling	7.4	0.25
Paraquat (0.84 kg/ha)		0.39
		0.64

weight of it needed to produce a given effect. Before drawing the conclusion that bottles and sacks should be made from polypropylene, it is important to remember that the end-user is concerned with price and suitability, not energy content. What it does illustrate is that polymers based on oil are energetically not unfavourable when compared with alternatives. Coal and cellulose are much less efficient as sources of chemical product than oil, and an energy-conscious world would probably use these for the basic energy needs and husband its oil reserves as a chemical feedstock in the period before non-combustion techniques for generating power become available.

Another illustration that energy economy is not always obvious can be taken from the field of agriculture.[4]

Table 6 shows the costs of cultivation using traditional methods of ploughing, harrowing, and sowing and how this can be reduced by methods involving chemical weedkillers despite the high intrinsic energy content of the weedkiller.

The whole of this treatment has been concerned with energy and has ignored the energy source. Clearly this is an over-simplification. Fossil fuels and fission fuels have only a limited availability. The renewable resources, essentially solar energy tapped via growing plants, wind, water power, and other means will one day be our energy and raw material source. How we use them in an energy-efficient manner to provide services that customers want is a problem for the next generation of research workers. It will certainly provide them with a worthwhile challenge.

Acknowledgement

The author thanks Dr. M. J. Weeks and Mr. A. McCulloch of the Mond Division Research Economics Section for their help in the preparation of this paper.

References

[1] For example: "Chlorine", Ed. J. S. Sconce, American Chemical Society Monograph No. 154.
[2] J. E. Lovelock, *Nature* 1975, **256**, 193.
[3] D. R. Morris and L. P. Hagar, *J. Biol. Chem.*, 1966, **241**, 3582.
[4] M. B. Green and A. McCulloch, *J. Sci. Food Agric.*, 1976, 27, 95.

A Chemical Challenge in Nuclear Energy

by J. S. Broadley; Head of Health and Safety Division, Dounreay
Experimental Reactor Establishment

Introduction

THE element plutonium is often described in the literature as the
"atomic bomb" element and consequently has been given a bad
reputation. It was named plutonium after the planet Pluto because
plutonium came after the element neptunium and the plant Pluto
came after the planet Neptune in the solar system; this name has
given the popular media the opportunity to refer to the element by
such titles as the Element of Hell and other such emotive phrases.
The element has been portrayed to the public as cancer-producing
which is also a very emotive subject. So, as you can see, plutoniun
has had more adverse publicity than most industrial materials.

I do not intend to try to minimise the challenge that working with
the element has introduced into technology; its properties demand the
utmost care, respect, and foresight. There is already considerable
experience in dealing with it safely; the nuclear industry early
recognised the need for a quantitative knowledge of the risks and its
properties are now better known than those of many other toxic
materials which have been in use for years.

Against this background I will try to show that plutonium is no
worse than many other materials, and that procedures have been
developed and risks assessed. These have made it possible for it to be
used safely in the nuclear industry.

Reasons for Interest in Plutonium

The primary reason for developing fast reactors is that they offer the
prospect of obtaining about 50–70 times more heat from uranium
than can be obtained with thermal reactors alone. This advantage
leads to lower nuclear fuel costs and a dramatic reduction in uranium
ore requirements. The fast fission type of reactor can use plutonium

as a primary fuel and at the same time produce from uranium-238 more plutonium than it uses.

This is not, of course, a contradiction of the second law of thermodynamics, since the overall entropy change is positive, but it is the conversion of a relatively useless material into one which can be used as a source of energy. Nor does the fast fission reactor offer us something for nothing, because although the reactor makes more fuel than it uses, it does require effort to extract the new plutonium from the initial fuel elements which had been used to fuel the reactor. For countries, which like Britain have to import uranium and have relatively small reserves of other fuels, this is a strategic as well as an economic gain.

There are many people who oppose fast fission reactors and who argue that other forms of energy are available and more acceptable.

A recent paper, from the Energy Technology Support Unit of the Department of Energy,[1] considered these other forms in detail and listed the contributions that new energy sources might make to Britain's estimated energy requirements in the year 2000 AD.

They estimate that the price of solar water heaters will have to fall by a factor of three before they are cheap enough to warrant encouraging their use. Solar space heating, while potentially more promising than water heating, faces an even steeper uphill struggle, and its growth rate will depend on the rate at which new houses are built.

Electricity-generating wind energy systems require no great technical breakthrough, but their best use might be to replace small diesel power stations. The limit for a fully developed wind power programme in the U.K. is estimated to be 10,000 generators each of one megawatt rating, feeding to the grid system.

Tidal and wave power are technically feasible, but would be prohibitively expensive in the immediate future. "The economic and technical factors," says ETSU, "should be kept under review to determine whether a more promising approach to the problem emerges in the future."

Geothermal energy suffers from technical and geographical problems. Also it produces low-grade heat rather than electricity. "The distribution and use of this heat in substantial quantities is a technical and economic problem common to the evaluation of the use of 'waste' heat from power stations." However, ETSU reckons that we know so little about Britain's geothermal prospects that some further investigation is warranted but again it cannot be considered an immediate source of energy.

Many observers have attempted to estimate the gap between the available fossil fuel resources and likely demands for energy based on estimates of future economic growth rates. Reasonably based studies[2] within the U.K. (which agree broadly with those of other authorities) indicate that in 2000 AD fossil fuel resources will have dwindled to such an extent that an alternative energy source capable of producing some thousands of Gigawatts – perhaps as much as 12,000 GW of some form of primary electricity will need to be installed, in the Western World. Since the potenial contribution of the sources of electricity reviewed by the ETSU to this total is likely to be minimal, the burden must fall almost entirely on nuclear power, if the standard of living is to be maintained.

This is the picture which has emerged after detailed studies in the U.K.; it is confirmed by similar studies in the U.S.A. It is generally accepted that nuclear energy is the only developed source which can fill the gap likely to exist at the year 2000 AD and consequently we must examine the supply of nuclear fuel.

In the long term, nuclear fuel supplies should create no difficulty. Considering firstly uranium, the total of "proven reserves" and "reasonably assured additional reserves" in western markets which are expected to be won at market prices up to $15 per lb, is some three million tonnes of uranium. If all this available uranium were to be used as fuel for thermal reactors, then shortages could arise by the end of the century. However, the large-scale use of fast breeder reactors will bring about some 50–70 times better utilisation of the power latent in uranium and the three million tonnes, for instance, could provide fuel for the estimated 12,000 GW for about 250 years.

Problems posed by Plutonium Technology

A fast reactor energy programme inevitably means that new chemical plants have to be built and operated to manufacture fuel elements, other plants have to be built to extract the manufactured plutonium chemically, and in addition there will be the associated facilities such as development and analytical laboratories, storage and waste recovery facilities.

Such a programme will increase the number of people working with plutonium. Also, since storage and transport are involved, this will have to be carried out in such a way as to provide the necessary protection of the public.

There are two main reasons why plutonium is considered to be hazardous:

(a) If sufficient pure material is available it is possible to produce a nuclear explosion; i.e., the element has a critical mass above which neutrons escaping from the nucleus have a multiplication factor greater than 1.

(b) The radiotoxicity of the element is high.

The Critical Mass

Now let us consider these hazards individually; the nuclear industry has recognised these problems from the beginning and has worked with the material to defined procedures.

There are no serious critics who would argue that industrial processes based on plutonium are not possible because of the dangers of criticality. Thirty years of experience has shown that by a combination of geometrically safe design, detailed managerial procedures, and strict material accountancy (no more strict than the methods used by banks to account for money), then it is possible to embark on the sophisticated technology required for plutonium with assurance.

I could, of course, go into much greater detail on this particular problem of plutonium handling, but since I would like to deal mostly with the aspect of plutonium technology where many consider the greater hazards lie, I will not elaborate on a topic which I feel has been technically and socially accepted.

Radiotoxicity

On the question of the toxicity of plutonium there have been many emotive statements and frequently the public are told that plutonium is the most toxic material known to mankind In addition, apparently quantitative statements have been made like the assertion that just one ounce of plutonium can cause 30×10^6 cancer deaths. These statements are very misleading and represent an over-simplification which cannot be justified.

As a heavy metal, plutonium is probably more or less as toxic as the other heavy metals in industrial use, the particular problem is its radiotoxicity. If plutonium is inhaled or ingested the majority is eliminated by natural biological processes; the remainder distributes itself throughout the body, and can lodge in the lungs, liver, or bone where in the extreme case (the bone) the retention period can be a lifetime. Plutonium is an energetic α-emitter and consequently subjects the host organ in the body to local irradiation, and the consequences could be the eventual production of a cancer many years (15–45) after the exposure. However, there has been no human case of cancer yet found which was due to plutonium, in spite of the fact that a number of early American workers at Los Alamos were seriously exposed. Nevertheless the people who work in the nuclear industry are very conscious of the possible dangers and work to internationally accepted standards.

International Standards and National Control

An organisation known as the International Commission on Radiological Protection, after many years of detailed study, poduced in 1959 recommendations for the maximum amount of irradiation that the various organs and tissues of the body can withstand without detectable hazard to either the individual exposed or to subsequent generations, this latter requirement being necessary because the germ cells of the body are the most sensitive and changes to the genetic material may be transmitted to future generations.

They have kept the situation under review, and with increasing use of radiation in almost every activity of modern society, the Commission has widened its responsibilities to advise over the whole field of radiological protection. It has produced recommendations with regard to permissible doses for exposure of radiation workers, for individual members of the public, and for populations.

There are also other international bodies with responsibilities in this field, United Nations Scientific Committee on the Effects of Atomic Radiation (UNSCEAR), International Atomic Energy Agency (IAEA), World Health Organisation (WHO), and Nuclear Energy Agency (NEA). As far as this country is concerned, the Medical Research Council (MRC) has the duty of determining the biological effects of radiation and the National Radiological Protection Board (NRPB) is a statutory body set up by legislation in 1970 to provide information and advice to industry or Government departments with responsibilities in relation to the protection of the public from radiation hazards. There is a continuing dialogue between members of these bodies and the International Commission on Radiological Protection (ICRP), and the recommendations of the Commission as interpreted by the MRC are officially accepted as the relevant standards for this country.

Various Ministries have responsibilities for radiological protection depending on the field of interest, e.g. licensing of installations, radioactive waste management and transport. Some have advisory committees, e.g., Nuclear Safety Advisory Committee; some have special inspectorates, e.g., Radiochemical Inspectors of the Department of the Environment and the Health and Safety Executive who are responsible for ensuring that statutory regulations are adhered to.

Recommendations of ICRP

The Commission makes recommendations in the form of Permissible Doses which will not be harmful to an individual. In the case of internal emitters these are used to derive the Permissible Body Burden, and air concentrations, in which an individual can spend a working life without harm, called a Maximum Permissible Concentration (MPC).

You may ask where the ICR obtained the data to make its recommendations. In the case of plutonium, ideally the MPC should be based on studies of humans who have been exposed to plutonium under working conditions and over an extended period of time. Because of the care taken, human data for plutonium are very scarce; however, for radium, another bone-seeking α-emitter, there is an accumulation of human experience over the past fifty years, which is the minimum time for selecting a concentration to which a man may be exposed as a chronic exposure over his working life. Since man has had years of experience with radium this is the basis of reference in choosing the MPC for similar α-emitting nuclides. There is a large group of people who were radium dial painters, and there were patients treated medically with radium, and persons using public water supplies relatively rich in radium; these have furnished the best sources of continuous human exposure from which to observe the effects of an internally deposited α-emitter.

In addition to this information which was specific for α-emitters, the Commission also had available to them a large body of evidence on human exposure to radiation. The following groups of people have been studied:

(1) The survivors of the atomic bomb attacks in the Japanese cities of Hiroshima and Nagasaki.

(2) Patients suffering from the arthritic disease, ankylosing spondylitis, who were treated with large doses of X-radiation.
(3) American and British radiologists who had been occupationally exposed.
These have been augmented by:
(4) Various animal studies, mostly on rats, mice, and dogs, exposed to radiation.

The doses received in all these cases were much higher than presently permitted levels and in applying the results to occupational exposures the ICRP made the pessimistic assumption that there is a linear dose—effect relationship. By this is meant that if there was evidence that when 1000 people were exposed to a dose of 100 rad and there were later 10 excess cancers found, they assume that if 1000 are each exposed to a dose of 1 rad there will be an excess of 0.1 cancer or 1 excess cancer per 10,000 man rads. It is likely that there is some small dose which is not harmful at all, but since this cannot be proved as the available statistics at high dose do not allow it to be demonstrated, the ICRP have chosen the most pessimistic assumptions in recommending the permissible levels.

Using data of this type the ICRP came to certain conclusions about how much radiation the various organs of the body could accept. In this country these quantities have been incorporated into Factories Act Regulations and have been laid down as maximum permissible doses and industry is obliged by law to remain below these levels. These doses are shown in Table 1.

In the case of lungs, bones, and liver irradiated by internal emitters the restriction required to achieve these doses is expressed as a maximum permissible annual intake, this limit being set at such a value that if workers were to spend fifty years at the maximum permissible annual intake then at the end of their working life they would still not have been exposed to an unacceptable amount.

Table 1: **Maximum permissible doses recommended by ICRP workers**

Gonads and red bone marrow and, in the case of uniform irradiation, the whole body	5 rems in a year
Skin; thyroid; bone	30 rems in a year
Hands and forearms; feet and ankles	75 rems in a year
All other organs	15 rems in a year

Protection of Workers

As these levels are set for a working life of fifty years, the quantities are as a consequence exceedingly small, and require the use of very special techniques to protect the working environment. The MPC for plutonium-239 in air in a working laboratory is 2×10^{-6} $\mu Ci/m^3$ (3.2×10^{-11} g/m^3), so all laboratory work involving plutonium is done in glove boxes which give an operator complete protection provided the integrity is maintained. When remote handling cannot be used, work is done in pressurised suits, which have endeared themselves to the popular media and become a symbol of the atomic energy industry. In fact very little work is actually done in these suits; their use is almost wholly confined to maintenance, which cannot be carried out by remote handling.

Estimation of Risks

Because of the present publicity being given to plutonium, the MRC has recently carried out an extensive study of its toxicity, looking at the problem from a statistical point of view, and estimating the risks which may result from exposure to its compounds.[3]

Most of the radiation workers around the world receive on average less then one tenth of the permissible level each year.[4] No harm has yet been demonstrated in these workers and there are no observations which tell us the actual risk consequent on such continued exposure, but statistical estimates of risk may be made using the mortality data which are available from the groups of people studied and adopting the ICRP principles, namely that there is no threshold dose below which there is no effect, and that the risk associated with irradiation of natural tissue is directly (linearly) proportional to the total accumulated dose received by that tissue regardless of the time over which the dose may have been received.

Information is accumulating which suggests that this procedure is bound to over-estimate the risk at lower exposure levels. This and all other numerical estimates of cancer risk for exposures at the recommended dose limits, must be nominal since they are derived on the basis of this hypothesis relating risk to radiation dose which has not been substantiated. The true risk could well be less and, in some people's view, very much less, and should be compared with the already present lifetime risk of 15–20% of naturally occurring fatality from cancer. The results of this MRC study are shown in Table 2. It can be seen that under the worst conditions the maximum risk is 15 in 10^4, for each permissible annual intake.

Table 2: Estimates for selected tissues of dose commitment per picocurie intake and risk per rem and of the total "nominal" risk of cancer from current values of permissible annual intake for plutonium-239

Organ of ref		Current permissible annual intake (μCi)	Dose commitment present estimate (Rem per μCi)	Present estimate of risk in individual organs (per million per rem)	Present estimate of risk in individual organs (per million per pCi intake)	Total "nominal" cancer risk from a permissible annual intake (per 10,000)
1 INGESTION						
(i) Soluble	Bone	40μCi (0.6mg)	0.4	5	2×10^{-6}	
	Liver		0.2	20	4×10^{-6}	
	Gut	—	0.1	20	2×10^{-6}	3
	Kidney		—	—	—	
	Gonads		0.02	25	0.5×10^{-6}	
(ii) Insoluble	Bone	200μCi (3mg)	0.01	5	0.05×10^{-6}	
	Liver		0.008	20	0.15×10^{-6}	
	Gut		0.1	20	2×10^{-6}	4
	Gonads		0.0006	25	0.015×10^{-6}	
2 INHALATION						
(i) Soluble	Bone	0.005μCi (0.08μg)	2000	5	1×10^{-2}	
	Liver		1000	20	2×10^{-2}	
	Gut		0.05	20	—	
	Lung		30	25	0.75×10^{-3}	2
	Kidney		—	—	—	
	Gonads		80	25	0.20×10^{-2}	
(ii) Insoluble	Bone		700	5	0.35×10^{-2}	
	Liver		400	20	0.08×10^{-2}	
	Gut		0.06	20	—	
	Lung	0.08μCi (1μg)	300	25	0.75×10^{-2}	15
	Gonads		40	25	0.10×10^{-2}	

The total nominal cancer risk given above is statistically the maximum possible risk and on the same basis could well be zero. In addition it must be noted that these figures are for a lifetime and are only per year if the intake is received each year, and care therefore has to be taken if comparisons are to be made. Obviously the nuclear industry carefully controls the situation by monitoring the environment and the people involved. Firstly the level of plutonium in the working environment is kept well below the permissible level and the monitoring of employees is carried out on a routine basis to check that the environmental monitoring and precautions have not been circumvented. On this basis and past experience it is reasonable to assume that on average radiation workers get no more than one tenth of the permitted dose each year[4] then statistically the maximum risk can be expressed as 1.5 per 10^4 /year (but could be zero).

There is at present no evidence from human populations of the genetic effects of radiation. No differences were found in a comparison of 30,000 children born to irradiated parents with 40,000 born to non-irradiated parents in Hiroshima and Nagasaki during the period 1948–53. In addition, investigations carried out into the health of populations in parts of the world where natural background radiation levels are much higher than elsewhere, up to about 1.5 rem/year, have so far failed to find evidence of any radiation effect.

Before comparing these risks with some others to which we are exposed I must emphasise that because these radiation risks are based on pessimistic assumptions, the Secretary of the ICRP has cautioned against the use of them in comparing the safety of operations involving radiation with operations involving other types of hazard as there is a real danger that such a comparison might lead to the adoption of a real risk to remove a supposed one.

Below are some recent statistics[5] relating to non-radiological risks:

Table 3: Fatalities per 10,000 persons per year

Road accidents	1.20
Home accidents	1.80
Coal mining	6.00
All Factory Act Workers	0.65
Pneumoconiosis (miners)	20.00
Lung cancer men 45–55 years	0.91
55–65 years	2.92
Heavy smokers 50–54 years	110.00

Industries which are commonly regarded as dangerous have annual fatality rates from accidents at work averaging from one to ten in ten thousand, or more, while industries which are commonly regarded as safe have annual fatality rates of less than one in ten thousand per year, which is about the same as the statistically maximum risk of cancer from the average of one tenth of the permissible annual intake previously discussed. It must be remembered that we are comparing an actual event which can take place immediately with a possible and maximum risk that may take place in 15–45 years.

Toxic Dose

In a recent paper from the U.S.A. the problem has been looked at from yet another point of view.[6] In this case the data have been used to calculate the total risk and to relate this to the quantity likely to cause cancer, not to the quantity which can be lived with without causing cancer. Using the data on the distribution of plutonium after inhalation and ingestion and assessing risks in a similar way to that adopted by the MRC, statistics can be obtained from the groups of people exposed to radiation, such as atomic bomb survivors, which allow this total risk to be estimated. Under the usual assumption of linearity, it is calculated that there could be one cancer death for every 1400 micrograms (85 microcuries) of insoluble plutonium-239 inhaled by humans, the insoluble compounds being the most hazardous.

This figure is of course obtained from a statistical assessment of data with a large population and does not mean that more than 1400 micrograms inhaled by a single person is fatal and less than 1400 micrograms is not; it means that if a total of N times 1400 micrograms is inhaled by a number of people much larger than N, we may expect about N eventual fatalities. The cancers, if any, would occur between 15 and 45 years after the radiation exposure, at an average age of about 55, so they correspond to an average loss of life expectancy of 15 years.

Plutonium obtained from reactor fuel cycles has important quantities of other plutonium isotopes. In Fast Breeder Reactor fuel, after a few cycles plutonium-239 represents only one seventh of the α-emitting activity in the plutonium mixture, whereas it contains 74% of the mass, so the mixture gives 5.4 times as much radiation dose per gram as plutonium-239. It is conventional to express toxic hazards in terms of micrograms, so to ensure that the hazard is not underestimated, we will express it as micrograms of "reactor-plutonium" which we define to be 3.0 grams per curie, or 5.4 times more radioactive than plutonium-239. The dose of "reactor-plutonium" which could statistically cause cancer, is then $1400/5.4 = 260$ micrograms.

It is customary to define the lethal concentration of a poisonous inhalant in terms of the amount that would prove fatal to 50% of those exposed after four hours (LC-50). In four hours an average man inhales 5 cubic metres (m^3) of air, hence LC-50 for insoluble reactor-plutonium based on cancer induction would be 0.036 mg/m^3.

The LC-50's for other materials are always based on short-term death. Some examples in mg/m^3 are cadmium fumes: 10, mercury vapour: 30, and phosgene: 65. There have been few studies of long-term cancer induction by chemicals, but such effects are known to exist for much lower concentrations in air than are lethal in the short term, there are no data available for a direct comparison, but it can be seen that the lethal concentrations of quite common substances are not all that much greater than the concentration of plutonium compounds which statistically may cause an eventual cancer 15 to 45 years later.

If plutonium is ingested in soluble form, only 3×10^{-5} of the quantity passes from the gastro-intestinal tract into the bloodstream, and under these conditions the toxic dose would be 2.3 grams of reactor-grade plutonium, or an LD-50 of 1.6 gram. The LD-50 figures for other substances are selenium oxide: 0.3 gram, potassium cyanide: 0.7 gram, mercury dichloride: 0.8 gram, and caffeine: 14 grams. All of these cause death within a short time.

Again, there seem to be no data on the amount of carcinogens that must be taken orally in order to induce cancer, and there is no known mechanism for plutonium taken orally to cause early death other than that with truly massive doses.

In Table 4 we summarise the cancer-causing doses by two main intake routes.[6] We may expect one cancer for every multiple of the indicated quantities that are taken in by humans. Because no threshold dose is assumed, then statistically the number of people over which the dose is spread does not matter as long as it is large. Common sense indicates that there must be an upper limit, otherwise individual doses become so small that it is not possible to believe that they would cause harm. If the population were infinite, in the extreme case the individual dose would be zero. For example, if a total of

Table 4: Summary of theoretical doses of reactor
plutonium and plutonium-239 which could statistically
cause one cancer

| | (in microgram intake) | |
	Reactor Pu	^{239}Pu
Inhalation	260	1400
Ingestion with food	2.3×10^6	12×10^6

14,000 micrograms of plutonium-239 were inhaled, be it by 10^3 or 10^6 persons, the statistical number who might die from cancer could be a maximum of 10 but could equally well be zero. Normally we would expect 2×10^4 deaths from natural cancers in 10^6 persons so it is doubtful if even the maximum statistical increase could be detected.

These toxicities are very much less than often supposed in popular discussion, and under no circumstances is there any reason for saying that plutonium is the most lethal substance known to man. The greatest risk is inhalation of the insoluble compounds, and since these are not volatile, widespread dispersion is not likely, in fact it is difficult to achieve. It is difficult to compare plutonium risks with other toxic risks because it does not cause immediate harm but even if we assumed that it did then there are biological agents that are orders of magnitude more toxic. Botulinus toxin is lethal in sub-microgram amounts, and anthrax spores are ten times more toxic again.

Therefore, while plutonium is indeed very toxic, its industrial use certainly entails no hazards which make it more socially undesirable than many industrial chemicals such as halogen compounds and the cyanides. It has received more detailed consideration by the nuclear industry than almost any other toxic substance has received from other industries, and even pessimistic estimates of its risks show them to be much less than modern technology accepts as the price we pay for industrialisation. To avoid risks completely is not possible; even in an agrarian society there must be some real, if small, risk associated with a plough and sickle.

Conclusions

In conclusion I would suggest that plutonium has presented industry with a challenge for several reasons.

The first of these is the attention that has to be paid to design and construction to ensure that plant can be safely operated without the fissile nature of the material causing concern. There is also the extremely low concentration permitted in the working environment because of the rigorous safety standards which the nuclear industry has imposed. This requires that the working environmental concentrations are at all times below 3.2×10^{-11} g/cm^3 and imposes a discipline not generally expected in the chemical industry.

Before such discipline could be rationally imposed it was necessary to have a real quantitative measure of the toxic risks. This type of approach has involved the nuclear industry in a more than usual amount of work on safety and has led to a good safety record. Additionally the rigorous control of operating conditions probably has a bearing on the statistics of the death rate for nuclear industry employees, which is lower in virtually every medical category than for the population at large as shown in the Registrar General's statistics. This applies to both our present employees and our pensioners.

References

[1] "Alternative Energy Sources for the UK", J. K. Dawson, *Atom*, No. 231, January 1976.
[2] "Meeting future world demands for Energy: The Role of Nuclear Power", R. L. R. Nicholson, *Atom*, No. 213, July 1974.
[3] "The Toxicity of Plutonium", MRC-HMSO, 1975.
[4] U.N. Scientific Committee on the Effect of Atomic Radiation, Report, 1972.
[5] G. W. Dolphin (NRPB), personal communication.
[6] "The Hazards in Plutonium Dispersal", B. L. Cohen, University of Pittsburgh, July 1975.

Human Energy Levels, Limits and Needs

by L. E. Reece and R. M. Kenedi; Department of Mechanical
Engineering, New South Wales Institute of Technology, Sydney, and
Bioengineering Unit, University of Strathclyde, Glasgow

Introduction

HUMANS use energy for diverse purposes. This paper explores two
of these — energy to maintain the normal body in health; and for
such a body to perform a spectrum of tasks involving mechanical
work.

For every individual there is a basic energy requirement to sustain
life — the "basal metabolic rate". This is measured by the rate of
energy exchange per unit of body surface area recorded under
conditions of rest and thermal neutrality (Slonim, 1974). Its value
can be broadly regarded as an indicator of the energy utilised to
maintain the tissues and thus sustain life.

In performing mechanical work it can be shown that there are
clearly defined limits to human *continuous* work rate capability —
these broadly correspond to around 4 times the basal metabolic rate.
Work at rates higher than these depletes the body's energy stores and
necessitates appropriate recovery periods (Parin, 1971).

The following points are of particular significance:

(i) There is considerable variability as to human capabilities and
corresponding energy needs. Different individuals undertaking
the same task can show variations in energy needs of the order
of 30%, while the same individual undertaking the same task at
different times exhibits up to 15% variation, (Parker *et al.*, 1973).
(ii) The mechanical efficiency of human task performance
appears low on first sight — around zero for mental work, 5%
for respiration, 10–20% for most muscular work and up to 30%
for the elite of athletes (Parker *et al.*, 1973). However, when it
is remembered that the work is produced virtually isothermally
at a temperature of around $37°C$, the values are impressive and

imply a most elegant energy processing mechanism. (The discussion of this mechanism is outwith the scope of this paper – the interested reader is referred in particular to Lehringer, 1971).

(iii) It is emphasised that ranking of tasks in increasing order of energy expenditure from some minimum value such as the basal metabolic rate is only a categorising device. It must be appreciated for example, that a state of minimum energy expenditure such as bed rest does not represent an intrinsically more "natural" tissue maintenance reference datum than any other arbitrarily selected condition. For example, immobilisation can in fact be destructive, producing exhaustion beyond permissible physiological limits (Parin, 1971). These and other factors such as the time rate of doing work, the environmental climatic conditions of temperature and humidity, etc., interact to produce limits within which human beings must remain if they are to continue in existence. In consequence the contents of the intimidatingly wide range of the relevant published literature (sample list of references appended) and the simplistic discussion that follows (the authors after all are confirmed engineering pragmatists!) must be regarded as pertinent only within strict limitations, although at present even these may only be dimly discerned. It is wholly essential that human dynamics and adaptive capability are never overlooked in this context otherwise hopefully postulated "scientific" concepts become rapidly transmuted into pseudo-scientific half-truths.

Tissue Maintenance and Muscular Work

The energy requirements for "tissue maintenance" can be considered to cover all biosynthesis, solute transport across cell membranes, and solute concentration together with the gross internal work of heart, lungs, and skeletal muscle in respiration, circulation, and body support under gravity (Lehninger, 1970 and 1971; Parin, 1971; and Kagi, 1964). For the average western human the basal metabolic rate is commonly quoted as being in the range of 0.9 to 1.4 k cal/min; a representative value may be taken as 1.25 k cal/min, and this is the figure used throughout this paper. Table 1 shows the tissue maintenance energy demands of various body components.

The mechanical work done by muscle cells in performing a task may

Table 1: (Stolwijk 1966.)

Body component	% of Basal rate	Rate of energy conversion for resting human (kcal/min)
Brain	16	0.20
Trunk core	56	0.70
Skin, fat, muscle compartment	18	0.23
Skeleton and connective tissue	10	0.12
		1.25

take place under two "limit" conditions — aerobic and anaerobic. The former obtains at relatively low time-rates of work when the cells in the normal course of events receive an adequate supply of oxygen and so the body's reserves are not depleted. The latter occurs at high time-rates of work and/or sudden work demands when oxygen cannot be supplied by the body sufficiently rapidly. This results in the accretion of an oxygen debt (depletion of the body's reserves) which has to be repaid at the termination of the exertion. (Parin, 1971). The body's energy expenditure capability (endurance) falls rapidly with increase in the time duration of work demand. It is only when the rate of energy expenditure falls to about 5 k cal/min that continuous steady-state work output is possible (Kagi, 1964). This figure is taken to represent the limit of aerobic work capacity.

Skeletal muscle is, however, equipped to function maximally at anaerobic levels for short-period "bursts". Table 2 lists energy utilisation rates considered typical.

A compendium of energy utilisation rates for some 95 activities ranging from rest through very light, light, moderate, heavy very heavy to extreme, culled from the sources listed in the references, is presented in the Appendix.

Table 2: (McCormick, 1967)

Item	Energy utilisation rate (kcal/min)
Basal metabolic rate	1.25
Maximal continuous rate (aerobic)	5.00
Maximal intermittent rate for normal man (anaerobic)	10.00
Maximal intermittent rate for trained athletes (anaerobic)	15.00–20.00

Energy Expenditure and Intake

The data presented in the Appendix indicate that most work of a continuous nature involves an energy expenditure rate of less than 5 k cal/min. In such activities, within the aerobic capabilities of the cells, steady-state conditions are quickly achieved in both working and resting periods, the appropriate physiological time constants for recovery being about 0.2 to 0.4 min for heart rate and around 10 min for rectal temperature (Murrell, 1965).

Energy production rates higher than 5 k cal/min are associated with manifestations of fatigue (lactic acid build-up in the body); continuous increase in heart rate (leading to exhaustion if the activity is maintained long enough); and a rather slow return to steady-state conditions at the end of the exertion as the oxygen debt is repaid.

It must also be remembered that normal work is not done under steady "static" conditions and that work-rate transients of both long and short duration can and do occur. Experience seems to show that in general no deleterious physiological effects obtain provided the average energy expenditure for the whole year does not exceed around 2500 k cal/day (Murrel, 1965).

A tentative assessment of wok and rest periods can be attempted by assuming the energy reserve of an average human individual (called upon if the work-rate demanded exceeds 5 k cal/min) as around 25 k cal. It can then be stipulated that the work period T should be limited to the time required to use up this energy, that is, $T = 25/(K-5)$ where K is the demanded work rate.

Murrell (1965) from his studies of human performance in industry suggested the following relationship for estimating R the necessary rest period per day in minutes:

$$R = T(K - S)/(K - 1.5).$$

Here T is the total working time (including rest, in minutes); K the actual average working rate over time T in kcal/min, S an agreed "standard" working rate (related to performance within aerobic limits) in kcal/min and the "resting" energy utilisation rate (representative of the basal metabolic rate) is taken as 1.5 kcal/min.

Well-motivated individuals will generally tend to work close to an optimum work-rate. The existence of such optima has been demonstrated, for example, in the effort expended in walking (Lehninger, 1971; Inman, 1968). In another instance (Hughes *et al.*, 1970) it was

Table 3: (compiled from Edholm, 1957; Food and Agriculture Organisation, 1949; Garry et al., 1955; Lehmann, 1958; Maver et al., 1969; Numajiri, 1969; Passmore et al., 1955)

	Energy utilisation kcal/per day		
Activity	Office work (clerks)	Light industry (truck drivers)	Heavy industry (coal mines)
Sleep	500	500	600
'Non' work	1300	1500	1500
Work	1000	1200	2500
	2800	3200	4500

shown that men expending around 7 k cal/min in carrying a range of loads up-hill, maintained their work rate constant by automatically amending their effort as the load carried was changed. Additionally rest by such well-motivated individuals is taken when required. The start of a rest period will often be deferred past the optimum since feelings of fatigue tend to lag behind its actual incidence as measured by blood lactate levels. It is pertinent also to comment here that if the necessary rest periods are not formally allowed, disguised rest periods of non-productive auxiliary activities take their place.

On the bases of the foregoing, typical energy expenditures per day in three different categories are shown in Table 3.

While it is possible to assess rationally the total daily energy required based on estimates of energy levels of utilisation as shown in Table 3, the actual energy intake in the form of food, for example, of individuals and of groups varies extraordinarily widely. A single example will suffice to show how confusing such figures can be.

Edholm (1957) reports a study of army cadets. A group of young men of comparable age and other characteristics, offered the same food and given the same range of tasks to carry out, showed a food intake of from 1500 to 7000 kcal per day for a range of energy expenditure from 2000 to 5000 kcal per day.

It is clear that there are a great variety of factors which influence both the energy expenditure and the energy intake figures. A random sample of such factors is as follows:

changes in work load due to mechanisation (Numajiri, 1969; Repka, 1974; Starek et al., 1973); operator stress (Dhesi et al., 1973; Neagu, 1973; Ostlund et al., 1964); work tools and techniques (Datta et al., 1973; Morrison et al., 1974); age and physical fitness (Ostlund *et al.*, 1964); diet (Berghoff *et al.*, 1970, Crowdy *et al.*, 1971); body temperature (ASHRAE Handbook; Parker *et al.*, 1973; Slonim, 1974; Starek *et al.*, 1973); skin microclimate (Slonim, 1974); environmental temperature and humidity (Wenzel, 1964). etc.

Summary

The essentially dynamic nature of humankind, its adaptability and self-surpassing ingenuity in enlarging its "needs" makes attempts at forecasting energy requirements an extremely "dicey" proposition. The foregoing discussion therefore serves primarily to highlight the extreme complexity of the problem. It is shown to be possible to estimate individual basic energy needs as around 2000 to 7000 kcal/ per day. These figures may be considered pertinent provided the human individuals concerned may be persuaded to remain docile enough not to aspire beyond such basic requirements.

Additionally, the bulk of the data available refer to Western individuals in normal health. This in itself is likely to be a source of error − most societies nowadays consist of significant proportions of the disabled and of the elderly whose energy requirements are likely to be different from and greater than those discussed here.

It seems to the authors that human energy needs, certainly in the long term, will be defined in terms of a range of values. The lower end of this range could possibly be one corresponding to the basic requirements discussed. The upper limit, however, could not correspond to the potentially insatiable human "need" but will most certainly be governed by limitations of the availability of resources at national and global levels.

References

American Society of Heating, Refrigeration and Airconditioning Engineers (ASHRAE), 1972. Handbook of Fundamentals; chapter 7.

Banerjee, B., and Saha, N., (1970): Energy cost of some common daily activities of active tropical male and females; Journal of Applied Physiology, August, 29/2, 200−203.

Berghoff, A., and Glatzel, H. (1970): Effect of forms of diet of different fat content on human organisms. 11. Energy metabolism and performance on the ergometer; (in German), T. R. C. Report No. BR-19035; abstract in R and D Abstracts.

Crowdy, J. P., and Haisman, M. F., (1971): Combat nutrition. The effect of a restricted diet on the performance of hard and prolonged physical work. T.R.C. Report No. T 72−03119.

Datta, S. R., Chatterjee, B. B., and Roy, B. N., (1973): The relationship between energy expenditure and pulse rates with body weight and load carried during load carrying on the level. Ergonomics, 16/4, 507−513.

Dhesi, J. K., and Firebaugh, F. M., (1973): The effects of stages of chapati making and angles of body position on heart rate. Ergonomics, Vol. 16, No. 6., 811–815.

Edholm, O. G., (1957): Energy Expenditure. Advanced Science, Vol. 13, 486.

Food and Agriculture Organisation of the United Nations (1949): Dietary surveys their technique and interpretation; Nutritional studies No. 4 Washington, U.N.

Garry, R. C., Passmore, R., Warnock, G. M., and Durnin, J. V. G. A., (1955): Studies on energy expenditure and consumption of food by miners and clerks, Fife, Scotland; Medical Research Council, Special Report, Series No. 289, London H.M.S.O. 1955.

Glick, Z., and Shavartz, E., (1974): Physical working capacity of young men of different ethnic groups in Israel. Journal of Applied Physiology, July 37/1, 22–26.

Hughes, A. L., and Goldman, R. F., (1970): Energy cost of "hard work". Journal of Applied Physiology, 29/5, 570–572.

Inman, V. T., (1968): Energy in ambulation. Department of Medicine and Surgery, BPR 10–9. Veterans' Administration, Washington, D.C.

Kay, C., and Shepherd, R. J., (1969): On muscle strength and the threshold of anaerobic work. Internationale Zeitschrift für Angewandte Physiologie. 27/4, 311–328: abstract in Aerospace Medicine.

Knuttgen, H. G., (1970): Oxygen debt after submaximal exercise; Journal of Applied Physiology, November, 29/5, 651–657.

Kagi, K., (1964): Die relative Wirkun von isometrischem und dynamischem Training auf die Ausdauer für dynamische Arbeit. Proceedings of Second International Congress on Ergonomics, Dortmund; Ergonomics Research Society.

Lehmann, G., (1958): Physiological measurements as a basis of work organisation in industry. Ergonomics, vol 1, 328–344.

Lehninger, A. L., (1971): Bioenergetics: the molecular basis of biological energy trans-formations, 2nd Edition, Benjamin, New York.

Lehninger, A. L., (1970): Biochemistry: the molecular basis of cell structure and function. Worth Publishers.

Lind, A. R., (1970): The lack of heat stroke in European miners working in hot climates. American Industrial Hygiene Association Journal; July–August 31/4, 460–465.

Maver, H., Kovacevic, M., and Grgic, Z. (1969): Energy expenditure of surface miners (Serbo-Croat). Arhiv za Higijenu Rada i Toksikologiju, 20/2, 167–172. Abstract in Excerpta Medica.

McCormick, E. J., (1967): Human Factors Engineering. McGraw-Hill, New York.

Morrison, J. F., and Blake, G. T. W., (1974): Physiological observations on cane cutters. European Journal of Applied Physiology and Ocupational Physiology. 33/3 247–254.

Murrell, K. F. H., (1965): Human Performance in Industry. Reinhold, New York.

Neagu, V., (1973): Ergonomic aspects of effort by workers operating soil compacting equipment in the construction of forest roads (Romanian). Revista Padurilon, May 88/5, 265–269 (C.I.S. Abstracts, CIS 74–2077).

Numajiri, K., (1969): Daily expenditure of workers at various jobs in industry. Journal of Science of Labour, 45/10, 569–587.

Ostlund, E. W., Lindholm, A., Sandberg, E., and Lindberg, B., (1964): Medical and ergonomic aspects of backache among certain groups of Swedish postal workers. Proceedings of Second International Congress of Ergonomics, Dortmund. Ergonomic Research Society.

Parin, V. V., (1971): Principal changes in the healthy human body after a 120 day bed confinement. (Abstract in Scientific and Technical Aerospace Reports). Report No. N71–19067 – January.

Parker, S. F., and Nest, V. (eds), (1973): Bioastronautics Data Book. Biotechnology Inc. Arlington, Virginia. 2nd Edition, NASA SP–3006.

Passmore, R., and Durnin, J. V. G. A., (1955): Human energy expenditure. Physiological Reviews. Vol. 35, 801–875.

Repka, I., (1974): The evaluation of the consumption of work when milking cows: (Czech). Provoni Leharsti, 26/7, 256–260.

Slonim, N. B., (ed), (1974): Environmental Physiology. Musby & Co.

Smola, J., (1973): Physical load in mining work; Zackranov; 1973; 10/4/2: (Abstract in Czechoslovak Bibliography on Industrial Hygiene and Occupational Diseases).

Starek, E., Borsky, I., and Strelka, F., (1973): Judgement of mechanical trimming of trees from the viewpoint of physical load; (Czech.) Lesnicky Casopis; 19/1, 39–46; (Abstract in Czechoslovak Bibliography on Industrial Hygiene and Occupational Diseases).

Stolwijk, J. A. J., and Hardy, J. D., (1966): Temperature regulation in man – a theoretical study. Pflügers Archiv für die gesamte Physiologie, 291, 129–162.

Tarriere, C., and Andre, A., (1970); Evaluation of the energy expenditure for various work postures and their effect on total energy expenditure (French). Conditions de Travail; June, No. 12, 25–44. Abstract in Occupational Safety and Health Abstracts.

Winget, H. G., (1971): Dissociation of effects of prolonged confinement and bed rest in normal human subjects; heart rate and body temperature. Proceedings of the 1971 Space-craft Center, Endocrine Program Conference, November 1972.

Wenzel, H. G., (1964): Untersuchungen des Erholungsverlaufes nach Litzearbeit. Proceedings of Second International Congress on Ergonomics, Dortmund, Taylor and Francis, London, 151–157.

Appendix

Energy utilisation spectrum for a range of human activities.

Activity		Energy utilisation rate kcal/min (including tissue maintenance)
Asleep	15–20 years of age	1.1
	20–30 years of age	1.2
	30–40 and beyond	1.3
Resting	lying fully relaxed	1.2
	lying moderately relaxed	1.3
	lying awake after meals	1.4

Very light activity

Seated	at rest	1.7
	watch repair	1.7
	office work (writing, typing, etc)	1.7–2.3
	driving car in light traffic	2.4
	riding in a car as a passenger	2.0
	routine flying of aircraft	1.6–2.2
	polishing gems	2.4
Standing	relaxed	1.9
	drafting	1.9
	peeling potatoes	2.1

Light activity

Seated	piloting light aircraft in rough weather	2.7
	instrument landing of aircraft	2.8
	piloting bomber aircraft in combat	2.9
	repairing boot and shoes	3.0

Activity		Energy utilisation rate Kcal/min (including tissue maintenance)
	at lecture	3.0
	driving car in heavy traffic	3.2
	driving motor cycle	3.2
	driving truck	3.3
	combat flying – fighter aircraft	3.8
	tractor driving	4.2
Standing	stream fishing	1.9–3.2
	entering ledgers	2.6
	engineering tasks (some movement involved)	
	medium assembly work	2.9
	welding	3.0
	sheet metal working	3.1
	machining	3.3
	punching	3.5
	machine fitting	4.5
	bricklaying	4.0
	washing laundry by hand	3.2–5.6
	ironing	3.2–5.6
Moving	golf, riding in cart and hitting ball	2.2–2.5
	golf, walking and hitting ball	2.2–4.0
	shopping (browsing)	2.2–2.8
	general laboratory work	2.5
	teaching	2.5
	bakery (cleaning tins, packing boxes)	2.2–3.2
	brewing (filling bottles, loading boxes on belts)	1.9–3.8
	cooking	2.5–3.2
	walking about room	3.0
	walking at level 2 mph	3.2
	shop assistant	3.2
	carpentry (machine sawing tables)	2.8–3.5
	garage work (vehicle repairs, replacing tyres,	
	raising car on jack)	3.4
	walking on level (3 mph)	4.1
	house cleaning	3.2–5.4

Moderate activity

Sitting	driving heavy vehicle	5.0
	rowing for pleasure	5.0
	cycling 8–11 mph	5.7
	cycling rapidly	6.9
Standing	foundry work (using pneumatic hammer)	4.7–5.4
	callisthenics exercises	4.7–6.4
	gardening	5.8
	chopping wood	6.2–7.5
	carpentry (sawing by hand)	6.3–7.6
Moving	dancing social	3.8–6.9
	walking on level (4 mph)	6.0
	crawling	6.1

Activity		Energy utilisation rate Kcal/min (including tissue maintenance)
	swimming breast stroke 1 mph	6.8
	swimming crawl stroke 1 mph	7.0
	table tennis	6.8
	tennis	5.6–7.2
	army drill	7.1
	swimming breast stroke 1.64 mph	8.2
	swimming back stroke 1.66 mph	8.3

Heavy activity

Sitting	cycling rapidly own pace	8.3
	trotting on horseback	7.1–9.8
	cycling in race (100 miles at 23 mph) track	9.8
Standing	shovelling sand	6.8–7.7
	carpentry, sawing wood by hand, planing by hand	8.8–10
	digging	8.9
Moving	skating at 9 mph	7.8
	playing soccer	8.3
	skiing 3 mph on level	9.0
	foundry work & tending furnaces	9.0
	climbing stairs at 116 steps/min	9.8
	squash	7.9–11.3
	basketball	7.9–12.0

Very heavy activity

Sitting	cycling at 13.2 mph	10.0
	rowing with two oars at 3.5 mph	11.0
	galloping on horseback	11.4
	sculling (98 strokes/min)	12.6
Moving	fencing	10.5
	squash	11.3
	basketball	12.00

Extreme activity

	wrestling	11.0–13.7
	marching on the double	13.3
	endurance marching	14.8–16.1
	moving over rough terrain in soft snow with 20 kg load	21.0

Can Human Energy Needs be met?

by C. R. W. Spedding: Department of Agriculture and Horticulture,
University of Reading

THE energy needs of the human population for food depend to some
extent on variations in individual need – but much more, of course,
on the size and structure of the population. Our individual needs
vary with our size, our physiological state, our way of life, the
climate, and the weather. What we desire or, in an economic sense,
demand, is another matter entirely. In developed countries, problems
due to overconsumption of energy exceed those due to shortage. The
variation in genuine need (as represented by energy expenditure over
24 hours) might vary from 18 MJ/day to 10 MJ/day, for an
exceptionally active man (65 kg) in a cold climate and a sedentary
man in a warm climate, respectively (F.A.O., 1975), and large
differences may occur between what is needed and what is actually
eaten by those able to purchase as much as they wish.

Even so, the over-riding consideration in answering the question
posed, in world terms, is the size of the population.

Clearly, at the present time, the world's population could be fed
adequately if there were no problems of distribution and if the
people who are hungry were not also appallingly poor. This
immediately answers the question in the affirmative for the existing,
and thus any smaller population, but it also casts doubt on the
relevance of the question. Put another way, it would seem that
meeting the energy needs of all the world's people may be more a
political or an economic question than a straightforward agricultural
one. This is almost certainly true, and larger-sized world populations
might make the political or economic issues even more difficult to
resolve, resulting in an exacerbation of mal-distribution and perhaps
raising prices still further out of reach of the very poor.

There is a very strong argument for the poor of populous regions
to have the means of producing their own food, as the only means of

ensuring that they are fed. They are, in the main, country people and members of farming families anyway.

Although I must now examine further the agricultural potential, and this is not the place to pursue the other arguments, it is very important to be clear about the differences between agricultural potential, agricultural achievement, and the final distribution of the products produced.

The question can be restated in the form "what size of population could the world sustain?", assuming that this can be achieved by producing a given total of edible energy. Or, as Georgesciu-Roegen (1971) put it, we should ask how long can the earth support a given population and what happens thereafter.

The total amount of edible energy does have to be in a form which people will consume (and people vary greatly in this, too) and some account has to be taken of the cost of producing it. This cost has to be sustainable as well and, of course, greatly influences who can buy and in what quantities: the cost may be measured in terms of money, misery, "support" energy, water, or work.

In recent years, much emphasis has been placed on the greater cost of animal products compared with crop products (see Table 1) and it is known (Duckham, 1974) that more people could be fed in the U.K. if fewer resources were devoted to animal production (Mellanby, 1975). Although the argument is really more complex that this (and I shall return to it later), it is nevertheless sensible to start with crop production in trying to estimate the potential output

Table 1: An illustration of the relative costs of animal and crop production, expressed in terms of the major resources

| | Quantity of resource required to produce 1 MJ of gross energy in the product | | |
	Land (ha)	Solar radiation (MJ)	'Support' energy (MJ)
Wheat	0.000017	563	0.19
Potatoes	0.00001	328	0.2
Milk	0.000114	3762	1.8
Eggs	0.0002	8017	12.8

Calculated on an annual basis.

Wheat, potatoes and milk calculations based on data in: Spedding and Walsingham (1975).

Egg calculations were made using a maize/soyabean meal ration and 'support' energy costs calculated by D. M. Bather, University of Reading.

of edible energy. Before doing so, let us examine the present position, in relation to feeding the world, and possible targets for the future.

The Present Position

There is at present a world food crisis, and this is not simply the result of one or two bad seasons. Even so, the general standard of health continues to improve and infant mortality to decrease.

Industrialised countries are producing more food than they can consume and developing countries have been increasing their agricultural production at more than 2½% per annum. The discrepancy between the food available to developed and developing countries (see Table 2) is enormous and getting wider.

Table 2: Food production (per head) in terms of wheat
equivalents* (from F.A.O., 1975)

Regions	1961−63	1971−73	Change
Developed countries	143	170	+27
Developing countries	49	51	+ 2

*This is one way of comparing production, whereby
commodities are weighted by price and converted to wheat
equivalents.

This means that the developed countries may have large reserves for bad years but the developing countries suffer very badly. At the present time, F.A.O. (1975) estimates that 61 out of 97 developing countries had a food deficit in 1970: in the Far East and Africa, 25% and 30%, respectively, suffer from significant undernutrition and, altogether, for that part of the developing world for which adequate information is available, malnutrition affects about 460 million people.

Yet large areas of land in Latin America and Africa are unused and, as we have seen, the potential for food production is very high. There are other constraints, however, such as animal disease in large parts of Africa, and lack of infrastructure and marketing channels, that should not be forgotten.

The immediate and short-term problems, therefore, are how to meet the food needs of poor people and, specifically, how to raise the present (2.6%) annual growth in agricultural production of the developing countries to the 3.6% required. By and large, the techniques and resources to do this exist but "the political will, the investment and the organisation are insufficient" (F.A.O., 1975). At "village" level, there are also problems of human will and competence, and resistance to change. Even so, it is the task of agriculture to produce within the given economic and social frameworks: agricultural research and development thus need to take these conditions into account and we do not always know how to improve existing agricultural systems technically.

Targets for the Future

The desirability of limiting population growth does not depend upon estimates of potential photosynthesis or food production or even on estimates of the maximum number of people who could be fed. There are many other reasons that might determine an optimum world population and no reason at all to aim at any kind of maximum number of people. In the short term, however, there would be nutritional advantages if population increases could be prevented from out-distancing food production, even though there is nothing whatever that can be done, by way of population control, that will influence the very short term (Bunting, 1974). It has been suggested that an achievable target for a stable world population would be 5.8×10^9 (Brown, 1974). The Population Council report for 1973 estimated that the world population would reach 5.9×10^9 by the year 2000 and that a continuation of replacement fertility thereafter would produce an ultimate stable population of 8.4×10^9 toward the end of the 21st century. McCloud (1975) has calculated that a population of 5.8×10^9 would need increases in grain yield in China, for example, from a current average of 1,800 kg/ha to 3,000 kg/ha, and in India from 1,100 kg/ha to 2,000 kg/ha. In Japan, however, an increase from 5,000 kg/ha to 7,000 kg/ha would be required, and in Egypt also an impossible yield of 7,000 kg/ha would be needed. However, there are large areas of the world that could export food and food could be better used than it is.

If animal production from grains were reduced, for example, very large quantities of feed grains (up to 100 million tons per year in N. America) could in theory be diverted to feed people (some 500 million persons at an Indian dietary level) (McCloud, 1975).

Targets for the future, therefore, involve decisions about the nature of our diet and, in particular, the amount of animal products consumed and the ways in which they are produced. First, however, it is necessary to consider potential crop production.

Potential Crop Production

The daily photosynthetic productivity for a specific geographical location· depends upon the crop surface available, latitude, season, and sky conditions (Monteith, 1972).

Taking these considerations into account, de Wit (1967) has estimated the potential production of the earth, in 10-degree latitude intervals (see Table 3). Based solely on the quantity of carbohydrate that can be photosynthesised per unit of land and the area available per person (after making allowance for urban and recreational needs, at 750 m^2/man), the figures show that the earth could support 146 billion (10^9) people, assuming that all the photosynthate produced could be harvested and used for feeding people. (If the non-agricultural needs are ignored, the earth could apparently support 1,000 billion people!) The land required, by affluent people, for urban and recreational use is so considerable that a yield increase of 30% per unit of land only raises the maximum number of people who could be sustained in theory by about 3%. Full use of the sea could add a further 20% but, as de Wit (1967) points out, the cost of maintaining such a large volume of water in a reasonable nutritional state would be prohibitive.

de Wit's conclusion is that the number of persons on earth is ultimately limited by the amount of space a man needs to work and live in in reasonable comfort and not by the production of food. Thus, eventually, overpopulation without starvation has to be envisaged, unless population growth is controlled.

There are, however, other factors besides photosynthesis that limit crop production, including others at a botanical level, such as distribution of the proceeds of photosynthesis and "sink" size, and losses due to pests and diseases.

More recently (Duckham, Jones, and Roberts, 1976), it has been estimated that only 2.8% of the possible world potential net photosynthate is actually formed in world farming. This is partly due to the fact that only 46% of the world's cultivable land is classed as cultivated (due to problems of accessibility or disease), only 70% of this bears a crop in any one year and only 70% of the growing season is actually used. Thus only 22% of the potential net photosynthate is actually used in the production of human food. The difference

Table 3: Potential productivity of the earth and the population it could support (after de Wit, 1967)

North latitude (degrees)	Land surface in ha (×10⁸)	No. of months above 10°C	Carbohydrate kg/ha/yr (×10³)	m²/man to support life (750 m²/man allowed for urban etc. needs)	No. men (×10⁹)
70	8	1	12	1556	5
60	14	2	21	1219	11
50	16	6	59	919	17
40	15	9	91	860	18
30	17	11	113	839	20
20	13	12	124	831	16
10	10	12	124	831	11
0	14	12	116	836	17
-10	7	12	117	835	9
-20	9	12	123	831	11
-30	7	12	121	833	9
-40	1	8	89	863	1
-50	1	1	12	1583	1
Total	131				146

between the potential (22%) and the achieved (2.8%) is considered to be due to losses, weather uncertainty, inadequate crop canopies and sheer bad husbandry. Furthermore, only about a third of the photosynthate formed in farming is recovered as potential human food (i.e. less that 1% of the initial potential figure) for direct consumption. There are thus enormous gaps between photosynthetic potentials and achieved levels of crop production.

The Costs of Crop Production

In practical terms, photosynthesis is never the only limiting factor, even for an area of land, and, for a man, possession of the land may require money that he does not have. When he has the land, however, soil has to be cultivated, crops have to be sown, watered, fertilised, protected, and harvested. Some of these activities require labour only but others require inputs that have to be purchased and may not even be available. Incidentally, the full use of manpower in agriculture, rather than labour-saving, is often what is needed in the developing countries: of the 3,000 million population of the less developed economies, at least 2,000 million are considered to be directly dependent on agriculture (F.A.O., 1975).

It has been estimated that, in the developing market economies, of the 200 Mha of potentially irrigable land, less than 100 Mha have been irrigated; one quarter of the total land surface is potentially arable, but only one-eighth has yet been brought under cultivation. This represents opportunity but also large costs, of water, of fertiliser, especially nitrogen, of capital, and, for example, of pesticides.

It is estimated that 25 million tons of N will be needed in 1985, compared with 6 million in 1971, and 11 million tons of phosphate, compared with 3 million. In the case of pesticides, it is estimated that there is a global deficit of 20–30% between demand and production now. It should be noted, however, that most plant growth in the world is still based on biologically recycled nitrogen.

These are illustrations of the problem: it would be difficult to establish the full costs of money and materials needed to approach anything like the photosynthetic potential of the world. So, although photosynthesis may not be the limiting factor to the size of population that can be sustained, food production is a much more complicated process and still presents problems. One of these is the proportion consumed directly and that processed by animals.

The Future of Animal Production

Animals serve many purposes throughout the world and their role as food producers has only become predominant where equipment and fossil fuels have substituted machine power for animal power. Whether it will be possible for less-developed countries to follow the same developmental route is now an open question.

Animals tend to be thought of as protein producers, but not all animal protein products are food, although animal products generally contain a good deal of protein. There is some justification, therefore, for thinking of the contribution of animal production to human food as characteristically proteinaceous, but it should be remembered that animal products also supply energy, minerals, particular amino-acids and flavour, as well as money and employment to those who produce them.

It is well known that, however desirable animal products may be, they cannot be regarded as essential and that more people can be supported per unit area of land if it is utilised for crop production than if it is used for animal production (Fig. 1). The idea of a pyramid of numbers is founded on the notion of herbivorous animals limited in number by the size of the plant production base on which they feed (and which must be much larger in biomass than they are). By the same token, the carnivorous must number only a fraction of the number of herbivores, since the latter live by eating the former (or each other). This ignores the substantial and successful group of omnivores (including Man), whose numbers can be greater than those

Biomass at different Trophic Levels

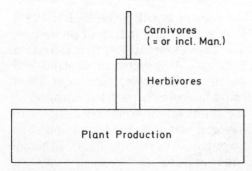

FIGURE 1   Simple diagram to represent the relative quantities of biomass that can be supported in the form of carnivores, herbivores and plants (from Spedding, 1976).

Potential Biomass of Omnivores

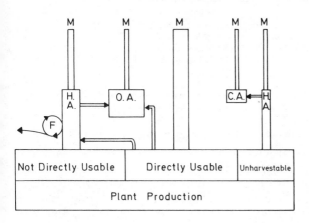

M ≡ Man   H.A ≡ Herbivores   O.A. ≡ Omnivores (other than man)
          C.A.≡ Carnivores   F ≡ Faeces

FIGURE 2   An elaboration of Fig. 1 to indicate the greater complexity of natural systems, in which omnivores utilise plant production by several routes (from Spedding, 1976).

of either carnivores or herbivores, because they can adjust their diets to maximise the use of all that is available (Fig. 2).

All this is greatly affected by the fact that Man cannot make direct use of the vegetation that can be produced in many areas. Large tracts of grassland, boggy and mountainous areas, do not produce food for direct human consumption but can produce feed for herbivorous animals. Ruminants, such as cattle and sheep, thus have roles as vegetation collectors (over areas that it would be impractical or uneconomic to harvest in any other way), as converters of fibrous feeds into those digestible by humans, and as concentrators of nutrients that are otherwise widely and sparsely dispersed.

Animal production may therefore be additional to crop production (rather than competitive) and may be complementary, as in many mixed farming systems. Animals can also be fed on the waste and by-products of settlement, agriculture, and industry (Table 4) and improve the overall efficiency of agricultural production by recycling waste: in this way, they may even contribute to the control of pollution and the promotion of amenity.

If Agriculture has to pay more attention to the use of wastes and by-products, it may be desirable to use a wider range of animals

Table 4: Waste and by-products used for animal feeding

Crop	Industrial
Sugar beet and other root crops, tops	Sugar beet pulp
Bean and pea pods and haulm	Brewers grains
Straw	Blood, meat and bone meals
Chaff	Fish meal
	Bran
	Meals from extracted oil seeds

including some well-known but barely agricultural animals (such as rabbits and guinea-pigs) and some far less well-known (such as earthworms, snails, and insects). These unconventional animals might only be the first stage in the production process, serving as feed for poultry, for example. One of the reasons for considering some of these unconventional animals is that it may be possible to economise on feed usage by employing cold-blooded animals that do not have to be fed such large amounts just to maintain themselves (and their body temperatures) during non-productive periods.

This same argument might lead to an expansion of fish farming in particular and aquaculture in general, based, for example, on prawns or mussels. The main feeds could be based on by-products and the advantages of invertebrate filter-feeders (such as shellfish) are that they can extract particles from large volumes of water and assist in pollution control of estuarine waters.

On non-croppable land, grazing animals can be kept and the areas available are very large indeed (8 Mha of rough grazing in the U.K., for instance). The reasons for land being in this category, however, may be edaphic, climatic, topographical, or economic and the same reasons will influence what animals may be kept.

In the majority of cases they will be ruminants. These animals, mainly cattle and sheep in the U.K., can make good use of fibrous feeds, including by-products, and they can use non-protein nitrogen.

The relative efficiency of energy and protein production per unit area of land by different agricultural animals has therefore to be related to the kind of land envisaged, and the answers will depend upon whether the land could grow either crops or grass or could only grow grass. Table 5 shows the kind of efficiencies obtained when arable land is considered, growing those feeds on which each kind of animal performs best. Table 6 illustrates the different order of magnitude obtainable on similar land by crops.

Table 5: Production of protein and energy by
animals (after Spedding, 1973; and Holmes, 1975)

Product	Protein kg/ha/yr	Energy MJ/ha/yr
Milk	126	10,300
Cheese	90	6,300
Beef (18 mth)	56	7,200
Beef (barley)	54	6,400
Lamb	27	3,300
Lamb (New Zealand)	62	7,500
Pig	66	9,700
Chicken (broiler)	96	4,800
Chicken (egg)	102	6,600
Rabbit	180	7,400

But land is by no means the only important resource. We have to be increasingly concerned about the very high levels of "support" energy used in the agricultural systems of the developed countries. Large quantities of fossil fuels are now used directly on farms and indirectly in the manufacture of inputs of such things as machinery and fertilisers. Energy is scarce and costly and we have to be concerned with the efficiency with which it is used, because Agriculture is unlikely to be protected from the high cost of energy supplies and the goods that use them.

Table 6: Production of protein and energy by crops (from
Spedding, 1973)

Product harvested	Protein kg/ha/yr	Energy MJ/ha/yr
Dried grass	700–2,200	92,000–218,000
Leaf protein	2,000*	–
Cabbage (edible)	1,100	33,500
Maize gran (N. America)	430	83,700
Potato (edible tuber)	420	100,400
Barley grain (U.K.)	370	62,800
Wheat (edible grain)	350	58,600
Rice grain (Europe)	320	87,900

*This is a high, experimental result and it is unlikely that more
than about 800 kg protein/ha would be obtained in practice.

Table 7 compares the efficiency with which support energy is used in agricultural systems. Clearly, this comparison favours crop

Table 7: Efficiency of
support energy use in
agricultural systems (from
Spedding and Walsingham,
1975)

	E
Wheat	4.6
Peas	3.2
Potatoes	3.5
Milk	0.62
Lamb	0.39
Beef	0.18

$$E = \frac{\text{Gross Energy in edible product}}{\text{Support Energy input to farm gate}}$$

production and, within animal production systems, grazing systems, especially on legumes, look most promising.

There are, of course, other important resources, including labour, capital, feed, and fertiliser. Feed costs represent a very high proportion of the total costs of animal production and the efficiency of feed conversion is rightly regarded as of great significance. However, it will be necessary to seek improvements in this without incurring large inefficiencies in the use of labour, energy or even capital, otherwise economic efficiency may be greatly lowered.

Nitrogen supplied as fertiliser is not always efficiently used by crops, but animals are not only very wasteful in terms of the nitrogen actually retained in the product but their inefficiencies are, of course, imposed on top of those involved in crop production

It is not surprising from the foregoing that animal products cost more to produce than do crop products: however, they also sell at a higher price per kg of protein (Holmes, 1975).

Ultimately, the factors that will determine the future of animal production, will be (a) demand for particular products: (b) the rewards for the producer (including aspects of land-ownership and a way of life); (c) the tolerance of the community of the production methods employed. The fact that other people could be fed on the foods used for animal production will not automatically cause them to be diverted: indeed, it does not do so now.

Conclusion

The energy needs of a human population depend both on the nature and quantity of the individual's diet and on the number of people. It may be doubted whether the majority will accept a diet that merely satisfies their needs (and certainly not one that only satisfied energy needs), unless forced to do so by relative costs and prices (or by unavailability). The problem of under-nutrition might then be exacerbated, since it is generally due to the fact that people do not have the money to purchase food, rather than to an absolute and inevitable shortage. Technical help is chiefly required to lower the cost of food production, by increasing the productivity per unit of land, capital, and "support" energy (and, in some cases, of water, for example), and to improve food production where it is wanted and within the existing or foreseeable political and social framework.

In so far as the question is a meaningful one, however, the food energy supply does not seem likely to be the ultimate limiting factor to population size. Other factors are likely to operate before this and there seems to be no good reason why population size should be allowed to increase to anything like these levels, assuming that it can be controlled.

References

Brown, L. (1974). "In the Human Interest – A Strategy to Stablise World Population". W. W. Norton & Co., New York.

Bunting, A. H. (1974). "Population, Agriculture and Poverty in the Developing World". Public Lecture in the University of Reading, 29th January 1974.

de Wit, C. T. (1967). "Photosynthesis: its Relationship to Overpopulation". In "Harvesting the Sun". Eds. A. San Pietro, F. A. Greer, and T. J. Army. Academic Press, p. 315.

Duckham, A. N. (1974). *Chem. and Ind.*, December 7, 1974.

Duckham, A. N., Jones, J. G. W., and Roberts, E. H. (1976). (Eds). Ch. 29 in "Food Production and Consumption: Human Chains and Nutrient Cycles". Elsevier, North Holland, Amsterdam.

F.A.O. (1975). Report of the Committee on Agriculture, Session III, Rome, 15–24th April 1975.

Georgesiu-Roegen, N. (1971). "The Entropy Law and the Economic Process". Harvard Univ. Press.

Holmes, W. (1975). Proc. 21st Easter School in Agricultural Science – "Meat" University of Nottingham. 1974, pp. 535–553.

Mellanby, K. (1975). "Can Britain Feed Itself?" Merlin Press.

McCloud, D. E. (1975). *Agronomy J.*, 67, 1–3.

Monteith, J. L. (1972). *J. appl. Ecol.*, 9, 747–766.

Spedding, C. R. W. (1973). *Agric. Prog.*, 48, 48–58.

Spedding, C. . W., and Walsingham, J. M. (1975). *Span*, 18 (1), 7–9.

Spedding, C. R. W. (1976). *Biologist*, 23 (2) 72–80.

Possible Effects of Human Activity on World Climate

by J. S. Sawyer; Director of Research, Meteorological Office

Introduction — Natural Climatic Variations

AS our Victorian ancestors colonised the remoter areas of the world they started meteorological observations in order to ascertain the nature of the weather which they might expect in their new homes. They thought that if they continued long enough the records would provide averages of weather variables which would define the climate. For this purpose the climate was regarded as something fixed. The day to day and year to year variations of weather were considered as temporary fluctuations around it. However, in the last few years it requires only a week or two of very cold or hot weather for the popular press to express concern that a climatic change has begun, and to seek some special cause for it. Before we can ask whether it is reasonable to seek such a cause in human activities, we need to ask how stable the world's climate is, and what natural fluctuations it had before man's increasing use of energy came on the scene.

Over most of the earth's history the world's climate as a whole has been as warm as, or warmer than, at present. There have however been some three colder periods which have had within them several glacial epochs during which ice sheets spread out from the polar regions as far south as the British Isles. Between the glacial epochs there were interglacials of duration measured in tens of thousands of years. The last glacial period ended about 10,000 years ago and we may regard the present as an interglacial period if we assume that another glacial will occur — and in the absence of an adequate understanding of the cause of glacials this is a reasonable assumption.

However, the timescale on which transitions from interglacial to glacial takes place is a long one. The climate in the past has remained in one of the phases, glacial or interglacial, for tens of thousands of years and even the most rapid changes between them

97

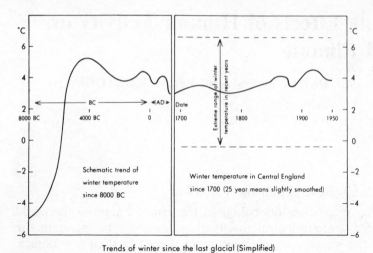

Trends of winter since the last glacial (Simplified)

FIGURE 1.   Variations of winter temperature in England since the last glacial (schematic).

were probably spread over many centuries. In thinking about climatic changes which may affect our lives or those of our children we are therefore more interested in what has happened on a shorter time scale. Figure 1 shows the broad trends of temperature in the British Isles since the last glacial. To display the significant points even here two time scales are needed. Over the last 2000 years or so the climatic temperature fluctuations have been quite minor compared with the variations from year to year. For example the variation of the 25 year average winter temperature in central England from the late 18th century cold period to the early 20th century mild period as about 1.2°C, whereas individual winters range from −0.3°C in 1962/63 to over 6°C. Nevertheless the small climatic changes of 1°C or less can be significant to agriculture, and to the economy more generally. It may be asked if such relatively small differences in the mean temperature over 25 years or so are not an accidental consequence of the random fluctuations from year to year, but careful statistical analysis shows that this is not so. Hence we are justified in seeking an underlying physical cause for these fluctuations over decades and centuries.

Unless we have a sound scientific basis for understanding these natural fluctuations, we are unlikely to be able to assess whether similar or larger fluctuations might arise from the increasing scale of man's activity on earth. The first step in assessing any possible human impact on climate is therefore to understand the way in which the climate is maintained.

Calculating the Climate

The atmosphere is an enormous heat engine. It receives more heat near the equator than towards the poles, but it loses heat more uniformly by radiation to space. The temperature difference between the equator and the poles drives the main systems of winds, and these carry the surplus heat from the equatorial regions towards the poles where outgoing radiation exceeds the income. The many processes which are involved are exceedingly complicated — the air motion is modified by the earth's rotation, heat is used in evaporation of water and released again in clouds, the clouds reflect some of the incoming sunshine and also blanket the outgoing radiation, and so on. However, all these processes obey the basic laws of physics and dynamics. These may be expressed mathematically and form a basis upon which the climate of the earth can, in principle, be calculated from the basic scientific laws.

A great deal of progress has been made in recent years towards calculating the world's climate in this way. However, it has been known for many years that the travelling depressions and anticyclones of middle latitudes play an essential role in conveying heat from the equator to the poles and in consequence they cannot be ignored in any attempt to calculate the heat budget of the atmosphere. Thus although the object of a calculation of world climate is to depict the average state over a long period of time, it has as yet proved impossible to carry out such a calculation satisfactorily without calculating the day by day changes arising from the passing weather systems.

A typical calculation of climate starts with an atomsphere of specified composition, with the distribution of land, sea, ice, and mountains also specified and with known incoming radiation from the sun. The initial state of the atmosphere is quite arbitrary, but the equations of physics and dynamics are applied at a mesh of some 5000 points at 5 or more levels. The integration of the equations forward with respect to time in steps of a few minutes describes the behaviour of the atmosphere day by day — not, of course, a forecast of any particular sequence, but a reproduction of the sequence of atmospheric states consequent upon the arbitrary initial conditions.

Computed January sea-level pressure chart
Average days 41-80   Exp. 90

(a)

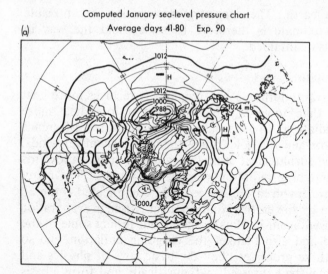

Observed January mean sea-level pressure chart
1873-1972

(b)

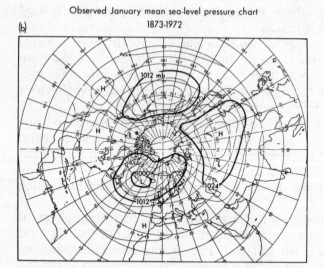

FIGURE 2.   January mean-sea-level pressure over the Northern Hemisphere (a) computed, (b) observed.

The calculated climate is obtained by averaging the calculated distributions over periods of 20 or 30 days. Such calculations are exceedingly lengthy even on the fastest available computers, but reasonably realistic simulations of the world's climate have been achieved. This is illustrated in Fig. 2(a) and (b). These show the computed chart of January mean-sea-level pressure over the northern hemisphere and the corresponding observed climatological chart. The main features are all present in the simulation – the Iceland and Aleutian low pressure areas, the Siberian and sub-tropical anti-cyclones etc.

With such a tool available to compute the earth's climate from first principles, we might well hope that it would be a simple matter to calculate the effect of any human interference with the processes involved. It might be thought to be merely a matter of introducing into the calculations a small change representing the man-made effects. Unfortunately thére are many complications to some of which I shall refer later, but first it is useful to look at the magnitude of possible human interference compared with the energies and masses involved in atmospheric processes.

Some Magnitudes of Atmospheric Quantities in Relation to Man-made Influence

Table 1 gives some typical magnitudes of the energies involved in atmospheric disturbances together with corresponding figures for the energies developed by human activities. It is clear that on a world-wide scale the direct input of energy from man's activity would have to increase at least one hundred-fold before it had much direct impact on the world-wide motion of the atmosphere. Even on a more local scale such as that of the British Isles, man's energy input is still very small compared with the energy sources driving the atmospheric circulation, but if we consider it reasonable to contemplate an exponential growth rate of 5% per year leading to a ten-fold increase in 50 years then man may well be providing heat sources of

Table 1: Some typical magnitudes of atmospheric energy and sources of man-made power.

Total kinetic energy of the atmosphere	7.5×10^{21} joules
World-wide industrial heat output (1970)	5.5×10^{12} watts = 4.8×10^{17} joules/day
Solar energy income	200 watts m^{-2}
Dissipation of energy of a large depression	100 watts m^{-2}
Total power consumption in the U.K. (1970)	1.5 watts m^{-2}

Table 2: The mass of the atmosphere and some of its constituents compared
with sources of pollution etc.

Total mass of the atmosphere	5.1×10^{18} kg
Total coal reserves	8×10^{15} kg
Total CO_2 in the atmosphere	2.5×10^{15} kg
Annual industrial production of CO_2	1.5×10^{13} kg
Total atmospheric ozone	2.5×10^{12} kg
Annual emission of NO_x by 100 supersonic airliners	6×10^7 kg per year
Total amount of NO_x above 15 km of the order of	5 to 10×10^9 kg

significance for the climate on a regional scale early in the next century.

Table 2 gives the masses of some of the constituents of the atmosphere. It is clear that man's capacity to pollute the world atmosphere will be limited by the available raw materials long before any substantial changes are produced in the concentrations of the main constituents – nitrogen and oxygen. Nevertheless certain minor constituents – notably carbon dioxide and ozone – play an important role in determining the heat balance of the atmosphere and earth's surface. The quantities of these in the atmosphere are not so much greater than the quantities of effluents produced by man's activities that we can regard them as unaffected. Ozone concentrations in the stratosphere are known to be sensitive to the concentrations of NO_x (that is NO and NO_2) and for this reason some relevant quantities are included in Table 2. I return to these matters laters.

Feed-back Processes and their Role in Determining Climate

Before attempting any assessment of the influence of particular human activities on climate, it is desirable to consider some of the factors which make such assessments particularly difficult and uncertain. Some of these may be illustrated by considering the problem of the response of the climate to a change in the heat output from the sun. If the earth were simply a solid body in radiative equilibrium in space, application of Stephan's Law would tell us that a 1% change in solar radiation would lead to a $0.7°C$ change in world temperature. However several important factors modify such a simple estimate. If we reduce the solar input, we reduce the temperature difference between the equator and the pole, and we reduce the intensity of the atmospheric circulation and the efficiency with which it conveys heat from the tropics to the polar regions. The polar regions therefore cool more than one would expect from purely radiative considerations. Moreover as the polar regions cool the area covered by snow and ice extends. This is important because a snow surface reflects much more of the incoming solar radiation than a typical vegetated surface (60 to 80% as against some 15%) so some 50 or 60% of the incoming heat may be lost which would otherwise have been absorbed. This results in an important "positive feed-back" process which enhances the effect of any potential cause of cooling. Estimating these processes in a semi-empirical manner a Russian climatologist, M. I. Budyko[1] prepared the curves which are shown in Fig. 3 relating the changes in the average temperature of the earth and its degree of glaciation to changes in the incoming solar radiation. The diagram shows how non-linear such relations may be, and suggest that with a fall of incoming radiation of less than 2% the earth might proceed to almost complete ice cover.

However, there are other "feed-back" processes which may be equally important and which may act to reinforce or oppose climatic change. Probably the greatest uncertainty is in regard to the effects of clouds. Like snow and ice, they reflect more of the sun's radiation than the underlying ground. In consequence an increase of the cloudiness of the atmosphere would lead to a cooler climate.

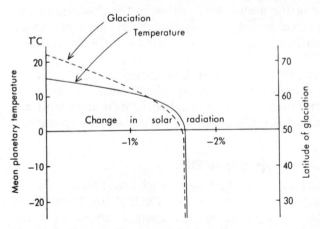

FIGURE 3.   The dependence of world temperature and glaciation on solar radiation from Budyko, ref. 1 .

However, we do not know whether a decrease of the incoming solar radiation would lead, of itself, to more or less cloud. However, from the ability of the climate to maintain itself within quite small limits over centuries despite considerable vagaries from year to year, one suspects that some stabilising influences are at work. Cloudiness variations may be one of these.

An important stabilising influence is, of course, that of the oceans. If all of the sun's heat which reaches the earth were used to heat all of the water, the rise of temperature would be less than 1°C in a year. In fact there is only a marginal imbalance between the heat reaching the earth and that radiated by the earth, and this can be absorbed by the oceans with little change in temperature. Year to year fluctuations in ocean temperature occur almost entirely in the top 100 metres or so of the ocean, but over longer periods of decades or centuries the heat storage and release from deeper layers must be taken into account. Transport and exchange of heat with these layers is controlled by the large-scale circulation of the ocean — itself driven mainly by the winds. Thus here we have another "feed-back" process between the climate and the oceans operating on the scale of ocean basins, and on a time scale measured in decades or centuries. The science of oceanography is not yet capable of describing these processes quantitatively. Thus the oceans provide another uncertainty in any prediction of climate. However we may be sure that deep-ocean heat storage will act to damp down any rapid changes of climate which might by initiated in the atmosphere, although the slowness of any response in the deep ocean may act to obscure any imbalance which may exist in the earth's heat budget and make it difficult to detect long-term trends.

A rather similar thermal inertia is imposed on any climatic warming in the neighbourhood of ice sheets such as those of Greenland and Antarctica. The heat required to melt any significant part of such ice masses could only be extracted from the atmosphere over centuries.

Effects of Artificial Heat Sources on Climate

Perhaps the simplest question which we can ask about man's possible influence on climate is in regard to the effect of his discharge of waste heat to the atmosphere. All the energy derived from the burning of fuel or from nuclear power sources ultimately finds its way into the atmosphere as waste heat whether it is discharged at the power station or generated at the place where the power is used. The effects of such waste heat need to be considered on several different scales.

On the scale of individual cities the heat generated may already exceed the incoming solar radiation — for New York (Manhattan) it is 630 Wm^{-2} compared with average net natural radiation of 93 Wm^{-2}. Such heating makes the city substantially warmer than the surrounding countryside when the winds are light and vertical transport of heat is impeded by relatively warm air aloft. Such conditions are most frequent at night in the cool seasons. The city may then be several degrees warmer than the surrounding country-side, but in most places such additional warmth is not unwelcome. During the day in summer when temperatures are higher there is usually a better ventilation of the city, and as the surface temperature rises heat is carried away upward freely by convection currents. Thus under the hotter conditions of summr the excess of city temperature over the surrounding country does not usually exceed 1°C, and this is contributed to by the reduced evaporation over the city as well as the artificial heat. Nevertheless with the increasing use of power for air conditioning the disposal of waste heat may well cause some inconvenience in cities located in tropical and sub-tropical areas of light winds.

Turning to the other extreme of scale, the world-wide scale, man's contribution to the atmosphere's heat budget appears quite trivial at present. Compared with an average net solar radiation at the ground of 100 Wm^{-2}, man's energy production averaged over the whole globe amounted to only 1.6 x 10^{-2} Wm^{-2} at the beginning of this decade. Thus it could increase sixty-fold before approaching 1% of the natural heat budget, at which stage changes of the order of 1°C might appear in world temperature. The uncertainties of any such estimate of the change in world temperature are great, but we may reasonably assume that there is room for a twenty-fold increase or more in energy use before any significant warming of the earth as a whole results.

However the discharge of waste heat is certainly not spread uniformly over the earth's surface, and one is led to ask whether the heat generated over limited areas such as Western Europe or the Eastern Seaboard of the U.S.A. can upset the atmospheric motions sufficiently to lead to a signficant change of climate. We have some measure of the amount of heat which would be necessary to do this because some of the natural variations from year to year appear to be due to additional heat supplied to the atmosphere from unusually warm patches of the ocean 1000 km^2 or so in extent. Over such areas the atmosphere may be supplied with an extra 100 Wm^{-2}. We may therefore assume that the discharge of waste heat over Western Europe at a rate of say 50 Wm^{-2} would produce a significant change of climate but not a catastrophic one. The climate would remain well within the normal range of variation from year to year but the bias to particular weather sequences would have a material effect on average conditions.

Currently the major industrial areas of the world such as Western Europe have a heat output of around 1 Wm^{-2} and we may conclude that a fifty-fold increase would lead to significant climatic changes extending far beyond the industrialised areas themselves. The effects of even a ten-fold increase would have to be seriously considered.

I have already mentioned the experiments which have been conducted to calculate the climate from first principles. Such experiments can be modified by including additional sources of heat. By carrying out the calculations with and without the source of heat one can form some judgement of the change in climate which might be brought about by the heat source. Fig. 4 illustrates the results of one such experiment in which a study has been made of the effect of

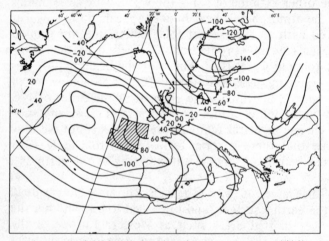

Atlantic energy park 41-80 day PMSL change (Waste heat experiment – mean 4 'controls') (mb)

FIGURE 4.   Mean-sea-level pressure anomaly introduced into calculated climate (winter) by a heat source introduced into the area shaded.

concentrating all Western Europe's heat output in a nuclear power generation area sited in the Atlantic off the South-western approaches. The total power generation is taken to be some fifty times the present level. The diagram shows the difference in mean-sea-level pressure between the calculations with the heat source and those without it. The differences in surface pressure are considerable and are comparable with the largest differences which occur between the same month in different years. It may be noted in passing that the winds over the British Isles receive a strong northerly bias from the additional heat source, reminding us that discharge of waste heat will not necessarily lead to a warmer climate everywhere.

It would be very unwise to put much weight on the results of a single experiment of this kind. There are many factors which have been left out. Nevertheless the experiment confirms that if the heat output of Europe were increased fifty-fold we might expect substantial climatic changes over a wide area of the northern hemisphere.

Carbon Dioxide and the Greenhouse Effect

There is one respect in which human activity has undoubtedly changed the composition of the world-wide atmosphere and in which it will continue to do so. This is in regard to the concentration of carbon dioxide. Carbon dioxide is a minor component of the atmosphere – only about 0.03% by volume – but it plays a significant part in the heat balance of the atmosphere because it absorbs and emits infrared radiation in parts of the spectrum for which the atmosphere is otherwise transparent. Carbon dioxide in the atmosphere has been monitored carefully at several places remote from sources of pollution and Fig. 5 shows the record from the summit of the volcanic mountain Mauna Loa in Hawaii. These observations are made in air above the trade-wind inversion which must have circulated widely through the atmosphere since it received any input from industrial effluents. The upward trend is apparent. The annual variation which is superimposed upon it is due to the annual cycle in the uptake of carbon dioxide by vegetation which is dominated by the growth of vegetation in the northern hemisphere in spring and summer.

The more-or-less steady annual increase of carbon dioxide in the atmosphere of about 0.7 p.p.m. per year is caused by the burning of

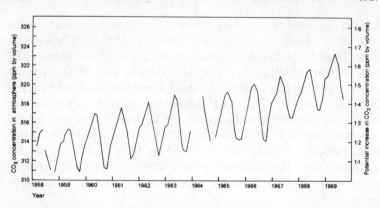

FIGURE 5.   Carbon dioxide concentration at Mauna Loa – monthly mean values. (from "Man's Impact on the Global Climate", MIT Press, 1970).

coal, oil, and other fuels. If all the carbon dioxide so produced were to remain in the atmosphere the rate of increase would be about twice as great as is observed. Part of the remainder is taken up by the oceans and part is probably taken up by vegetation, but the relative proportions are uncertain. The natural reservoirs of carbon which take part in the cycle of carbon dioxide with the atmosphere are shown in Fig. 6. The oceans as a whole hold a great deal more carbon

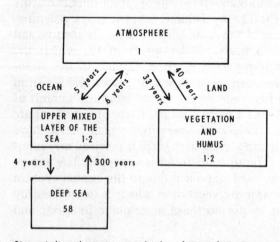

Figure indicated content as multiples of atmospheric content

FIGURE 6.   Natural reservoirs of carbon dioxide (based on Craig[3]).

dioxide in solution than exists in the atmosphere, and if the additional CO_2 which man adds to the atmosphere were shared between atmosphere and ocean according to their capacities, the rate of increase in the atmosphere would be very slow since the oceans hold sixty times as much as the atmosphere. However CO_2 is not shared in this way for two reasons. Firstly the rate of transfer of carbon dioxide to the oceans is quite slow and particularly from the upper layers to the deep ocean − mixing between the upper layers and the deep ocean requires a period of centuries − and secondly because of the complex chemical buffering processes which control the carbon dioxide equilibrium at the sea surface. These involve the carbonates of magnesium and sodium dissolved in the sea water. In consequence an increase of 0.6% in the carbon dioxide content of the sea corresonds to a 10% increase in the partial pressure of the gas in the atmosphere above it.

The world-wide industrial output of carbon dioxide has increased exponentially over recent decades at about 4% per annum. If an exponential increase in fuel consumption continues we may expect that about the same fraction of the carbon dioxide produced will remain in the atmosphere as hitherto. This leads to a prediction of an increase of some 25% in atmospheric carbon dioxide by the turn of the century − a value approaching 400 p.p.m. If the use of fuel does not increase so rapidly a rather smaller fraction may remain in the atmosphere as the longer-term mixing with the deep ocean removes some of the gas. However so long as man continues to burn fuel on anything like the present scale a continued increase in atmospheric carbon dioxide is inevitable.

We must therefore ask what effect this may have on world climate. Carbon dioxide is responsible for the so-called "greenhouse" effect which helps to reduce the heat loss from the earth. It operates thus. In the wavelength bands in which carbon dioxide is an absorber, heat is radiated from the earth and absorbed by the air above after it has passed through sufficient CO_2. This CO_2 radiates again, some heat goes upward and is absorbed by a higher layer, again radiated upward and so on until ultimately it reaches a layer above which there is insufficient CO_2 to prevent its escape to space. The more carbon dioxide there is in the atmosphere the higher we must go to find such a layer and the colder it will be. The colder this effective radiating layer the less heat it will radiate, and the more heat will be retained by the earth, thus allowing world temperature to rise until a balance is again reached.

Estimating just how large such a rise in world temperature will be is a complicated process. Not only have the radiative properties of all atmospheric gases and cloud to be considered, but also the changes which may come about because of higher temperatures. The water vapour content is likely to increase for example, and water vapour will contribute additionally to the "greenhouse effect". Probably the best available estimate of the effects of increase in carbon dioxide in the atmosphere are those of Manabe and Wetherald.[2] Their calculations suggest that the increase of 25% in carbon dioxide concentration would lead to an increase in average world temperature of $0.6°C$ – an amount which would not be distinguishable from the natural fluctuations of world temperature but which would nevertheless be of economic significance.

It is however desirable to remember the uncertainties of any such estimate. As indicated earlier there are many "feed-back" processes within the energy exchanges of the climate system which we do not fully understand. Some of these have been taken into account by Manabe and Wetherald, but others have not. Reference has already been made to the effect of the polar ice sheets which reflect the incoming solar radiation and reduce the available heat as the temperature falls and the ice area expands. Similarly, as temperature rises, snow-covered areas contract and more heat is available to warm the earth. Another "positive feed-back" arises from the carbon dioxide itself. As temperature rises, less carbon dioxide can be dissolved in the ocean, and the partial pressure in the atmosphere may increase, thus contributing to further warming. On the other hand there may be stabilising processes yet to be discovered, associated for example with variations in cloudiness. The relative stability of world temperature over long periods encourages the belief that unstable feed-back processes are not dominant. However estimates of the effect of carbon dioxide change in world temperature such as that given above – $+0.6°C$ by the year 2000 – can be regarded as no more than an indication of the possible magnitude.

The Stratosphere and the Ozone Layer

A great deal of interest has recently been generated in regard to possible effects of man's activities on the stratosphere and one may ask why there should be such concern over this rather remote region of the atmosphere. However there are several reasons why the stratosphere may be particularly sensitive to pollution. First the quantities of key constituents — ozone in particular — are not so large as to be beyond the possible influence by the effluents of man's activity. Secondly, the exchange of air between the stratosphere and the lower atmosphere is slow — mixing being a matter of years — so that there is time for pollutants injected into the stratosphere to accumulate. Thirdly, there is no scavenging of pollutants by cloud and rain such as helps to clean the lower atmosphere.

Although the ozone content of the stratosphere amounts at its maximum to only a few parts in a hundred thousand parts of air, it has two important effects. First, the maximum of temperature to be found around the 50 km level, where the air is some $50°C$ warmer than in the lower stratosphere, is due to the solar radiation absorbed by ozone. Second, the absorption of ultraviolet radiation by ozone prevents harmful ultraviolet radiation reaching the earth's surface. Thus any substantial change in the amount of ozone in the stratosphere might therefore be a cause of some concern.

Ozone is formed in the stratosphere by the photochemical dissociation of molecular oxygen, when subject to the incoming solar radiation and the subsequent combination of the oxygen atoms with oxygen molecules to form O_3. However the ozone concentration depends upon a balance between a large number of chemical and photochemical transformations which lead to a rate of destruction of the ozone which balances its formation. Reactions involving hydrogen and nitrogen atoms are known to be important. In unpolluted conditions the hydrogen is supplied by water vapour and methane, and the nitrogen atoms by nitrogen oxides. Recently it has been suggested that chlorine (or bromine) atoms if injected into the stratosphere might have to be taken into account in the ozone balance.

More than 50 different chemical reactions are believed to play a significant part in determining the ozone concentration but the problem does not end there. Although at levels above 40 km photochemical equilibrium is reached in a matter of hours, at levels below about 15 km, where much of the ozone is found, photo-chemical equilibrium would only be reached in a matter of years. The observed distribution of ozone is therefore partly determined by its formation mainly around 30 km and above, but also by its transport by the air currents which result in a net transport of ozone downward into the troposphere where it is ultimately destroyed at the ground. Figure 7 illustrates some of the processes involved.

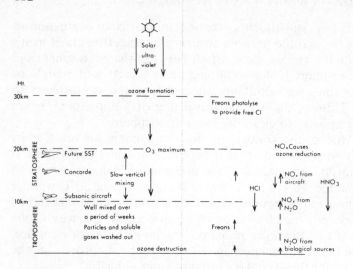

FIGURE 7.   Some factors affecting the ozone layer.

The chemical equilibrium of the ozone layer might be disturbed if the natural concentration of NO_x (that is nitrogen compounds containing odd numbers of nitrogen atoms – NO and NO_2) were increased. The natural content of these gases in the stratosphere has been measured only recently and been found to be very low – around 1 part in 10^9 – but sufficient to play an important role in the ozone photochemistry. NO_x is produced in aircraft engines when air is heated to high temperatures and discharged into the atmosphere in the exhausts. The level at which the aircraft fly is important in regard to their effect on the ozone layer because the NO_x which they produce would be most effective if diffused to the ozone maximum around 20 km. For this reason supersonic aircraft at 16 to17 km are likely to have more effect than subsonic aircraft at a little above 10 km. Such vertical diffusion is a slow process.

A considerable number of attempts have been made recently to calculate the ozone loss which might arise from the operation of fleets of supersonic airlines. These calculations are based on some 50 or more chemical reactions taking into account the diurnal cycle of solar radiation. They have to assume rather arbitrary rates of vertical diffusion of the ozone and of the nitrogen oxides, and so far the complexity has prevented any account being taken of the systematic motions of the air in three dimensions which give rise to geographical distributions of the upward and downward motions.

There is some disagreement among the various estimates which have been made. Calculations carried out in the Meteorological Office suggest it would require the operation of about 600 aircraft similar to Concorde to cause a 1% reduction in ozone above middle latitudes of the northern hemisphere. Such change would be quite undetectable against the natural fluctuations which exceed 30% from day to day and are believed to have changed by as much as 10% world-wide over a period of years. Although estimates of the effect by other scientists are several times greater, there is clearly no cause for concern in regard to the flights of the small number of supersonic aircraft currently planned. However, the matter may need to be kept under review if very much larger fleets of aircraft, whether subsonic or supersonic, were planned to fly in the stratosphere.

The effect of ozone reduction that has caused most concern arises from the additional dosage of ultraviolet radiation which would be received at the ground. There is some statistical evidence that the number of cases of skin cancer increases as exposure to solar ultraviolet increases. A 1% reduction in ozone would lead to a 2% increase in the ultraviolet dosage, and it has been suggested that this might lead to a few per cent increase in the number of cases of skin cancer – although, of course, such an effect might also be brought about by a 2% increase in the time spent out of doors.

Calculations carried out with numerical simulations of climate indicate that the climate at the ground is not likely to be sensitive to any possible artificial fluctuation of the ozone layer. The mass of the atmosphere at the ozone levels is small and disturbances do not readily propagate downward through a stably stratified atmosphere.

Aircraft are not the only possible source of nitrogen oxides in the stratosphere. Indeed the principal natural source of NO_x is believed to be in biological activity at the ground which produces nitrous oxide, N_2O. This is diffused upward to the stratosphere where it is transformed photochemically to NO_x. It has been suggested that the use of fertilisers in agriculture will increase the production of nitrous oxide and hence provide another potential source for man-made disturbance of the ozone layer. Quantitative evaluation of the effect has not yet been carried out. Incidentally it may be of interest to note that the odd nitrogen atoms are believed to leave the stratosphere ultimately as nitric acid which reaches the troposphere and is finally washed out by rain.

A further possible threat to the ozone layer, which has been extensively discussed recently, arises from the Freons which are discharged into the atmosphere from aerosol cans and from refrigerators when they are dismantled. In the atmosphere these carbon—halogen compounds are very stable and with very low solubility in water are not washed out by rain. It has been suggested that they will diffuse upward into the stratosphere where they will photolyse under the effect of the solar radiation at wavelengths which are filtered out before they reach low levels. The free atoms of chlorine may enter into the reactions controlling the ozone balance and be another possible cause for ozone depletion. There is some doubt as to whether the calculations so far carried out truly represent the processes which will operate. However one aspect makes a full evaluation of the matter highly desirable. This concerns the time scale on which such a process might operate. Since the Freons appear to be almost inert in the troposphere their concentrations will build up slowly over the years. Their effect on the stratosphere will, however, develop more slowly because it will take several years for the Freons to diffuse upward to around 30 km where they may photolyse and affect the ozone concentration. Thus if an adverse effect of Freons were noted and production were stopped (or reduced) any effect on the ozone layer would be maintained and indeed would increase further for many years after the cause was removed.

The Effects of Climatic Change

In considering some of the various possible man-made climatic changes, I have compared them with some of the natural short-term climatic variations of climate which occur over a period of a few years, decades, or centuries. Clearly man has learned to live with such fluctuations but how important are they economically? This is a question which it is appropriate to ask as agriculture and industry become more carefully tuned to make the maximum possible use of the climate and other climate-derived resources such as water.

Some parts of the world are more sensitive to climatic fluctuations than others. We heard a great deal about the devastating effects of drought in the Sahel in the early 1970s. Figure 8 is a rainfall map of Africa which shows that this strip of territory south of the Sahara

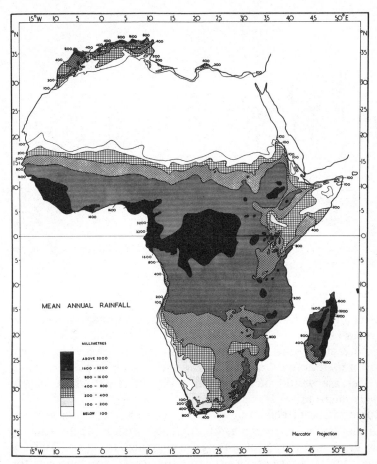

FIGURE 8. Rainfall map of Africa: mean annual rainfall. (Reproduced from "The Climate of Africa", by courtesy of the Oxford University Press).

lies in a region of very rapid transition of rainfall regime from north to south. Only a small shift in the latitude of the rainfall belt can produce a substantial change of the local rainfall. That such shifts take place over periods of a few years is apparent from the rainfall record reproduced in Fig. 9. There is some evidence that such shifts are associated with anomalies of the large-scale atmospheric circulation resulting from anomalies in the heat input from the oceans of a magnitude similar to those which I discussed earlier as responsible for year to year variations in weather. Thus any human activity which

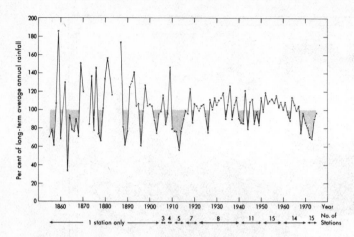

FIGURE 9.   Annual rainfall in the West African marginal rainfall areas expressed as per cent of long-term average.

produces changes in the atmospheric circulation comparable with the natural year to year fluctuations, has the potential for serious economic effects in such sensitive areas as the Sahel. As we have seen effects of human activity are far below such a scale at present, but a ten-fold increase would be approaching the threshold where significant effects might arise.

To illustrate the effect on agriculture nearer home, I reproduce in Fig. 10 a map showing the areas of England suitable (a) for growing maize for grain and (b) suitable for growing maize for silage. Maize is responsive mainly to temperature and the difference between the two boundaries is equivalent to a difference of a little over $0.25°C$ in mean summer temperature. It can be seen from this that the change of $0.6°C$ which might arise from the effects of carbon dioxide at the end of the century (twice the amount responsible for the difference between these boundaries) could have a quite significant effect on the boundaries of the areas over which various crops may be grown.

As a further indication of the significance of small temperature changes one may note that a $1°C$ temperature change is roughly equivalent to one week's additional snow lying in areas with occasional snow cover — enough to affect the agricultural work plan.

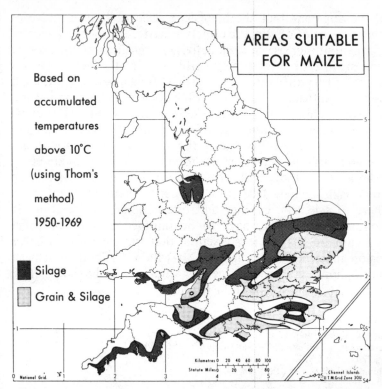

Based on
accumulated
temperatures
above 10°C
(using Thom's
method)
1950-1969

Silage

Grain & Silage

AREAS SUITABLE
FOR MAIZE

FIGURE 10.   Areas of the United Kingdom climatologically suitable for growing maize
(from Hough[4]).

Concluding Remarks

There are many aspects of man's potential impact on climate which I
have not touched upon. Some of these are not connected with
energy use or chemical problems. Large-scale irrigation has the
potential to change the energy balance of a region on a scale greater
than current industrial activities. Other agricultural activities also
change the reflectivity of the surface. After a snowfall the difference
between the heat absorbed by a forest which has shed the snow from
its canopy and from snow covered fields is particularly large. There is
also the possibility that pollutants may affect precipitation processes
in clouds or affect their reflectivity.

It will be apparent that the increasing scale of human activities makes the assessment of climatic effects a matter for serious concern. If an exponential increase in such activities continues at the present rate some significant effects may arise early in the next century. However, it will be difficult to detect such effects, because, although of economic significance, they may still be below the level of natural fluctuations of climate. It is thus essential that we should attempt to trace the chain of cause and effect quantitatively through the climatic system. As we have seen the necessary calculations are expensive and difficult. However the foundations for them are being laid. I hope that they will attract scientists of the necessary intellectual calibre and dedication to carry them through in an atmosphere of scientific enquiry and international co-operation. If ever economic restrictions have to be imposed because of some suspected climatic hazard, it is essential that the scientific basis for the decision must be above challenge. It will be difficult to achieve this, and I hope that the necessary studies will be adequately supported in nations throughout the world.

References

[1]   M. I. Budyko, *Tellus*, 1969, **21**, 611.
[2]   S. Manabe and R. T. Wetherald, *J. Atmospheric Sci.*, 1967, **24**, 241.
[3]   H. Craig, *Tellus*, 1957, 9, 1.
[4]   M. N. Hough, *ADAS. Q. Rev.*, 1975, **18**, 64.

Crops and Fertilizers: Overall Energy Budgets

by J. A. Tatchell, Imperial Chemical Industries Limited, Agricultural Division

Energy Analysis

IT is becoming generally recognised that we not only consume energy directly as fuel, but that any production of material or product involves the consumption of energy. Energy analysis assesses all the energy used in a manufacturing process, starting from the energy used to win the raw material, adding the energy used in transport and further processing, and tracing the various flows through the manufacturing process to the final product.

Materials which are not fuels, e.g., limestone, iron ore, or phosphate rock, are assumed to have no energy content in the natural state. Energy input starts when they are mined or quarried. On the other hand a fuel has an inherent energy content in the natural state, but further energy is used to win or transport it, and there may be processing losses, so that when it is burned the energy which has been consumed is greater than its conventional calorific value.

Table 1 traces the energy input to electricity generated from coal: coal production uses 1% of the coal output for its own purposes and the equivalent of 1.7% as purchased electricity. Including transport, about 1.035 units of energy are required to produce 1 unit of coal energy. The CEGB uses coal at 31% thermal efficiency to generate electricity and there is about 4% loss in transmission and distribution to industry. There is thus an input from the coal of 3.48 GJ for each GJ of electricity generated. Other energy was used to manufacture the power station, and in theory the amount could be calculated step by step starting with the manufacture of steel. This process would be extremely laborious, so an average figure of energy per £ expenditure is used, based on the total U.K. energy usage divided by the gross domestic product. The writer also uses this

119

Table 1: Calculation of primary energy input to electricity

		Primary energy
Primary fuel (coal in the ground)		1
Coal mining and transport	Usage 3.5%	1.035
Electricity generation	Efficiency 31%	3.34
Transmission and distribution to industry	Loss 4%	3.48
Energy in power station equipment	+0.15	3.63

Total input 3.63 GJ/GJ of electricity (13.1 GJ/MWh)

figure to allow for the energy associated with labour, on the grounds that any employee uses considerable energy, e.g., in the home and in personal transport. In the case of electricity generation these additional inputs are relatively small and increase the total energy input to 3.63 GJ/GJ.

Where substantial steam loads and electricity loads occur together, back pressure generation can be used, giving an efficiency of about 70% (1.43 GJ/GJ).

Energy Input to Fertilizers

The fertilizer production flowsheet (Fig. 1) shows the main inputs and the intermediate products used in making the actual fertilizers.

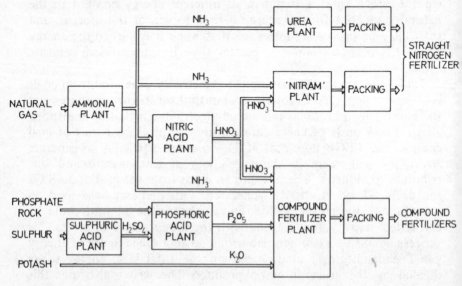

FIGURE 1   Fertilizer production flowsheet.

Table 2: Energy input to fertilizer raw materials and services

Natural gas	1.032 GJ input/GJ of CV.
Electricity	13.1 GJ/MWh (5.1 where a large steam load is associated with the electrical load).
Steam	3.3 to 3.9 GJ/tonne
Phosphate rock	2.2 GJ/tonne
Potash	6.2 GJ/tonne
Sulphur	1.45 GJ/tonne
Fixed costs (1975 values)	0.1 GJ/£.

The direct energy inputs are natural gas and electricity, together with steam whose energy input can readily be derived from the fuel used. Phosphate rock and potash both involve energy usage in mining, processing, and transport, which can be calculated from published data. Sulphur is produced by partial oxidation of H_2S removed from sour natural gas. The process is exothermic and little external input is needed. In fact the H_2S has a significant calorific value (about one-third that of natural gas) so it could be considered as an energy input, but in practice it would be impossible to use it as a practical fuel due to the SO_2 effluent, so it is valued as a waste product with no energy value. Production of the raw sulphur therefore involves only the energy input for services and for the capital invested in the plant, but there are further inputs involved in transport. Table 2 lists all the basis inputs associated with the flowsheet. The next stage is to calculate the inputs to the intermediate products. Table 3 shows the materials usage and the corresponding energy inputs including the inputs of steam and electricity, together with the fixed and capital costs. In the case of nitric acid and sulphuric acid, steam is produced from waste heat and the energy input is negative. Phosphoric acid needs considerable amounts of electricity and steam, and back pressure generation is assumed.

Table 4 shows the completed calculation of the energy inputs to typical fertilizers. It will be seen that nitrogen involves far larger inputs than the other two elements, also that ammonium nitrate needs about 10% less energy input per unit of nitrogen than does urea. The inputs to P and K are considerably less than to N.

Energy into Agriculture

Table 5 shows the total energy consumed in agriculture in the U.K., which totals 250 m GJ per annum, about 2.7% of the national total. 29% of the agricultural energy is used on fertilizers.

Table 3: Inputs to intermediates

	Ammonia	Nitric acid	Sulphuric acid	Phosphoric acid as P_2O_5	Fertilizer packing
Material usage/tonne product:					
Natural gas	46.0 GJ				
Ammonia		0.285 tonne			
Sulphur			0.330 tonne		
Phosphate rock				2.9 tonne	
Sulphuric acid				2.6 tonne	
Energy inputs GJ/tonne product from:					
Natural gas	47.5	14.3			
Ammonia					
Sulphur			0.5		
Phosphate rock				6.3	
Sulphuric acid				-3.5	
Steam and electricity	1.6	-1.0	-2.1	5.7	0.6
Fixed and capital costs	1.1	0.5	0.2	2.3	0.4
TOTAL	50.2	13.8	-1.4	10.8	1.0

Table 4: Inputs to typical fertilizers

	"Nitram"	Urea	Compound fertilizers			
			15.15.21	22.11.11	9.25.25	17.17.17
Material usage/tonne fertilizer:						
Ammonia	0.220	0.593	0.097	0.143	0.058	0.110
Nitric acid	0.807		0.355	0.520	0.213	0.403
Phosphoric acid (as P_2O_5)			0.155	0.113	0.258	0.175
Potash (as K_2O)			0.216	0.113	0.258	0.175
Energy input from: (GJ/tonne fertilizer)						
Ammonia	11.1	29.8	4.9	7.1	2.9	5.5
Nitric acid	11.0		4.9	7.1	2.9	5.6
Phosphoric acid			1.6	1.3	2.8	1.9
Potash			1.3	0.7	1.6	1.1
Steam, electricity, and oil for drying and coating	2.0	5.2	2.0	2.0	2.0	2.0
Fixed and capital costs	0.2	0.6	0.4	0.4	0.4	0.4
Packing	1.0	1.0	1.0	1.0	1.0	1.0
Total (GJ/tonne bagged fertilizers)	25.3	36.6	16.1	19.6	13.6	17.5
Inputs to useful elements						
MJ/kg N	72.3	78.5	81.9	78.9	84.7	80.8
MJ/kg P_2O_5			14.1	13.4	14.9	13.7
MJ/kg K_2O			8.2	7.7	8.6	7.9

Table 5: Primary energy consumed by U.K.
agriculture 1973

	GJ × 10⁶	per cent
Solid Fuel	4.1	1.7
Oil	84.0	34.1
Electricity	33.1	13.5
Fertilizers	71.1	29.0
Agrochemicals	1.3	0.5
Machinery	52.0	21.2
Total	245.6	100

Source: Joint Consultative Organisation for Research
and Development in Agriculture and Food. Report
No. 1: Report of the Energy Working Party. Dec. 1974.
Reproduced by permission of the A.R.C.

The agricultural industry is complex, and like the chemical
industry produces many intermediate products which are further
processed. The fertilizer is used on arable crops and on grass, but
only part of the arable crops are sold as such. The remainder,
together with all the grass, are further processed through animals
producing dairy products, meat, eggs, and wool. A further complication is that some animal feed is imported. Making reasonable
allowance for these factors I have calculated that the net food output
from U.K. farming in 1973 was about 8.5 million tons of cereals,
meat, sugar, and dairy products and about 9 million tons of potatoes
and vegetables (Table 6). Valuing this food purely in energy
terms − by the number of calories it contains − the output of U.K.
agriculture is about 125 million GJ, i.e., about half the energy input.
I discuss the significance of this figure later.

Table 6: Net food production from U.K. agriculture

	Million tons
Cereals for food	2.2
Cereals for beer and spirits	1.6
Sugar from beet	0.8
Meat (liveweight)	2.1
Milk − as solids	1.3
Eggs	0.5
Potatoes	5.5
Vegetables	3.2

Total food energy content − about 125×10^6 GJ.

The Effect of Fertilizers

The majority of the energy input to agriculture is used for working the land, for sowing and harvesting crops, also in providing machinery, buildings etc. These inputs remain virtually constant whatever amount of fertilizer is used on the land. It is therefore reasonable to consider the effect of the fertilizer separately, and to try to equate the energy input to the fertilizer with the increased output produced by its application.

There have undoubtedly been large increases in crop yields in the last 50 years since artificial fertilizers started to be used. For example wheat yields have at least doubled (Fig. 2). Not all this increase is due to the use of fertilizers, other major reasons being improved varieties and farming methods, but the new varieties have in fact been bred according to their response to fertilizers.

Field tests on experimental farms can show the effect of fertilizers under controlled conditions and Fig. 3 illustrates the type of result obtained. The increased crop yield, or response, tends to decrease with larger applications, the graph being represented either as a curve or by a straight line with a point of inflection. In practice many tests

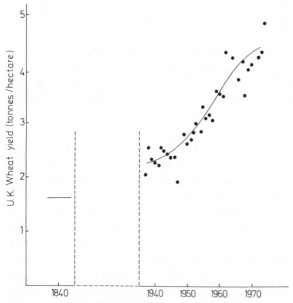

FIGURE 2   U.K. wheat yield.

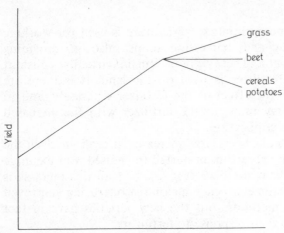

FIGURE 3   Typical fertilizer response. (Source: G. W. Cooke, "Fertilizing for Maximum Yield", 2nd Edn., Crosby Lockwood Staples, 1975. Reproduced by permission of the Copyright holder).

are needed as the yields are affected by temperature and rainfall during the growing season, and by the initial condition of the ground which is itself determined by its use and treatment during the previous season and by the weather during the previous winter.

Response curves can be derived for any of the three major plant foods, N, P, and K, and indeed for minor ones as well. However, nitrogen is the main promoter of extra growth, and the required phosphate and potash can readily be applied. Also the energy inputs to phosphate and potash are relatively small, so attention will be concentrated on the effect of nitrogen application.

Figure 4 shows the response of winter wheat to nitrogen application based on tests at Jealott's Hill Research Station. 17 kg/ha of nitrogen plus P and K were drilled with the seed, and the larger applications of N made in early May. The results are for one particular variety over four years, and as would be expected there is significant variation from year to year. The average curve shows a nearly linear response to the spring applications up to about 100 kg of N per acre. These results are characteristic of wheat and barley, but give rather bigger yields than are achieved on the average farm. The average U.K. yield of wheat in 1974 was 4.37 tonne/ha with a fertilizer application of 92 N, 45 P_2O_5, and 40 K_2O (kg/ha). This point is shown in the Figure 4, and assuming the same proportional

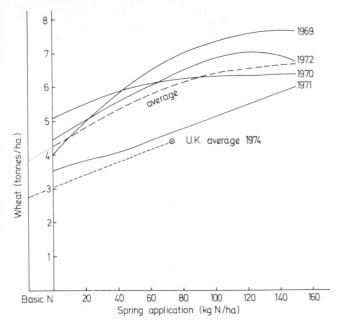

FIGURE 4   Fertilizer response of winter wheat. (Source: Jealott's Hill Research Station).

response as in the tests, the yield without fertilizer would be 2.78 tonne/ha. This is higher than the actual yields in the past when little artificial N fertilizer was used (e.g. 1.6 tonne/ha in 1840) as would be expected if fertilizers are not the only cause of increased yield.

In energy terms these figures shows that an application of 7.7 GJ of energy as fertilizer produced an increment of 1.59 Te of wheat with a food energy content of 24 GJ, corresponding to 3.1 units of food energy per unit of fossil energy.

Figure 5 shows similar tests on grass, where response is linear up to much higher rates of N application. The response is affected by the amount of clover in the sward, particularly at low rates of fertilizer application. However, the full advantage of introducing clover cannot always be achieved; for example grass grown for hay will tend to stifle the clover, so an average curve has been taken as typical of U.K. conditions.

The extra production of grass through fertilizer application contributes to production of meat and milk, but the relation is relatively complex as there are many different feeding systems, most

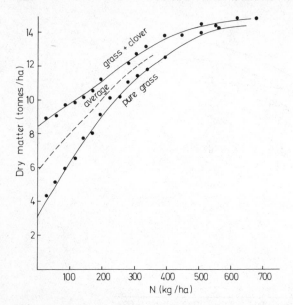

FIGURE 5   Fertilizer response of grass. (Source: D. Reid *J. Agric. Sci. (Camb.)*, 1970, **74**, 227–240. Reproduced by permission of Cambridge University Press).

of which involve more than one type of food. With cattle the output may be both milk and meat, but in these calculations it is reasonable to consider the two outputs separately.

Milk Production

The I.C.I. Dairymaid Scheme records the performance of over 1800 dairy herds in England and Wales and comprehensive data are published. Cows are fed with grass either by direct grazing or as hay or silage, with a supplement of concentrate. The proportions of grass and concentrate vary considerably depending on farming practice such as stocking rate and rate of fertilizer application. Table 7 shows the average figures for the I.C.I. Dairymaid herds during 1975.

The response curve shows that for the average nitrogen application rate about 45% of the grass yield is due to the fertilizer. Similarly if the concentrates are assumed to be wheat grown under average conditions, about 35% of the concentrates would be produced as a result of fertilizer application. It can then be calculated that the primary energy input as fertilizer is 5.53 GJ/1000 litres extra milk production, and the ratio of food energy output to fertilizer energy input is 0.51.

Table 7: I.C.I. Dairymaid herds

Average annual figures

Yield 4596 litres/cow*
     0.478 ha/cow
     280 Kg N/ha (134 kg/cow)
     1.22 tonne concentrates/cow.

Energy input to fertilizer 134 x 72.3 MJ/cow (9.68 GJ).
This produces 50% of the grass consumed.
So equivalent input for full output is   19.4 GJ
1.22 tonne concentrate* needs 4.88 GJ/tonne i.e.   6.0 GJ
                                      25.4 GJ

i.e. 5.53 GJ/1000 litres milk.

Food value of milk 380 kcal/pint (2.81 MJ/litre) so
food energy output/fertilizer energy input = 0.51

*Calculation neglects output of calves, also uses wheat
as characteristic of concentrates.

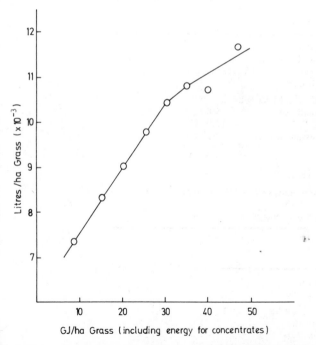

FIGURE 6   Milk production. (Source: I.C.I. "Dairymaid" scheme).

Figure 6 shows a detailed analysis of the results from 1683 herds, which also shows the effect of increased fertilizer application. The graph includes an allowance for the fertilizer needed for the different concentrate usages and shows an input of 7 GJ of fertilizer energy input per thousand litres of incremental milk production, which agrees reasonably well with the previous calculations.

Meat Production

Feeding systems for beef cattle cover nearly the entire range from wholly grass to wholly cereal rations. Tables 8 and 9 show calculations for two typical systems using figures from the Meat and Livestock Commission, the first being mainly grass and the second wholly cereal. The fertilizer energy input per pound of extra liveweight gain is a little less where cereal feeding is used. This appears surprising, as it is normally considered extravagant to use potential human food to feed animals. However in fertilizer terms the N is used rather more efficiently in growing cereals than in

Table 8: Semi-intensive grass beef

2 seasons grazing plus winter on concentrates.
Liveweight gain overall 943 lb (428 kg).
Average stocking rate 2 beast/acre over 2 seasons (2.47/ha year).
Concentrates usage 0.68 tonne/beast.

Assume 200 Kg N/ha year: i.e., 81 kg N/beast
N produces 42% of grass and needs   5.86 GJ
— equivalent for full output is   13.9 GJ
0.68 tonne concentrate (assume barley)   3.3 GJ
                                          ――――――
                                           17.2 GJ

i.e. 40.2 GJ/tonne liveweight.

Carcass weight 56% of liveweight, so 71.8 GJ/tonne meat.
Food value of carcass 10 MJ/kg
so food energy output/fertilizer energy input is 0.14

Table 9: Cereal fed beef

Feed: 1.95 tonne
Liveweight gain: 0.35 tonne

Fertilizer input to feed 1.95 × 4.88 = 9.52 GJ
i.e., 27.2 GJ/tonne liveweight
      48.6 GJ/tonne carcass
so food energy output/fertilizer energy input is 0.20

growing grass, so that where the land used to support animals is capable of growing cereals it is probably best to do so. However in many areas grass is the only practical crop.

Discussion of Results

Table 10 summarizes the results of the calculations of incremental food energy output per unit of fertilizer energy input and shows that in the case of cereals the ratio of food energy to fertilizer energy is greater than one. In fact if the straw is taken into account, about five units of energy are produced for one unit of fossil energy input. The extra is, of course, solar energy which has been trapped and concentrated in the process. It has been suggested that we should "grow" fuel in this way, and theoretically the energy needed for the fertilizer could be provided from part of the output, so giving a net output from an entirely solar input.

However, this is not the important point. What we have achieved is to turn fossil energy into food energy and although they are both conventionally measured in heat units they are by no means equivalent. Table 11 shows a variety of different things which each contain the same amount of energy as a gallon of petrol. It is clear

Table 10: Output/input ratios

	Energy input from fertilizers	Incremental food energy output	Ratio output/input
Wheat	4.84 GJ/tonne	15 GJ/tonne	3.1
Milk	5.53 MJ/litre	2.81 MJ/litre	0.51
Beef carcass	50–70 GJ/tonne	10 GJ/tonne	0.14–0.20

Table 11: Energy equivalents

2	weeks sunshine (on a square metre)
26	lbs straw
14	lbs coal
1	gal petrol
30	lbs bread
96	pints milk
38	lbs steak
300	pints beer
24	bottles whisky

All can provide 155 MJ of heat.

that there are very great differences in the quality of these different forms of energy, though admittedly it is not easy to put them in order. In fact the value will differ in different circumstances. Anyone who was hungry would agree that the food was of the greatest value, though a motorist stranded on his way home after a good dinner might prefer the petrol. Neither could make much use of a pile of straw or indeed some sunshine to meet their particular needs.

I have tried to compare food and fuel energy by considering the choices made between the two by someone at subsistence level. The minimum subsistence diet could comprise mainly bread, with only a little extra protein and vitamin foods. The minimum cost of this diet at late 1975 prices would be around £2 a week, compared with the average expenditure on food of about £5 per week. At this time the average expenditure on domestic energy was £1.1 per head per week. I assume that the first priority would be given to the £2 worth of basic food, and that the next 50 pence available would tend to be used on heating. If more money were available the choice would probably be to improve the diet by replacing some bread by more palatable animal products such as meat and milk, so raising the food expenditure to around £4 per week, before bringing the fuel expenditure up towards the national average. Table 12 lists the energy inputs associated with these choices, and it is seen that the 2700 calories of basic food energy is valued 4 times as highly as 7000

Table 12: Choices between food and fuel

Priority	Choice	Cost/ week	Energy content/ day
1	Minimum diet (Mainly bread)	£2	2700 cal.
2	Minimum Heating (40% of average)	50p	7000 cal.
3	Improved diet* (70% bread, 30% animal)	£4	2900 cal.
4	Improved heating (80% of average)	50p	7000 cal.

(*Average is 45% animal, cost £5, 3000 cal/day).
Choices 1 and 2: 2700 Cal bread valued equal to (7000 x 2)/0.5 fuel
    i.e. 10 x
Choices 3 and 4: Replacement of 700 cal bread by 900 cals meat is
                is valued at (7000 x 2)/0.5 fuel
   i.e. $900 \equiv 28000 + (700 \times 10)$
   i.e. 39 x

Table 13: Output/input ratios, allowing for quality of food energy

	Ratio output/input in crude energy terms	Quality factor	True ratio
Wheat	3.1	10	31
Milk	0.5	40	20
Beef	0.14–0.20	40	5.5–8

calories of space heating fuel, i.e., a calorie of basic food energy is valued at 10 times the value of a calorie of fossil fuel. In the same way it can be shown that the energy in animal food is valued at about 40 times the energy contained in fossil fuel.

Table 13 re-calculates the ratios of fertilizer energy input to food output allowing for these quality factors. The picture is completely changed and shows that even where meat was apparently produced inefficiently, we are in fact getting a good return from the use of fossil energy.

Even this is not the whole story. The basis of all these calculations is the principle that the amount of land is fixed, and that the application of fertilizer produces an increment of food production, whose value is then compared with the energy input associated with the fertilizer. It is, however, sometimes argued that the extra land is in fact available and should be used to produce the extra food without the use of any fertilizer energy. But in this case extra energy would be used to work the increased acreage of land. In simple terms, fertilizers represent 29% of the energy input to agriculture. If this fertilizer produces 29% of the total yield, and if the other inputs are proportional to the acreage used, it would use the same amount of energy to produce the same food on a greater area if fertilizers were not applied. In more detail (Table 14): half the total oil input to agriculture is used in tractors and farm machinery and from Table 5 it can be shown that these involve 38% of the energy use in agriculture. Allowing for greater use on arable land, the input associated with working this land is about 10 GJ/ha. It has previously been shown that fertilizer needing 7.8 GJ/ha provides 35% of the total wheat yield, so that if the fertilizer were not used 55% more land would be needed which would involve 5.5 GJ of extra energy input – 70% of the saving of fertilizer energy.

One final point: there are those who suggest that our whole

Table 14: Energy for cultivation versus fertilizer energy

U.K. figures	GJ x 10^6
Fuel usage on tractors etc. (½ of 84)	42
Energy input to machinery	52
	94
	Mha
Agricultural land: Arable	7.3
Grass	4.8

Assume arable needs twice use on grass.
Energy used on arable (94/9.7) = 9.7 GJ/ha (say, 10).

Average fertilizer use on wheat is 92 kg N/ha involving energy input
7.7 GJ/ha (including P and K), and providing 35% of total yield.

If fertilizer is not used, need 55% more land, involving 5.5 GJ/ha
i.e., 70% of the fertilizer energy saved.

approach is wrong and that because meat involves more energy use
we should eat less of it. This is a valid point of view, but has little to
do with agricultural efficiency. There is a fundamental difference
between improving the efficiency of making a product and stopping
using the product altogether. Our reason for using energy has always
been to improve the standard of living and we still assume that this
will continue. The aim should surely be to achieve this improvement
with less energy input, not to reduce standards.

Conclusions

I have tried to show that the small amount of the national energy
(3%) used to produce food – and the even smaller amount used to
produce fertilizer – is very well justified.

If allowance is made for the much higher "quality" of food
energy, the extra output is many times the input of fertilizer energy.
This extra food is being produced from the same area of land, and
even if more land were available it would need nearly as much energy
to work the extra land as to apply fertilizer to a smaller area.

Clearly there is still scope and need for improvements both in
making fertilizer and in using it, but there is no need for fundamental
change.

References

[1] "The Energy Input to a Bag of Fertilizer", I.C.I., 1974.
[2] G. W. Cooke, "Fertilizing for Maximum Yield".
[3] Jealott's Hill Research Station, "Guide to Field Experiments", (Annual publication).
[4] "Effects of a Wide Range of N Application on Grass with and without Clover", D. Reid, *J. Agric. Sci. (Camb.)*, 1970, 74, 227–240.
[5] "Prospects for Dairy Farming in 1976", I.C.I. Farm Advisory Service.
[6] "Report of Energy Working Party", Agricultural Research Council, 1974.
[7] "Cattle Facts", Meat and Livestock Commission, 1972.
[8] "U.K. Dairy Facts and Figures", Milk Marketing Board, 1975.
[9] "Agricultural Statistics", H.M.S.O., 1973.

Energy Conservation in Biology

by R. J. P. Williams; Inorganic Chemistry Laboratory, Oxford
University

Introduction

IN this article I shall take conservation of energy (in biology) to refer
to its relatively short-term purposeful preservation from destruction
and wasted use. There is of course no continuously increasing energy
store on earth due to biological systems. Biology has really but one
source of energy, the sun, and the utilisation of this energy is a
central theme in the whole of life. Both the reflection and
re-radiation of light from the earth are losses (inefficient capture)
and the ultimate degradation of light to heat is an inevitable and final
energy loss in the life process associated with growth and death, and
it is not possible to conserve this heat loss. Putting the energy input
and output together there is therefore no ongoing conservation of
energy by life in its totality, for life is in an approximately
steady-state energy and mass relationship with its surroundings:

light from the sun → life → heat (of the earth)
matter from the earth → life → matter to the earth.

Much of life is not sustained directly by the light from the sun but
engages in the digestion of other living forms which themselves are
ultimately dependent upon the sun's energy. It is usually true
therefore that one form of living matter can become an energy store
for another, but this is not a purposeful storage activity of any form
of life, except for rare examples such as by man himself, and this
"feeding" activity can reasonably be included within the above
steady states.

In passing, note that the stores of oil, gas, and coal in the earth
due to the destruction (degradation) of living matter at high pressure
are not conserved forms of energy usable by biological systems
generally, but represent accidental losses, the waste of living

137

materials some long time ago. (In this respect they are not to be compared with the oxygen of the air: see below.) By burning these materials man is returning chemicals to the life cycle while "using" their energy, but it would appear that life generally is quite unable to do this. Note too that man's problem in building a technology based on energy from these sources, which means that he, a biological object, has found a temporary energy store, is that they are exhaustible and man will ultimately have to go back to direct harnessing of atomic energy, e.g. of the sun, thus returning to an energy economy common to other forms of life. Storage of the sun's energy is life's business: coal, oil, and gas are accidental products and would remain as waste but for man's ingenuity).

In the above steady state, life is a constant energy store, but it is clearly beyond the scope of this article to deal with the total conservation in life itself. Instead I shall look at the activity of an individual biological system which represents a fluctuation within the steady state. At first sight it would appear to be best to take a single whole organism and to describe how it sets aside energy stores for the various activities in which it must engage subsequently. Unfortunately our understanding of the complexity of organisms with their dependently functioning parts is rather limited and I shall confine my attention therefore to the activities of single cells.

The material of all cells is formed by uphill (in a thermodynamic sense) reactions and thus there is a retention of energy in growth materials such as DNA, RNA, and essential functional proteins and polysaccharides during cell life-times. I shall not treat conservation of energy in cells in this general way, for it does not represent a deliberate conservation by a cell in order to assist later activity. Rather I shall look at one cell and ask how can it conserve energy by certain steps in its own history which will assist the cell at some other phase of development. Thus the conserved stores of those cell materials, e.g. fats, saccharides such as glycogen, some proteins, and some inorganic materials, to be used later in synthesis and activity, are the chemical forms of conserved energy to which I shall be referring.

Biology conserves energy in these synthesised chemicals, but they are also a store of chemical elements, for life needs materials as well as energy for growth. Thus the materials in which energy is stored must have been "chosen" so that a good variety of elements is present. A principal element which must be conserved is carbon,

Table 1: Storage of some elements

Element	Form of storage
Carbon	Fats, Sugars, (Protein)
Hydrogen	Fats, Sugars
Nitrogen	Protein, Amino-acids
Oxygen	Bound to myoglobin, (air)
Phosphorus	Polyphosphates, Creatine phosphate, Phosphovitin, Bone
Calcium	Bone which can be re-sorbed
Iron	Ferritin

Note also the storage of compounds such as transmitters and hormones in a great variety of vesicles.

which is used in all biopolymers, and fats and sugars are the major stores of it in well-known carbon pathways of life cycles. For each required element there is such a pathway and a quick glance at the paths reveals the storage mode, c.f. Table 1. The free energy in the store of each chemical ΔG is related to ΔG^0, the free energy of formation of the chemical from elements in some chosen standard states, and to the concentration of the chemical if it is in solution. We shall be concerned with the producion of this overall ΔG. Now that the sense in which I use the idea of energy conservation in biology has been outlined, I must go back and examine the connection between the light input from the sun and the stores of chemicals in the cell, not forgetting that biology is forced to use particular elements in these chemicals as they are a required part of later synthetic pathways.

The trapping of the radiant energy of the sun is photo-assimilation, and turning it into a synthetic chemical form is photosynthesis. Photosynthesis is really a dark reaction not different from other dark reactions of biology. It has two major steps:

Oxidation/Reduction: $\quad H_2O \longrightarrow$ bound$-H_2 + \frac{1}{2}O_2$(air)

$$CO_2 + 2H_2 \longrightarrow (HCOH) + H_2O$$

Condensation of (HCOH): $\quad ROH + ROH \longrightarrow$

$$R_2O \text{ (sugar and fats)} + H_2O.$$

This scheme hides the fact that although the initial disproportionation of water to bound-H_2 and oxygen is driven directly by light, the energy requirements of the two subsequent steps are not provided directly by light and therefore there is a need for a part of the light energy to be conserved in some relatively transient form and chosen materials, so that it can be used to drive such reactions as are represented by the second and third equations above. Before turning to this problem, notice that the outstandingly simple stores of conserved *light energy* in chemical form are therefore the oxygen of the air, and the H_2 bound together with CO_2, i.e. as stated above, concentrated forms of sugars and fats. Energy and chemicals (H,C,O) are put into storage by the same reaction system.

The oxygen of the air can be re-used by biological systems to generate additional storage of energy. Thus by the correct assembly of catalysts the action of oxygen on combined hydrogen is used to drive the formation of pyrophosphate (the energy-rich chemical bond of the biochemist) in oxidative phosphorylation.

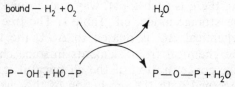

Combined pyrophosphate – as adenosine triphosphate (ATP) – is the usual (temporary) energy store, mentioned above, of biology. Some of this pyrophosphate is also formed directly from light in a step known as cyclic photo-phosphorylation, Fig. 1, which is an alternative way of using the energy of light.

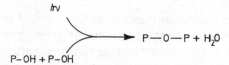

The subsequent reverse transformation, hydrolysis of P–O–P, drives the dehydration of many chemical species while itself returning to phosphate, and this is the basic mechanism of carbon dioxide fixation and of condensation polymerisation of amino-aids, nucleotides, and sugars giving proteins, DNA, RNA, and poly-saccharides. This step is the immediate utilisation of transiently stored energy for growth. The hydrolysis of P–O–P also occurs in the utilisation of stored energy for work such as in movement (muscle contraction) in which the store is dissipated (largely as heat) and in the concentration of some chemicals in which the use of

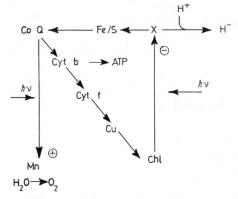

FIGURE 1   The photo-reaction of the chloroplast. The paths of charges are shown. Note ATP formation.

P—O—P energy results in a third form of energy conservation through the generation of a gradient of concentration as in a concentration cell. (P—O—P is the required transient chemical form even in the initial capture of CO_2 (and N_2) and its incorporation in sugars, mentioned above).

The essential biological energy conservation can be seen to be the initial steps of photosynthesis in the chloroplast and of oxidative phosphorylation in the mitochondria, Fig. 2, and the subsequent steps are conventional though complicated downhill chemistry. The total amount of ATP in a cell is never very large and most energy is stored after passage through ATP which is thus a temporary small store of immense importance and which is held in a steady-state relationship with the initial energy supply and the larger energy stores:

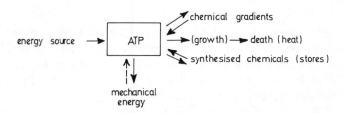

There is no great mystery in the energetic relationships of the right-hand side of the diagram, but we shall see that at the present time the initial synthesis of ATP is poorly described. In the next

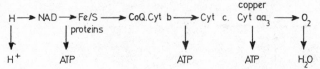

FIGURE 2   The cytochrome chain of mitochondria. The path of electrons is shown. Note the sequence from Fe/S to copper is the same as in the chloroplast as cyt. f and cyt. c are very much alike. The mitochondria use the oxygen from the chloroplast.

sections the initial steps between light or redox energy and ATP formation, so-called photo-phosphorylation and oxidative phosphorylation, will be discussed.

Photosynthesis: the Chloroplast

We can start the description of biological energy transformations with the action of light on organised photo-absorbing pigments of green plants and algae. Energy transfer within membrane-bound photo-systems leads to little loss of radiant energy before the photo-reaction system converts the photon into a diradical pair, and at this stage the energy is captured as a separated pair of charges. Before following the charge migration the essence of this photo-capture machine can be drawn out, as in Fig. 3.

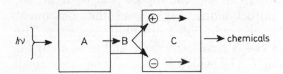

FIGURE 3   The photo-capture unit. A is a large congregation of photo-absorbing pigments (Chlorophylls). B is a special centre for converting photon energy into a charge-separated unit, and C is the storage for small amounts of charge from B and contains Fe/S centres. The whole unit replaces X in Fig. 1, and is in a membrane.

A is a light-capture device and all light absorbed by it is funnelled to B, by energy transfer. B is a reaction centre where the light produces a diradical which we shall write as + −. The flow of + and − separately away from B leads to initial storage of charge in C. In bacterial photo-capture systems there is an electron-transfer path connecting A and C in a single protein which has a chain of cofactors bound within it. This is the unit B.

A → [chlorophyll dimer P-700 $\xrightarrow{\quad}$ "pigment" $\xrightarrow{\quad}$
$\qquad\qquad\qquad\qquad\quad\downarrow\qquad\qquad\qquad\qquad$ quinone.Fe] → (C)
$\qquad\qquad\qquad\qquad\quad +$

This protein is well characterised. From Fe the electrons flow into a small electron-storage unit which is composed of several iron-sulphur, Fe/S, proteins, in C. It seems likely that green plants have a very similar light-capture device leading to charge separation, followed by flow to a depot of Fe/S proteins which store the negative charge in part. The negative charge can be used to pick up H^+ from water, giving bound reducing equivalents as "bound-H_2", and the "bound-H_2" is no longer necessarily associated with the membrane reaction system drawn above.

Apart from the flow of the "−" unit away from the reaction centre we must follow the + unit. Here there are a variety of consequences all of which follow from a forward flow of electrons to fill the positive hole + and terminate in the production of stored sulphur or oxygen (air):

Clearly, to generate either sulphur from sulphide or oxygen from oxide requires a four-electron reaction. Thus there must again be storage of several charges just prior to O_2 or S_n generation. Such storage systems are known, for there are the various multi-centre sulphur−iron proteins, which can synthesise sulphur, and a manganese protein (2−4 Mn atoms) which can make oxygen. (These proteins have units similar to the electron-storage assemblies of nitrogenase which must carry out the multi-electron reduction reaction,

$$N_2 + 6H^+ + 6e \rightarrow 2NH_3$$

The production of sulphur as a waste product follows, and originally oxygen too must have been waste! In fact some biological systems can use the sulphur − man included. In the above equations O^{2-} and S^{2-} are visualised as arising from H_2O and H_2S and their reaction leaves H^+ in solution, either aqueous or in the membrane.

If the overall reactions are inspected we have now the following energy conservation:

$$h\nu + H_2O \longrightarrow O_2 + \text{'bound } H_2'$$
$$h\nu + H_2S \longrightarrow S_n + \text{'bound } H_2'$$

and we should now be able to calculate efficiencies for the light reactions, but it is found that the system is more complicated. As mentioned above, during the course of light absorption pyrophosphate is also observed to be produced as ATP (Figure 1) and this reaction is brought about in some way by the flow of charge from one place to another (see later). The overall photosynthesis energy storage is difficult to assess.

The Mitochondrion: Oxidative Phosphorylation

The reacton of oxygen with bound hydrogen (both generated by photosynthesis, as above) can also be used to provide energy which is stored temporarily as pyrophophate, ATP, as described above. This reaction occurs in the mitochondrial membranes of plants and animals.

$$\tfrac{1}{2}O_2 \; + \; bound-H_2 \qquad\qquad H_2O$$

$$P-OH \; + \; HO-P \qquad\qquad P-O-P + H_2O$$

Now the reaction system which captures the energy as pyrophosphate is very similar to the multi-enzyme electron conduction system, C, found in the chloroplast (Figs. 1 and 2). The essence of the mitochondrial reaction is the ability of O_2 to act as a sink for electrons and therefore it acts as a source of 4+ charges for a metalloprotein to which it is bound, while at a distant place in space bound-H_2 gives electrons and protons. Thus we find as one common feature of the chloroplast and the mitochondrion the presence of electron carriers, metalloproteins, which act both to store and to transfer electrons. All the metalloproteins in both systems are linked together in complex multiprotein units and all are located *within membranes of the organelles i.e. within nonaqueous media.* The purpose of this structure is not fully understood but some findings about it will be described below.

Returning to the mitochondrion, between the sites of generation of 4+ and of 4− there is a long series of electron carriers, and it is the potential energy drop of the electrons within the chain from bound-H_2 to bound O_2 that is conserved by converting this potential, redox energy, to P−O−P bond formation, Fig. 2. The system is efficient and can be looked upon as a fuel reaction, bound-$H_2 + \tfrac{1}{2}O_2 \rightarrow H_2O$, for which $\Delta G = -30$ kcal per electron driving the formation of P–O–P from phosphate which has an estimated ΔG of +10 kcal per mole. In fact, three or four P–O–P bonds are made for each two electrons dropping through the potential difference, and the overall conservation of energy is some 50%. Both the mito-chondrion and the chloroplast devices for conservation of energy as pyrophosphate can now be written in several steps of the kind

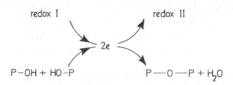

Such energy conservation requires a coupling device between redox reaction and condensation. There is now general agreement about the overall nature of the coupling but there is great confusion in the language which is used to describe it and little knowledge of the precise steps involved; see below.

At this stage it is good to summarise the energy conservation from the light energy. In the chloroplast the two major steps are 1 and 2 which occur to different degrees

1. $H_2O \longrightarrow$ bound-H_2 and free O_2(air)

   $(H_2S \longrightarrow$ bound-H_2 and free $S_n)$

2. P–OH + HO–P $\longrightarrow$ P–O–P.

Thus the reactions pick up particular elements, initially hydrogen and phosphorus, and bind them subsequently into the larger molecules of biology, which are energy stores. There are two types of conservation – one of chemicals and the other of energy insofar as the chemicals are stored through chosen "energy-rich" bonds. The free oxygen plus bound hydrogen can be used to make more pyrophosphate in mitochondria, but equally important is the use of bound-H_2 plus the energy of pyrophosphate to capture carbon dioxide, making sugars (again in the chloroplast)

$$P–O–P + CO_2 + \text{bound } H_2 \longrightarrow (CHOH)_n + 2P–OH$$

The sugars of the plants can be further reduced to fats and this transformation of bound-H_2 and CO_2 leads to a storage of the chemical elements (H and C) and of energy, that of C–H and C–OH relative to CO_2 and H_2O. Overall, carbohydrates, fats, and oxygen are the energy conserving chemicals and bound-H_2 and pyro-phosphate are an intermediate storage for their formation.

For the non-biochemist it is important to note that once pyrophosphate and bound-H_2 can be formed then the capture of other elements (CO_2 and N_2 for example) can be accomplished and conservation of energy and chemicals in such forms as sugars, amino-acids, fats, etc. is readily brought about by conventional though complicated reactions. At the end of this article the scheme of glycolysis and its reversal is outlined to illustrate further the point that pyrophosphate and chemical stores are also readily reversible.

Coupling of Electron Transfer to Phosphorylation

It can be seen that the essential initial steps of energy conservation are those of coupling between redox reactions and condensation of phosphate to pyrophosphate. This coupling is not easy to understand for it requires, apparently, coupling of one-electron reactions (redox) with two-electron reactions (acid—base conden-sations). In 1961 I pointed[1] to the following features of the electron-transfer paths in both the photo-driven phosphorylation and the mitochondrial phosphorylation systems. (i) The reactions were confined to separate phases away from water, the membranes of the chloroplast and the mitochondrion, and that (ii) there was an organisation of the electron carriers within the phases. Such an organisation is essential in order to prevent the formation of a short-circuit between the separated charges, e.g. see Fig. 3, before chemical reactions were driven; for otherwise, of course, energy would be dissipated as heat. A two-phase (or a multi-phase system) is of great advantage for such systems in that it prevents the ready diffusion of charges together and it is here that the metallo-proteins are so vital in that they permit diffusion of electrons but not protons. A third required feature of the system was that (iii) the passage of the electrons through a potential drop was compulsorily connected to alternating changes in proton concentration in the membrane by the nature of the electron-transfer path. At each stage of P–O–P production the path was thought to be a series of reactions of the type:

bound-H_2 $\longrightarrow$ $2H^+ + 2e$(site I)

$2e$(site I) $\longrightarrow$ transfer through metalloproteins $2e$(site II)

$2e$(site II) $+ X + 2H^+$ $\longrightarrow$ XH_2 $\longrightarrow$ (site III)

XH_2(site III) $X + 2H^+ + 2e$ $\longrightarrow$ $2e$(site IV) where XH_2 is a new form of bound-H_2. Thus at several steps the initial bound-H_2 is re-formed at a lower potential only to be dissociated again into $2e + 2H^+$. It is the $2H^+/2e$ charge separation that is used in some way to produce P–O–P. As electrons cannot drive condensation reactions it was suggested further that it must be a coupling to the proton flow which did the work of pyrophosphate formation,

$$2H^+ + 2P–OH \rightarrow P–O–P + (2H^+)H_2O$$

in the course of which the H^+ was stabilised by hydration or dilution. The essence of the problem is then the exact nature of the coupling between H^+ concentration changes and phosphate condensation which is known to require a complicated protein or series of proteins.

Purple Bacteria

Before attempting to describe further the coupling device, there is one other way in which light energy can be conserved in biology. It is found in certain "purple" bacteria where, on the absorption of light, a carotene pigment in a membrane undergoes a conformation change together with a change of pK_a of one of the groups of the carotenoid/protein complex.[2] Thus here the light reaction in the membrane is

$$h\nu + RH^+ \rightarrow R^* + H^+$$

where R* is R in a changed conformational state of high energy. This is an acid-base reaction immediately and not a redox disproportionation reaction driven by light, and energy is now stored in an acidified medium, either the membrane or an aqueous surrounding phase, and as conformational energy in a membrane. The return of R* to RH^+ can be made to drive a chemical reaction.

A plausible way of relating this device to that of mitochondria and chloroplasts is to propose the following scheme:

$$h\nu + RH^+ \longrightarrow R^* + H^+ \text{ (site I)}$$

$$H_2O \text{ (site II)} + R^* \longrightarrow RH^+ + OH^- \text{ (site II)}$$

which generates the charge gradient from (site I) to site II). Movement of the proton down the gradient can now be used to drive the formation of P–O–P using the same coupling proton as before. In order for such a device to work the conformation change would have to release H^+ in one direction (to site I) and take up H^+ from another direction (from site II) since it is required again that the proton passes through the enzyme device which makes pyrophosphate. Once again the minimum requirements are the correct assembly of proteins (enzymes) in a system which prevents ready return diffusion of H^+ to the site of its production without it having to pass through the coupling device. Thus if this description is correct it is the organisation of multienzyme systems which allows energy to be conserved in these devices.[1]

Two further points may be of interest. Firstly the action of light on the purple membrane can be likened to that of the absorption of light by the eye. All storage of messages as in vision, memory, etc., is a form of energy conservation but these topics cannot be covered here.

A second point concerns the energy conserved temporarily in the membrane of the purple bacteria through the conformation change. Such *mechanical* energy storage occurs in the membranes of the mitochondria and chloroplast too when they are energised by charge-storage. In a labile system such as a series of organised proteins in a small structured membrane phase, it is not possible to store charge without altering conformation and it is undoubtedly true that the conformational energy store as well as the charge store has a part to play in the energy conversion. I shall not refer to these conformational changes in detail because it will not be possible to follow them at an atomic level for a very long time to come. Hence their exact significance is unknowable (by me).

Fundamental Systems of Energy Conversion and Conservation

The fundamental features of chloroplast, purple membrane and mitochondrial energy conversions are seen to be:

1. Separation of charge.
2. Conversion of positive charge to give protons in one part of space.
3. Use of protons to carry out formation of pyrophosphate as they flow through a coupling device.

The reactions occur in organisations associated with membranes and there have been several attempts to describe how they occur. The first scheme, Fig. 4, which I shall describe shows the proton gradient to be between the membrane phase in which it is generated and a solution on one side of that membrane. In other words a charge is built up in the membrane, which established a potential difference between it and the surrounding fluids. Discharge of this potential gives P—O—P. (The proton generated in the membrane is the reagent for dehydration of phosphate to pyrophosphate, the real coupling device).

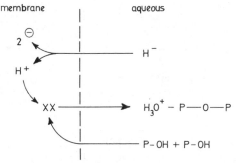

FIGURE 4   One scheme proposed for coupling. Note that the proton drives pyrophosphate formation in the unit XX.

XX is the coupling protein, called the ATP-ase. A somewhat different scheme which uses both sides of the membrane can be written in the following way:

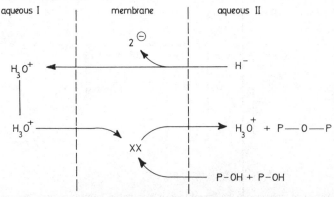

FIGURE 5   A second coupling scheme. Note that again the proton drives ATP formation in the unit XX.

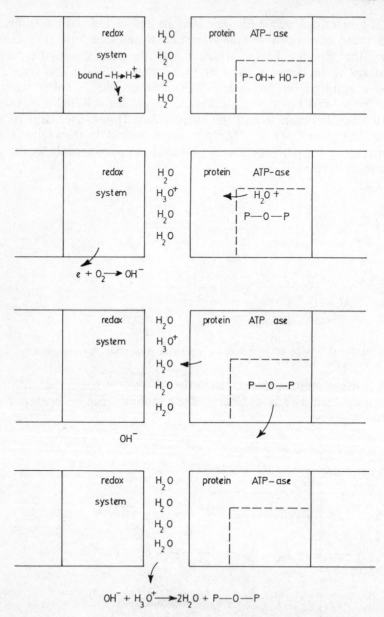

FIGURE 6   The series of charges in the membrane which could be used to link proton production from redox centres with ATP formation. There could be conformational changes and minor leakage to outside solutions.

Table 2: Details of the enzyme for the manufacture of pyrophosphate in ATP

	Mol. Wt	Sub units	Function
Component F_1	360,000	$\geqslant 5$	ADP + P $\leftarrow$ ATP Water soluble
Component F_0	80,000	>4	Membrane protein which binds other units together
Inhibitor	10,000	1	Inhibits F_1
F_1/F_0 peptide		1	Binds F_1 to F_0

See P. W. Postma and K. van Dam, *Trends in Biological Sciences*, 1976, 1, 16.

The energy storage across a membrane can be likened to osmotic energy and this model is called the chemi-osmotic model, Fig. 5.[3] No description was given originally[1,3] for the coupling step in either of these schemes, as the coupling enzyme was known to be extremely complex, Table 2. The present author has suggested the scheme of Fig. 6 for the coupling, which is a dehydration path. It does not involve direct attack of the proton on the phosphate groups, but an alternative direct scheme has been proposed by Mitchell;[4] Boyer[5] and Slater[6] having developed the possibility of driving ATP formation by protein conformational changes. Be these schemes right or wrong, the immense complexity of the protein, Table 2, which generates the energy capture in the form of ATP (pyrophosphate) makes it likely that it will be a long time before this step of conservation is understood and possibly all the ideas contain some of the truth.

As the initial energy store of separated charge is in several forms, it may well be better to express it in a general equation

$$\partial \Delta G_i = \partial(\Delta G_i{}^0 + RT \ln[H^+]_i)$$

where the subscript i refers to the different phases and ΔG^0 to different standard chemical potentials of protons in the phases. At equilibrium all phases have the same ΔG_i but on energising the system they store energy differentially following changes in both $\Delta G_i{}^0$, which can take into account both electric potential, chemical binding and conformational changes, and in local changes of $\ln[H^+]_i$ In this steady state, transfer of H^+ from one phase to another could be used to create P–O–P, for in the steady state each phase is at a different proton energy ΔG_i.

Coupling to Other Cations

It might be thought that it would be a simple matter to determine $\ln[H]_i$ but this proves to be very difficult. The internal volumes of chloroplasts and mitochondria are very small and the protons can exchange with many other ions. At the present time it would appear that when the membrane is energised only some of the energy is to be found in changes in $\ln[H^+]_i$ in the aqueous media and it is probably not in the electric double layer but is associated with bound protons attached to the membrane and with gradients of other ions and their bindings.

The interaction between the proton gradients and the ion gradients is best seen in the chloroplast. It would appear that in the resting state (no light) the "inner face" of the chloroplast membrane is bound heavily by magnesium ions and it is thought the binding is to proteins of the membrane. Figure 7 gives an impression of the situation. On energisation, the magnesium moves into the outer solution and the suggestion arises that the protons bind to the inner reaches of the membrane in place of magnesium ions, Fig. 7. The energy store must now be stated as a sum of hydrogen ion and magnesium ion free energies. In other systems the hydrogen ion could be used to move other cations either from bound positions in membranes or across membranes.

Strikingly the plant cell does not use ATP, CO_2 and H_2O to make sugars in the absence of magnesium ions outside the chloroplast in fairly high concentration. Thus the action of light in transporting Mg^{2+} ions to the place in which these dark reactions occur could

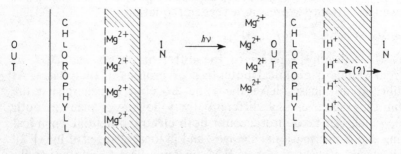

FIGURE 7   The movement of protons in the chloroplast is known to be coupled to the movement of magnesium ions and there is a diffusion barrier to the escape of protons. These facts favour the scheme of Fig. 4 over that of Fig. 5.

produce a deliberate coupling of the light and the dark reactions. In the dark the return of Mg^{2+} to the inner face of the chloroplast membrane would switch off the dark reactions in the outer phase.[7]

Mitochondrial energy goes from proton gradients to a control of calcium ion (not magnesium ion) concentrations and this movement has precedence over ATP formation. Thus the mitochondria may control their aqueous surround by removing calcium before ATP synthesis much as the chloroplast controls its surround by generating magnesium ions in its surrounding fluids.[8] Just as magnesium ions are known to bind to the chloroplast membrane, so calcium ions bind strongly to the mitochondrial membrane. It will now be appreciated that it is impossible to break down the free energies ΔG_i of different states of the membrane into conventional $RT\ln[H^+]_i$ and potentials. Moreover this discussion draws attention away from the proton states as energy storage modes to the states of other cations

Energy → proton + other cation gradients.

The purple membrane of halo-bacteria is quite anomolous in these respects in that, when exposed to light, it can make the solution outside the cell either acid or alkali depending upon whether the medium is acidic or alkaline, and yet it makes pyrophosphate (ATP) in both cases.[9] In fact it can make ATP from light when there is no observable pH change, which demonstrates that chemi-osmosis is not the mechanism in this case. The significance of this membrane has yet to be determined for it belongs to a living organism which stores very large amounts of potassium chloride while living in a sodium chloride medium. It may be that the problems posed by the purple membrane are not the same as those posed by mitochondria and chloroplasts, and that the parallels between this system and the other two are quite other than have been described so far.

Metal Ion Gradients as Stores

It is difficult to store (electronic) electricity and the devices used by biology for storage of electricity are really just electrolytic batteries. (Man will be forced to invent very similar efficient devices very soon). The ions M^+, and less importantly Ca^{2+} and Mg^{2+}, are separated across interfaces or membranes by processes described above giving rise to energy storage in the form of concentration cells. For each ion the free energy store is related to

$$\Delta G = RT\ln[M]_I/[M]_{II}$$

Table 3: Ion contents of some cells, 10^{-3} mol dm^{-3}

System	Na_i	Na_o	K_i	K_o	Mg_i	Mg_o	Ca_i	Ca_o
Red blood cell (human)	15	143	152	5	2.5	1.0	10^{-3}	3.0
Squid nerve	10	460	355	10	20	53	10^{-4}	10
Skeletal muscle (frog)	10	108	120	5	15	1.0	10^{-4}	2.0

Note. "i" stands for in cell and "o" stands for the outside bathing fluid of the cell.

where $[M]_I$ and $[M]_{II}$ are the concentrations in aqueous phases I and II separated by a membrane in all cells. Table 3 gives some of these gradients. Unfortunately the cell membranes are not very efficient diffusion barriers, so that the maintenance of these gradients is very energy-demanding. Most of the food used by animals is in fact used in maintaining the gradients, but at any one time the total energy store of the gradients is very large indeed.

In some of these processes such as the storage of calcium ions in muscle cell sarcoplasmic reticulium or in storage of sodium and potassium ions across the endoplasmic reticulium of all cells (but note nerve cells especially) the ion gradients follow the generation of ATP. It has been shown by Glynn,[10] as predicted by Davies and Ogston,[11] that this reaction can be driven backwards, i.e. gradients of sodium, potassium, and calcium can be used to make ATP. But in others it is thought that the storage in ion concentration cells follows directly from the energy changes in the membrane and may be directly coupled to H^+ generation in the membrane.

Such movement of material across membranes by reactions closely associated with them is not confined to the movement of inorganic ions and in fact any chemical can be pumped into the cell. Thus the uptake of chemicals such as sugars, amino-acids, etc., can be driven and the chemical storage of materials for growth achieved at least in part. Thus provided that there are complicated and *regulated* coupling devices the energy intake of a cell can be switched to many purposes which can take priority over ATP formation or follow it.

The function of the ion gradients is manifold, for although they represent an energy store which could be switched back to metabolism this is not usual. Rather the relaxation of the gradients is used to send messages (nerves), and to trigger action (muscle contraction and hormone release). It would appear that the ion gradients are also associated with the storage of information (memory) and in the control of osmosis (water movement). Thus ion gradients are the most rapidly usable forms of energy store and in this respect may take precedence over ATP which is relatively slowly hydrolysed.

The Membrane Conformation as an Energy Store

Now we must look back at the membrane itself. The ion-gradient across the membrane will generate asymmetry within the membrane. The asymmetry arises as some metal ions, notably calcium, interact much more strongly than others with the membrane head-groups.[12] As a consequence of the large calcium gradients (10^{-3} M outside and 10^{-7} M inside cells) there is a preferred orientation of the components of the membrane either toward (binding calcium) or away from (binding magnesium) the solution with the highest calcium ion concentration. The membrane then adopts a stereochemistry which is clearly an energy store similar to a capacitor.[12] Other components such as proteins are also thought to be arranged in preferred ways across the membrane. This organisation of the membrane is a conformational storage form of energy. It is well known now that changes in the state of energy absorbed by the membrane or its surrounding component solution affect the topology of the membrane.

The relationship of the energy source to initial charge separation and ATP formation is now more complicated than appeared earlier for we must now write:

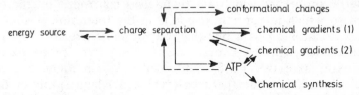

Certain steps (shown dotted) are virtually irreversible in some cases and only reversible to limited degrees in others. The degree of reversiblity remains a mystery in many of these steps.

Now that the general ideas of energy storage modes have been described a few words will be added on the nature of the enzymes involved.

Some Details of the Enzymes[13]

We return now to the membrane-bound enzymes in order to find out how they operate. The starting point is the development by the action of light of a very local charge separation. It is necessary to guide the charge along a path but biological systems do not have wires. In their place they have evolved complicated metalloproteins. Electrons pass from metal ion to metal ion over many tens of Ångstroms. Now such a conducting device differs from a simple metal wire for it obviously has a capacity (the number of metal ions in the chain is the maximum charge capacity if all metal ions are one-electron redox centres) and it can also operate as a switch-control for, on receiving the electron, the protein can change geometry and its interaction with another protein will alter. The nature of metalloenzymes needs further description.

The case of cytochrome c is the most fully documented, and n.m.r. and crystallographic studies provide the following picture of this protein. The metal ion sits in a porphyrin complex not far from the centre of the protein, where on redox change, Fe^{II} to Fe^{III}, the metal environment undergoes a small stereochemical change. This change is reflected by a small conformational change of the surface of the protein.

The important feature here is that the passage of current (charge) is associated with geometric changes in this conductor. If the geometric change is prevented then charge cannot pass at all or is seriously hindered. (The adjustment of the ligand atoms of the metal by the protein to give the best possible energy for the reaction processes has been called an entatic state of the metal complex.) Each metlloprotein of the "wire" can thus act as a switch controlled by geometric properties which are themselves controlled by the other groups to which the protein is bound in the total biological device. While cytochrome c is a one-electron protein there are proteins of higher capacity, which contain many metal ions. Some bacterial ferrodoxins have two $Fe_4 S_4$ units embedded in them, and some cytochromes have four (perhaps even eight) heme units in them. Most of the metalloproteins of the photosynthetic and mitochondrial apparatus (Fig. 1 and 2) have many more than one $Fe_4 S_4$ (or $Fe_2 S_2$) unit. Thus these units act as charge storage devices and they can be likened to small condensers. Undoubtedly the flexibility of the internal groups of proteins assists the flow and the control of the flow of charge through these assemblies.

Simple Equivalent Circuits

It is easy now to draw out circuit diagrams representing the energy conservations described above. Figure 8 shows the initial source of

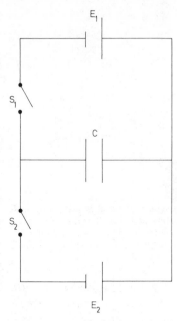

FIGURE 8   An equivalent electric circuit for any one of the three particles of oxidative phosphorylation. The battery E_1 is the initial chemical reaction; C is a sink for electrons and or protons and is therefore a capacitor, and E_2 is a second chemical cell which is driven by the discharge of C. S_1 and S_2 are conformational switches which allow the separation of the charging and discharging of the capacitor. Wires are electron transfer proteins. There is no problem over the reversing of the electron flow, which simply depends on the potentials at E_1 and E_2. E_1 can be thought of as a redox cell, whereas E_2 involves a dehydration reaction that is coupled to a redox change and gives P–O–P.

charge as a chemical battery which transfers electrons through a switch to a store in a condenser. In effect the condenser can be just a large number of metalloproteins in a membrane. This charge can be used to drive other chemical storage forms shown here by the formation of P–O–P (ATP), proton gadients (electrolytic cell), or gradients of other ions and materials, Fig. 9.

Reconstruction and Models

The aim of the chemist should be to simplify and then reconstruct models of these devices. The leading exponents of this approach are Jagendorf[14] and Racker[15] in America and a group in the Institute of Electrochemistry in Moscow.[16] Jagendorf and Racker base their model systems on views of the energy storage where there is no need

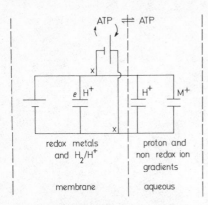

FIGURE 9   An elaboration of Fig. 1, to show that a variety of connections can be made to the initial energy source and that they are competing methods of storing energy. In chemosmotic theory, Fig. 5, the production of proton gradients takes priority over all other energy stores. Note the connecting role of the proton in all forms of energy store; this is made possible by the fact that it is the only mobile redox "metal".

to control the membrane phase and have been able to show that ion gradients of various kinds can generate ATP as in the early views of Davies and Ogston[11] and the more recent views of Mitchell.[3] Although the efficiency of these processes is quite unknown the success of the approach has lent support to the concept of osmotic energy as a transient storage mode. Members of the Russian group[17] have shown that ATP can be synthesised by reactions in a two-phase system so that there is evidence for the possibility that it is the *membrane storage* which is linked to ATP synthesis. The experimental tests of the theories,[18] which are as yet indecisive, are becoming extremely sophisticated. However, many more experiments are required to define the system fully, as can be seen from a reading of the proceedings of a recent meeting on "Electron Transfer and Oxidative Phosphorylation".[19] All these experiments point to ways in which man could make energy-capture devices modelled on biological systems.

Energy Conservation in Chemical Transformations: Glycolysis

The reactions of sugar to give alcohol and carbon dioxide or to give acetic acid are disproportionation reactions:

$$C_6H_{12}O_6 \longrightarrow 3CH_3CO_2H$$

$$C_6H_{12}O_6 \longrightarrow 2C_2H_5OH + 2CO_2$$

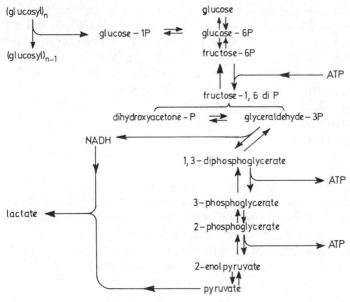

FIGURE 10   The path of glycolysis.

Such reactions are downhill and therefore present the opportunity for energy conservation. Biology has a masterly chemical scheme for handling the problem known as glycolysis, Fig. 10. (In general there are quite a number of such schemes in biology while in industry virtually all the energy of such processes is lost as heat).

The essence of the scheme is to carry out the disproportionation reactions of sugars in steps while gradually rearranging the oxidising and reducing equivalents in the original sugar molecules. Starting from the alcohol groups of the sugar the reaction takes place along two paths *simultaneously.*

$$\left[\diagdown \!\! \begin{array}{c} \text{CHOH} \end{array} \right]_n \begin{array}{c} \nearrow \\ \searrow \end{array} \begin{array}{l} -\text{CHO} \longrightarrow -\text{CO}_2\text{H} \longrightarrow (\text{CO}_2) \quad \begin{array}{l}\text{Oxidation}\\ \text{(acidic)}\end{array} \\ \\ -\text{CH}_2\text{OH} \longrightarrow \text{CH}_3\text{OH} \longrightarrow (\text{CH}_4) \quad \begin{array}{l}\text{Reduction}\\ \text{(basic)}\end{array} \end{array}$$

Note that certain carbon–oxygen units become acidic on oxidation, while others become more basic on reduction, in the disproportionation reaction. The esters of –OH groups are less stable (thermodynamic sense) the more acidic the $-OH$ group becomes, i.e. stability falls in the series $CH_3OP >.CH_2(OH)OP_2 > HCO \cdot OP$. Thus if the starting material of a reaction is an ester of an alcohol, i.e. an ester of a weak acid — for example the phosphate ester, CH_3OP — then the reaction to $HCO \cdot OP$ is energetically uphill as far as the ester bond is concerned, but is overall downhill due to disproportionation above. While phosphate cannot be transferred to another phosphate from CH_3OP since this transfer is a downhill reaction from $HCO \cdot OP$

$$HCO \cdot OP + P-OH \rightarrow P-O-P + -COOH.$$

In this way pyrophosphate, the usual transient energy store of biology, is made, but this reaction can only occur if the downhill energy $(-\Delta G)$ of disproportionation can be coupled to the uphill production $(+\Delta G)$ of P–O–P. This is brought about by starting glycolysis with phosphate esters of alcohols (sugars) which are made from sugar and phosphate by a reaction which requires little free energy. During subsequent disproportionation the reactions of the $(CHOH)_n$ unit, a process which is favourable, the reactions are *guided* so that the phosphate remains on carbon atoms which undergo *oxidation*, and thus disproportionation energises phosphate bonds. The sequence of glycolysis in Fig. 10 outlines the chemical scheme which is a major source of energy for anaerobic life. It will be appreciated that it is the choice of catalysts (enzymes) which has produced this energy conserving path. These enzymes are quite well-known, water-soluble, and the crystal structures of many of them are available. I point to one other feature of them only, although there are many subtleties: the enzymes are under control and the scheme is reversible. Energy is taken out close to equilibrium.

This mode of energy capture is not complicated and is only given here to show how energy can be transferred to a conserved form by a set of designed transfer reactions in free solution. In some cells the energy is not stored as pyrophosphate but as a phosphate condensate of another group, e.g. in muscle a major store is creatine-phosphate.

Here the unstable (energy rich) bond is a phospho-amide. The reason for storage in phosphate condensates is probably one of ready kinetic control over their hydrolysis. If glycolysis runs backwards it will produce from sugar a store of polymerised sugar, glycogen. On the other hand should it run forward. to acetic acid in the presence of oxygen then the mitochondria oxidise the CH_3COOH to CO_2 and H_2O and the energy is captured as ATP, cf. mitochondria. Finally, should glycolysis run to CH_3COOH in the presence of excess reducing capacity the acetic acid will be converted into fat by polymerisation and reduction to $CH_3(CH_2)_nCOOH$. The last step is reversible. Thus all the energy stores are connected.

References

[1] R. J. P. Williams, *J. Theoret. Biol.*, 1961, **1**, 1.
[2] E. Racker and W. Stoeckenius, *J. Biol. Chem.*, 1974, **249**, 662.
[3] P. Mitchell, *Nature*, 1961, **191**, 144.
[4] P. Mitchell, *FEBS Letters*, 1974, **43**, 189.
[5] P. D. Boyer, *FEBS Letters*, 1975, **50**, 91.
[6] D. A. Harris and E. C. Slater, *Biochim. Biophys. Acta*, 1975, **387**, 335.
[7] J. Barber, in "Topics in Photosynthesis. The Intact Chloroplast", ed. J. Barber, Elsevier, Amsterdam, 1976; to be published.
[8] M. D. Brand, C.-H. Chen, and A. L. Lehninger, *J. Biol. Chem.*, 1976, **251**, 968.
[9] W. Stoeckenius and co-workers, *Biochim, Biophys. Acta*, 1976, to be published.
[10] I. M. Glynn and S. J. D. Karlish, in "Energy Transformations in Biological Systems", Ciba Foundation Symposium No. 31, 1975, p. 205.
[11] R. Davies and A. G. Ogston, *Biochem. J.*, 1950, **46**, 324.
[12] R. J. P. Williams, *Ann. New York Acad. Sciences*, 1974, **227**, 98.
[13] R. J. P. Williams, *Trans. Biochem. Soc.*, 1973, **1**, 1.
[14] A. T. Jagendorf, in "Bioenergetics of Photosynthesis", ed. E. Gornidj, Academic Press, New York, 1975, pp. 413-493.
[15] E. Racker, *Trans. Biochem. Soc.*, 1975, **3**, 27.
[16] I. I. Boguslavsky, A. A. Kondrashin, I. A. Kozlov, S. T. Metelsky, V. P. Skulacher, and A. G. Volkov, *FEBS Letters*, 1975, **50**, 223.
[17] L. S. Yaguzhinsky, L. I. Boguslavsky, A. G. Volkov, and A. B. Rakhmaninova, *Nature*, 1976, **259**, 494.
[18] W. Junge and W. Ausländer, in "Electron Transfer Chains and Oxidative Phosphorylation", ed. E. Quagliarello *et al.*, North Holland, Amsterdam, 1975, p. 243.
[19] "Electron Transfer Chains and Oxidative Phosphorylation", ed. E. Quagliarello *et al.*, North Holland, Amsterdam, 1975.

Ideas and Ideals for the Education of Chemists at Universities

by C. Kemball; President, Royal Institute of Chemistry

THE number of full-time students in British universities increased by nearly 140% between 1938 and 1962.[1] Since then, as a consequence of the Robbins report on Higher Education,[2] this number has doubled again in a much shorter time. I want to consider carefully whether we have been successful in conserving standards at universities since the Robbins report was accepted in 1963. If there are criticisms to be made, perhaps it is not inappropriate that they should be voiced by an academic. I shall be expressing personal opinions about a subject which concerns me deeply and, on this occasion, I am not attempting to act as a spokesman for the Institute.

My discussion will be limited in the main to the factors influencing the teaching and training of chemists. I shall not be dwelling upon present financial difficulties nor on the current debate about the level of financial support merited by universities – important though these topics may be. I want to look at problems at a more fundamental level and consider whether changes have been occurring which could inflict serious and possibly irreversible damage on our system of education of chemists at universities. In preparation for this address I have been speaking with many from universities, expert in the sciences or engineering, as well as with a number of senior industrial chemists. From the latter in particular, I gained the impression that it was time for a self-critical exercise to be undertaken by university chemists. So the purpose I hope to achieve by a provocative discussion of some of the developments and trends which have occurred is to initiate a debate in which chemists will be able to consider constructively such remedies as may be necessary. If changes are needed, it is vital that chemists in universities should be prepared to act to put their houses in order and not wait for solutions to be imposed from outside or from above.

Before we consider in detail the problems of chemists and chemistry, we ought perhaps to remind ourselves that the benefit which should be gained from a university education is more than the demonstration of a student's ability to pass examinations and acquire a degree. The university should provide an experience that enables each student to develop his personality and his intellect to the full. Much that J. H. Newman set out in his lectures on "The Idea of a University" in Dublin in 1852 applies with equal force today.[3] He claimed that a university training is "the education which gives a man a clear conscious view of his own opinions and judgements, a truth in developing them, an eloquence in expressing them, and a force in urging them". I wonder what proportion of present-day graduates exhibit all these qualities.

The Robbins proposals for an expansion of higher education were welcomed widely and the guiding principle "that all young persons qualified by ability and attainment to pursue a full-time course in higher education should have the opportunity to do so" was warmly accepted. The doubts that have arisen in recent years are centred on two questions. Firstly, while the idea of providing an increasing proportion of the population with some form of tertiary education was and is attractive, the proposal that the university sector should expand at a comparable rate is now less obvious. The question put another way is whether it was justifiable to increase the size and number of universities without contemplating a greater range in the character and status of these institutions – as found for example in the universities and colleges of the U.S.A. Do we have an unworkable arrangement if 45 universities are adopting Oxbridge as their ideal? Assuming that a substantial expansion of the university sector was appropriate, the second question is whether the proposed rate of expansion and the consequential perturbations associated with such rapid expansion should have been accepted.

Staffing

Many problems and difficulties have arisen from the very rapid rate of change in the number and size of universities following the Robbins proposals. Let us consider staffing. The rate of expansion was so great that, for a period of about three years, the recruitment of staff for science departments took a substantial percentage of the output of good quality Ph.D's and postdoctoral fellows. Too much of the intellectual "cream" was drawn back into university teaching and far too little entered industry. This led to the first phase of disillusionment in industry with the new situation created by university expansion. There is also little doubt that, in addition to the recruitment to university positions of many with great talents, some of lesser calibre were brought in at the same time. Jobs which ought to be held only by the most dedicated and able became too easy to get. Surely this rapid expansion introduced a potential weakening of standards. But even if this last statement is challenged, the evils of the subsequent stagnation cannot be denied. The period of rapid expansion was followed by one in which recruitment to university staffs was very small. Subsequently, under the influence of recent financial difficulties, recruitment became almost negligible. For the last two or three years there have been hardly any vacancies for the really outstanding young scientists who should be entering university teaching now to provide the intellectual leadership of the future. Unless some action is taken to open up recruitment on a modest scale the damage could last for a generation or longer. Many chemistry departments have an unfortunate age distribution. Too many came in at much the same age and have reached or are reaching the top of the lecturers' scale together. Promotion that might have occurred under normal circumstances is now more difficult and this fact does not help morale. The average age of the staff is tending to rise and the recruitment of new blood is not sufficient to maintain vitality.

Before we leave the problem of staffing at universities we might dwell on two related problems concerning organization and tenure. One of the facets of modern society is an increasing dislike of hierarchical systems and a tendency to introduce more and more consultation into the processes of decision-making. A movement too far in these directions inside universities would be potentially weakening. Intellectual leadership and inspiration can all too easily be stifled by a surfeit of committees. While consultation and government by consent are essential, the introduction of increasingly complex and complicated democratic processes inside universities can be taken too far. A university teacher should be prepared both to accept and to give leadership.

Ideas about tenure need to be revised. Let me quote from the editorial in *Nature* "Good for people, bad for science" of 10th July 1975 which included these words 'The pressures in recent years have been rather obviously towards increasing job security in universities (the Civil Service is already about as secure as the priest-hood) . . . Such pressures ought to be firmly resisted and, if anything, there should be serious discussions about reversing the trend". I believe that the A.U.T. with its emphasis on equality of treatment in regard to tenure for all grades is not serving the best interests of the universities nor in the long run of its members. The most serious problem is the pressure for tenure for those starting a career as university teachers. It is a mistake to suppose that brilliance at the immediate postdoctoral stage necessarily guarantees a successful career on the university staff. In every university there should be a post of demonstrator or assistant lecturer with tenure limited to five years. Some, but only some, would win promotion to a lectureship and there might well be some flexibility in departmental establish-ments to ensure that the best could be retained. Let us remember that some of the most coveted awards for the new Ph.D — research fellowships at Oxbridge — are positions of limited duration; they provide an opportunity to blossom and develop but without a guarantee of a permanent post.

But equally the present concept of full tenure to the retiring age for lecturers and professors may need some reconsideration. The possibility of science professors stepping down at age 60 from positions of departmental responsibility and making way for younger men is well worth considering. If such professors at 60 are successful they are likely to be spending too much time outside their departments or their university — if they are not successful they may be impeding developments inside their departments. It should be possible to devise a system by which there is a diminution of their responsibility inside departments without appreciable loss of status or salary for the final few years before they retire. Some of course may be able to perform a useful function as Deans or Vice-Chancellors — these positions being sufficiently remote from the frontiers of teaching and research that their occupants have limited opportunity to impede progress!

Chemists Entering Industry

I have referred already to the immediate consequenc of the Robbins expansion which reduced the flow of research chemists into industry and diverted too many of the better graduates back into the university system. The cry from industry that it was not finding enough able scientists was noted in the 1968 Swann report on the

Flow into Employment of Scientists, Engineers and Technologists.[4] Clearly some of the statistics upon which this report was based related to the abnormal years when the university expansion was distorting the regular pattern of employmnt and hampering industrial recruitment. As a consequence, some of the criticisms of the lack of attention in university courses to the requirements of industry were undoubtedly too strong, particularly in regard to the training of chemists. This was one of the conclusions of the Eaborn report published in 1970 by the Royal Institute of Chemistry.[5] But the ironic factor was that soon after the publication of the Swann report the pendulum had swung back once again and the new generation of Ph.D's seeking industrial posts because university recruitment had declined were faced with falling demand from industry because of the economic crisis of 1968. There is no doubt at all that the stop-go recruitment policy of industry associated with the crises of 1968 and 1971 sent messages thundering back to the schools and discouraged many from considering a science or technology degree. The image of the technological revolution was distinctly tarnished.

We must not let preoccupation with these oscillations in the recruitment patterns and with the impact of the economic crises deflect us from considering one vital consequence of the Robbins expansion. If the output of graduates increases dramatically as it did in chemistry and other subjects, there must be a corresponding change in the pattern of employment of graduates. Many young people expected good jobs merely through the possession of a degree and were disappointed when these jobs did not materialize. This should have been obvious from the start because from it followed the inevitable consequence that some graduates would find themselves in jobs previously held by non-graduates. Undoubtedly this was a further cause for some of the disillusionment which filtered down to the schools. It does make one wonder whether the continuing expansion of the facilities for degree work inside and outside universities is necessarily serving a useful purpose.

Returning to the present, what industry requires now is not more chemists but better chemists — chemists who are self-propelled, who show initiative, who are alert and interested in applying their knowledge to the kind of problems industry faces. The mere possession of a degree in chemistry, no matter how hardly won, does not guarantee a young man or a young woman a place in industry. Qualities of intellect and personality which ought to be associated with the graduates of a good university matter tremendously. If a growing proportion of our output of graduates does not have these qualities then our standards are falling.

Quality of Entrants and the Nature of the Honours Degree

I have heard my colleagues in chemistry departments in Scottish universities complain that the standard of their first year classes has declined in the last decade. The phenomenon is not confined to Scotland as is apparent from the views assembled by the late Professor J W. Linnett on the capabilities of current entrants to university chemistry courses. There seems no doubt that with more spaces (or should I say too many spaces?) to fill in chemistry departments, the standard of the lower end of the intake is less good than it was. To what extent this results from the attraction of potentially good students away from chemistry to other disciplines or from poorer preparation of the pupils at school must remain a topic of debate. However, the decline in the quality and ability of the classes to cope with chemistry is real enough and perhaps more marked in recent years. The quality of undergraduate performance may also reflect a lower commitment to study associated with a loss of the sense of privilege as numbers expanded.

The wider ability range of those entering coupled with some decline in motivation has led to pressure for more and more tutorials and for novel means of putting the subject over to make it more palatable. Some of these developments may be desirable but others are undoubtedly bringing us to a situation that Newman described in these words "Learning is to be without exertion, without attention, without toil; without grounding, without advance, without finishing". We all of us know the good effect that a brilliant and hardworking group can have on an otherwise undistinguished class but we are beginning to see the other side of the coin now when the inadequacies of the poorer students spread upwards and poison the attitude of the top. If too many are concentrating solely on meeting the examination requirements, study in depth is bound to suffer and standards will fall if they have not already done so.

We ought to be more critical than we have been about the content of our honours courses in chemistry. We have a situation where a greater percentage of those studying chemistry will not practise it afterwards and where a smaller percentage (and perhaps it should be an even smaller percentage than now) will carry out postgraduate work in chemistry. Of course we should continue to foster the idea of a study of chemistry as an education in itself but we must recognize that some of our present courses do not take sufficient cognizance of this concept. Too often we as chemists have failed to adjust our approach to teaching to take account of the expansion of our discipline. We have allowed ourselves to become too specialized, we have listened too carefully to those who claim that the honours chemists must know A and B and C *etc.* and we have attempted to include too much recent knowledge. There has been overloading — not necessarily in lecture time — but in the number of facts and concepts that have been stuffed into our students. There has been insufficient time for independent study and for allowing students to develop their own ideas in depth. We expect the students to carry out independent reading but we make it difficult for them to do so. To quote Newman again "I will tell you, Gentlemen, what has been the practical error of the last twenty years, — not to load the memory of the student with a mass of undigested knowledge but to force upon him so much that he has rejected all".

The problem of containing the honours course is not easy. Of course the student must be brought up to the frontiers of knowledge in some areas of chemistry but more attention must be paid to the foundations and the scaffolding of his knowledge and less to the fads and fashions of individual members of staff (professors included of course!). We have a marvellous subject to teach but we throw away our opportunities.

The Training for the Ph.D. Degree

Postgraduate education now takes many and varied forms but in this address I shall confine my remarks to training in research for the Ph.D degree. Many might agree with the advantage of hindsight that the numbers undertaking research in chemistry in universities were expanded too greatly — but opinions would differ on the extent of the over-expansion. Several years ago, to be offered an opportunity to start research training was an honour and a privilege — now entry has become too easy. Perhaps the extent of the expansion of research places was unwise and, with this inflation, the currency of the Ph.D. has become tarnished if not actually debased. In some cases students of little more than average ability have been retained in universities for three further years and their entry into useful jobs in the wider world has been delayed. A proportion of the projects initiated by some members of staff have had neither significant value for research training nor any marked intrinsic interest. There have been pressures which may have tended to weaken the standard of the upper second class honours degree – the level of performance required by the Research Councils for a student to qualify for a research grant. Departments naturally are anxious to keep up their research numbers and examiners are anxious not to deny students showing any potential the opportunity to undertake research and so the borderline between upper and lower second acquires undue prominence at examiners' meetings. If real competition to acquire finance for research training was restored, the acquisition of an upper second need no longer be maintained as an artificial and sometimes inappropriate hurdle for the prospective research student.

There have undoubtedly been problems associated with the developing complexity of research. Sometimes the techniques and machinery to be mastered have been so demanding that the average research student has had little time and energy to develop his own ideas during his three years. In other cases, the building of some intricate apparatus has consumed so much time that the acquisition of results is compressed into the final term. This has the consequence that an important part of the education and training associated with the digestion and analysis of results and the subsequent testing of hypotheses is omitted. In other branches, including organic chemistry, there are problems associated with the provision of a sufficient range of expensive equipment with adequate technical assistance to give the facilities considered desirable for modern work.

I believe that the status of the research student has fallen and that it has to be improved. Entry must be more competitive but once accepted the research student has to be better financed and, above all, the rewards for the well-trained Ph.D. have to be increased. Fewer people should be kept for research training which should be recognized as a privilege. The first year should be probationary but the emoluments should increase during the three years. A limited number of students should be encouraged to study for a Ph.D. as a worthwhile education in depth even if they have no thoughts of a career involving research. But most research students will be aiming for a subsequent career beginning with some content of research and development although often not in the narrow specialization of their Ph.D. work. There are arguments to support the idea that the normal period of research training might be increased from three to four years but with a more drastic cut in the number of research grants available.

I believe that the extraordinary emphasis on the part that course work should play in Ph.D. training in the recent report on Postgraduate Training by a Science Research Council working party is unfortunate. If the calibre of the people we encourage to undertake research training is high enough and if we allow them adequate leisure they will broaden and deepen their own knowledge. We cannot expect a research student to be deeply involved and dedicated to his research problem, cope with a complicated array of compulsory courses and have the time and energy to develop his own intellectual capacity to the full. I have little sympathy with those who decry the specialized nature of much Ph.D. research. Their criticism is misdirected. They are failing to distinguish between the nature of the research which must often be specialized to be worthwhile and the characteristics of the individual undertaking the work who ought to be a man of parts and not a narrow minded specialist. Perhaps this confusion arises because we in the universities have accepted some of too low calibre as research students.

One problem associated with the increased complexity of research has been the demand from university teachers for postdoctoral assistants to maintain and devlop techniques. There has been a tendency for these posts to proliferate and consume too high a proportion of the output of Ph.D's. Some who have occupied these positions have had little opportunity or the necessary drive to develop their own independence. If we are prepared to accept that some contraction of the chemical research in universities is inevitable and possibly desirable, we might expect to see fewer but reasonably paid postdoctoral workers with appointments running for up to four years. Such carefully selected postdoctoral workers would have better opportunities to establish their own lines of work within research groups and provide the seed corn for the next generation of university teachers.

The Difficult Decisions

It is not a difficult exercise to look back over the last 20 years and find aspects of the university education of chemists which can be criticized, but to attempt to chart the way ahead is a daunting prospect.

First of all I believe that we should be rather cautious about how far we go in attempting to persuade schoolchildren to study chemistry at university. Of course it is right to ensure that they know what an interesting and important subject we profess, but we ought not to conceal that it demands real effort and we ought to settle for fewer but better quality entrants to chemistry departments. If we have the courage to tighten up on standards of entry we shall strengthen the profession in the long run.

The same criteria apply with even greater force with respect to the percentage of honours graduates encouraged to stay on for research. A gradual decrease in this percentage provided it is accomplished by raising the status and prospects for chemistry Ph.D's should not be regarded as a retrograde step.

The real problems are concerned with the fact that there are too many chemistry departments all trying to maintain not only good honours degree courses but active and flourishing research schools. It is no longer feasible, and perhaps it never was, to think of some 60 university chemistry departments having full-scale research schools and the difficulties of the situation are not eased by the existence of 30 polytechnics and the central institutions in Scotland, many with aspirations of a similar kind. Whether we like it or not, neither the talent nor the finance is available to feed so many research schools and the process of concentration which has already begun is likely to continue. We must accept that the presence of too many people involved in research in establishments of higher education is one of the ways in which there have been too many non-producers in the country. If we attempt to spread the finance and facilities available for research over too many centres we shall weaken dangerously our potential for future scientific growth and leadership. There must be an increasing concentration of resources at chosen centres.

How do we diversify our university chemistry departments? Some may find an attractive role by increasing collaboration with and possibly even merging with allied departments either in the direction of physics and engineering or towards the biological end of the spectrum. But perhaps a more fundamental change in attitude is needed by recognizing that excellence in teaching is something to be fostered as strongly as excellence in research. Some chemistry departments might be encouraged to develop in the "liberal arts" direction with emphasis on the quality of their undergraduate teaching and general scholarship but with limited research activity. A deliberate effort would have to be made to increase the respect and kudos associated with good teaching. Those involved in "liberal arts" departments should be accorded conditions of work which compare favourably with those at centres where research is concentrated and they might qualify for more generous conditions of tenure. They should also be given good opportunities with appropriate financial arrangements to take sabbatical years at universities with active research schools. Facilities should be provided to make regular collaboration with neighbouring research centres easier than it is at present.

Perhaps it is worth mentioning at this stage that the movement of staff between universities should be made more attractive and stimulated as an important counter to the stagnation that may otherwise afflict us. This idea is worthwhile for its own sake quite apart from any question of changing the character of some chemistry departments. There should be positive encouragement and generous dislocation allowances for staff, aged say 40 to 45, who are prepared to move to the same grade in another University.

The myth that it is desirable for all university teachers to be active in research *throughout* their career must be challenged. Intense contact with research for a period of years is a *sine qua non* for a university teacher but the arguments that each individual must have continuing personal contact with research have been overstated. The contrast between the contented and useful older teacher with an alert mind capable of modernizing his teaching as required and the unhappy and agitated middle-aged man using up his energies struggling to keep a mediocre research effort from sinking is probably a picture that is known to many of us. The system ought to permit the middle-aged university chemist to opt out of the research game without loss of face.

How much influence should we expect from outside to induce us to diversify the character of our chemistry departments? The Science Research Council already has an influence in concentrating research potential and it is doubtful whether more power should be given to a single organization. The U.G.C. can exert some influence of a gentle kind but the effect is somewhat attenuated when transmitted through the barrier of university autonomy. But as I said at the beginning chemists must be prepared to put their own house in order. The recent history of the Canadian universities in the province of Ontario provides an example of the problems of rapid growth and the consequential reaction. The cycle of events started with an increase in the number and size of universities in Ontario and the method of financing led to a marked rise in the provision of graduate places. Then a reaction followed and under external pressures several universities were required to curtail their Ph.D. programs. Do we have a warning here about the turn of events that might occur in Britain?

At one stage I wondered whether the profession of chemistry itself in the shape of a unified CS/RIC might have some role to play in the rationalization of the large number of chemistry departments that we appear to have. On further consideration this idea is less attractive. First of all unification is not likely to occur before 1980 and the process of adjustment by university chemists to new circumstances must begin soon. Second it would take time to establish confidence in the ability of a unified CS/RIC to evolve the necessary machinery to even out the pressures from various sectional and sometimes conflicting interests of universities, polytechnics, industrial reformers, educational enthusiasts and chemists active in a variety of disciplines of teaching and research. Nevertheless there may be some action that can be taken now to open up the debate inside the profession in order to see what ideas could emerge of value to the U.G.C.

Summary

With regret I come to the conclusion that standards associated with the teaching and training of chemists in universities may have declined in certain respects. I believe that the serious thoughts which we are giving in this symposium to the conservation of resources should include some consideration of the university sphere as that part of our educational system which is of the greatest importance for the future of this country. Remedies to correct the present trends will not be easy to apply and they must be gradual if they are to be acceptable and avoid exacerbating the problems. Too rapid changes in the size and organization of universities, in the expansion or contraction of scientific research, and in the supply of financial support for these activities, bring repercussions which have to be recognized and include some potentially serious effects on standards. As the Vice-Chancellor of Bristol wrote in a recent article "It takes a long time to build up first-class educational institutions and the nation is fortunate to possess so many. It takes almost no time at all to weaken them fatally".[7]

Notes and Bibliography

[1] Numbers rose from 50 000 in 1938–39 to 118 000 in 1962–63.
[2] Higher Education, Cmnd. 2154 (October 1963).
[3] see for example Select Discourses from The Idea of a University by J. H. Newman, Ed. May Yardley, C.U.P., 1931.
[4] The Flow into Employment of Scientists, Engineers and Technologists, Cmnd. 3760 (September 1968).
[5] The Committee of Enquiry into the Relationship between University Courses in Chemistry and the Needs of Industry, The Royal Institute of Chemistry, 1970.
[6] Postgraduate Training, Science Research Council (September 1975).
[7] A. W. Merrison, The Education of Ministers of State, The New Universities Quarterly, p. 1, Winter 1975.

Nature's Assets — an Elementary View*

by P. F. Corbett; Corbett Industrial Consultancy Limited

Introduction

In reviewing Iain Macleod's biography of Neville Chamberlain in 1961, Roy Jenkins wrote two sentences which I have always feared could equally apply to many of us who attempt broad reviews of multidiscipline areas. "Mr. Macleod writes with a scrupulous accuracy. Yet there is a constant impression that he is writing close against the frontiers of his knowledge". The inclusion of the word "elementary" therefore in the title is by way of disclaimer — rather than pun!

I am not attempting a review, but merely giving a "view" of Nature's assets. It is a personal view and therefore a biased and a prejudiced one. Moreover it is formed out of experience rather than deep academic understanding. It is on the whole one of optimism — which may be unusual (and even unpopular) at a time when ignorant men are prophesying doom and sensible ones are competing with each other in cynicism.

I believe, in spite of every shred of evidence to the contrary, that man is a resourceful, enquiring, hardworking and imaginative animal. Whether he is always wise is debatable, and whether he has always used Nature's assets for the best purposes, or even for the best reasons, are matters of opinion and judgement and not of fact.

Chemists are no better, but certainly are no worse, than other men. They have helped to use Nature's assets to improve man's standard of living and change his environment. Much is talked about the environment and most of it by people who really do not accept that man's natural environment is the forest and swamp, and do not

*Published by permission of the Copyright holders, Corbett Industrial Consultancy Limited, to whom requests for permission to reproduce extracts should be addressed.

understand that it is technology – applied science – that has moved him from these!

Over the centuries man has learned to understand and use Nature's assets, and chemists (and others) have created wealth so that all men, and not just a few, have access to the material and cultural benefits that derive from the intelligent harnessing and utilisation of all such resources. These assets include, of course, man himself: the development of his mind and memory by education and experience is perhaps the greatest asset of all.

Man has widened his geophysical environment whilst he has been widening his intellectual one. He has crossed rivers and mountain ranges, cleared forests and grown crops, made roads, canals, railways and artificial lakes, charted and crossed oceans, explored the stratosphere and ocean beds and landed on the moon! Every new step forward has followed some new product of science and/or technology: a bigger or a faster ship, train, plane or rocket; a cheaper or more reliable or more efficient source of power; some new material developed specifically to accommodate the new conditions into which man was thrusting either himself or the appliances assisting him in his pursuits.

His control over heat and light has reduced to insignificance the difference between night and day, the seasons, and his own position on the earth's crust relative to the orbital movement of the earth round the sun. It would seem that by utilising Nature's assets to his own advantage, man, to a very large extent, can control his own progress and his own environment.

Changes in Resource Needs

This process of social and technological change has been continuous over a period of about ten thousand years and for most of this time man lived, everywhere, in an agrarian economy. Over the last 150 years, however, those living in N.W. Europe and N. America have been changing their economy into an industrially based one: more recently the inhabitants of Russia, Japan and parts of Australasia have begun to do the same. This change has been most significant because, using the classification of the old parlour game, an agrarian environment is based on resources of animal and vegetable origin: an industrial one requires those primarily and essentially of mineral origin.

Using this elementary classification, I wish to advance the view that because animals and vegetables are reproducible by sexual and photosynthetic processes, a knowledge of these processes and our own requirements should, with good husbandry and good sense, enable us to produce and continue to produce such resources of these classes as we need. Their availability is limitless. (This presupposes the solution of a whole host of political, economic and distribution problems well outside the scope of this Paper – the point is that we can control our animal and vegetable resources if we have the will to.)

Minerals however are the products of earlier high-temperature, high-pressure chemical reactions or the results of very long-range degradation processes. They may be changed in form, new sources may be found, but they cannot be reproduced: their availability is limited.

The change from an agrarian to an industrial economy therefore begins to limit our freedom to perpetuate our resources. Our quality of life is now restricted by the availability of minerals. This restriction is applicable not only to a new set of materials additional to those we previously had, but (due to inter-related developments arising from industrialisation) applies also to materials which could still come from the animal and vegetable sector. We have replaced wood and its products with plastic; soaps from animal fats and vegetable oils with mineral oil-based detergents; cotton, flax, etc. and hides of animals with synthetic fibres; natural manure with synthesised fertilisers; the sap of rubber trees with synthesised materials; the wide range of quadrupeds (which we can call generically "beasts of burden") with tractors and trucks, made from and powered by mineral resources. We have shifted almost the whole of our resource needs from the animal/vegetable (limitless) sector to the mineral (limited) sector. Except for food and drink our dependence on minerals is almost complete: even in the case of these obviously "natural" resources, we must consider the vitally ancillary requirements of the products of mineral resources for containing, preserving, distributing, and cooking.

The Consumption of Minerals

If it is accepted that the availability of minerals conditions our life-style, then the way in which we are using them should be examined.

Before about 1800 our mineral requirements were simple – the base metals copper, lead, zinc and tin and the precious metals, gold and silver. These – with some readily available salt deposits – produced the early chemistry and metallurgy in which great scientific discoveries were made and our scientific tradition began to develop. Iron ore, coal, cement and sulphur were the new requirements of the Industrial Revolution. Since about 1910, pressures predominantly from war-based economies stimulated the use of chromium and manganese for stainless steels, aluminium and magnesium for low-density high-tensile materials, and nickel, tungsten and molybdenum for many new ferro-alloys.

Since 1945, firstly the demands of reconstruction in Europe, Russia and the Far East, and secondly the social demands of all peoples who saw the War as a watershed between semi-poverty and pseudo-affluence, have placed unprecedented demands on the mineral extractive industries. We may have given an "increased standard of living" to a wider section of the population but we have used up much material from our limited sector of Nature's assets.

Table 1 lists some 30 minerals which account for over 90% of the world's mineral production (a full list would be at least twice as long). For convenience I have sub-divided these so that a few group comparisons can be made of the rates at which consumption is

Table 1: Major metals and minerals

A. Iron ore	F. Nuclear
B. Base metals	Uranium
Copper	G. Electronics
Lead	Mercury
Tin	H. Chemical
Zinc	Bromine
C. Precious metals	Fluorspar
Gold	Phosphate
Platinum	Potash
Silver	Pyrites
D. Light metals	Salt
Aluminium	Sulphur
Magnesium	J. Industrial
Titanium	Asbestos
E. Ferroalloys	Cement
Chromium	Gypsum
Manganese	Talc
Molybdenum	K. Abrasive
Nickel	
Tungsten	

Table 2: (Proportionate) increases in production

1955 = 1

Groups	Actual 1970	Projected 1985
A Iron ore	1.6	2.5
B Base metals	1.6	2.8
C Precious metals	1.6	2.0
D Light metals	3.8	10.0
E Ferroalloys	1.7	3.5
F Nuclear	(4)	(30)
G Electronics	2.5	3.2
H Chemical	1.8	3.4
J Industrial	2.3	5.0
K Abrasive	1.9	6.5
Total all groups	1.9	3.7

currently increasing (Table 2). It will be seen that we are already consuming these materials at double the rate at which we were consuming them in the years immediately after World War II, and we can expect to double consumption again by the time those now at University are established in their profession, contributing to society's needs, and expecting in return further increases from society's services.

We should perhaps ask ourselves whether we have the resources to meet these anticipated needs. The answer is "yes" if, (a) we are considering the situation in 1985 in isolation and (b) if we confine our predictions to the needs of current consumers only. I will return to both these points, but before then I draw your attention to the results of a few predictions (Table 3) for sixteen metals – all reasonably basic to our every-day needs.

The current rate of consumption has been divided into the known (i.e. published) reserves, and assuming the consumption rate to be constant, the date (to the nearest five years) has been postulated at which current reserves might be depleted. These dates are given in Column A. Consumption rates, though, have not been constant; they have been exponential. Assuming the average compound growth rate over the period 1960–1970 (shown in Column C) can be extrapolated forward and apply unchecked until current reserves are used up, then an even more dramatic series of forecasts (Column B) may apply.

Table 3: Dates at which current reserves could be
exhausted (nearest 5 years)

Metal	A	B	C
Aluminium	2145	2005	8.1
Chromium	2550	2065	3.2
Cobalt	2125	2015	4.6
Copper	2010	1995	3.3
Gold	1990	1985	2.5
Iron	2400	2045	3.8
Lead	1990	1985	2.9
Manganese	2150	1985	4.5
Mercury	1985	1985	-0.3
Molybdenum	2070	1995	8.1
Nickel	2110	2000	8.7
Platinum	1995	1985	0.5
Silver	1990	1985	1.8
Tin	1995	1985	4.2
Tungsten	2015	2005	0.5
Zinc	1990	1985	6.2

A Assuming future consumption at current rate
B Assuming uninterrupted exponential growth at (C)%.
C (Average) compound growth rate, 1960–1969

Let us examine the validity of these deductions. The consumption figures are more or less reliable: governments need to collect them for taxation or planning purposes, and the industries concerned do not consciously send in incorrect returns. However, there is no valid reason for any such close check on reserves, assessments of which find their way into the literature in a variety of ways: many perpetuate each other's errors or confirm each other mistakes. Also definitions of reserves are relative; what is uneconomic one day, is economic under different conditions of supply and demand. A new technology may change the basis of assessment; different industries, and even different companies in the same industry, may have different interpretations of proved, possible and probable reserves.

This is one series of errors. But, perhaps of more importance, any calculation of depletion which ignores the certainty of new discoveries, also ignores man's insatiable lust for exploration and enquiry, which has moved him, over the last few thousand years, from forest and swamp on to the moon.

New Sources and Techniques

Minerals must clearly be looked for in new areas. Not every area of land, and hardly any of the sea bed, has so far been explored: and it should be remembered that three-quarters of the earth's surface is covered by water of various depths. We all know from recent experiences in the North Sea that a few hundred or so feet of water and about 2 miles of other rock covered deposits containing new sources of fuel of which we have only become aware within the last 10 years. Similarly recent and commercial discoveries of fuels have been made in other Continental Shelf areas in other parts of the world. About 30 million square miles of seabed is covered by less than 200 metres of water. The oil industry has successfully operated in these depths and with this experience, the mineral industry also has a new and potential area (which is nearly three times the area of Africa) in which to seek out new sources.

On land we must surely accept that under the Arctic and Antarctic ice there is a distribution of minerals similar to that so far found in temperate or tropical areas. Of course these difficult working environments require new techniques and special equipment and materials of construction – but much has already been done here also.

Techniques for better mineral extraction must be used. One such is to use controlled underground nuclear explosions to crack up ores from which metals can be extracted by selective leaching techniques. Many neglected spheres of inorganic and physical chemistry must come back into their own. As an immediate measure, steps should perhaps be taken to limit the research work devoted to organic and synthetic chemistry, and replace it with inorganic and physical chemistry slanted to metallurgical problems.

Some Immediate Needs

Assuming however that all goes well and that new sources are forthcoming, the tasks ahead appear challenging, when the quantities involved are examined. To do some predictions it is necessary to assume (a) that the projected requirements for 1985 are correct (and unless there is some political or economic calamity this is a fair assumption. Technological forecasts are usually correct five years ahead and nearly always correct seven years ahead) and (b) that to produce at this projected rate in 1985 the industry needs to be assured of a 25 year back-up in supplies. This is not an unreasonable assumption – certainly anything less than 15 years would be economic folly. Some probable deficiencies for a few selected metals are given in Table 4, firstly in actual quantities, and then as a comparative index of the known reserves of 1970. Taking all mineral resources in total, as a broad conclusion we can say that if we wish to

Table 4: New sources required to ensure 1985
production, and 25 year "back-up"

	Million tons (approx)	Approx % 1970 Reserves
Copper	60	20
Lead	80	100
Molybdenum	3	100
Tungsten	2	450
Zinc	250	350

continue at our present rate of consumption we need to find, in the next 20 years, rather more reserves of minerals than have been discovered in the last 200!

Whose Needs?

Moreover it cannot be assumed that future demands for minerals will arise solely from those already consuming them. It is important to remember that the people with high standards of living occupy only about 8% of the total land area of the globe and constitute about 13% of the world's population.

The possible pressures on already scarce supplies can be illustrated by examining the per capita consumption of fuel, which is a very sensitive index of the goods and services at our disposal. It reflects, in broad terms, the average standard of living of the country as a whole. Table 5 gives some data from which it will be seen that the affluent 13% consume about 50% of the total world consumption of energy. It is almost axiomatic that similarly they consume about 50% of the world's total production of metals and minerals. What is to happen when seven-eighths of the world's population seek the affluence

Table 5: Annual energy consumption

	Population millions	Per capita tons coal equivalent
United Kingdom	55	5.2
Common Market (average)	250	4.5
United States	200	10.8
World (average)	3,450	1.7
Rest of World i.e. excluding Europe and U.S.	3,000	1.0

currently enjoyed by the other one-eighth? Or if Europeans seek further to emulate their American cousins who on average consume twice as much energy and other resources as they do? Approximately one-third of the world's resources are used by the 200 million inhabitants of North America, leaving the remaining two-thirds for the use of about 3,200 million people. Expressed another way the average American citizen consumes 8 times more energy and raw materials than the average for the rest of the world.

Energy

Energy is a fascinating subject and some of its magic will be revealed in other papers.* All I want to say at this stage is that combustion is an oxidation process, and that the controlled oxidation of a wide range of naturally occurring materials – wood, coal, shale, petroleum oil, natural gases – and their derivatives, have provided us with all the light, heat, power, and energy we have not received directly from the sun, and the movement of the wind and water.

As our need for energy increased so our production and consumption of fuels increased; our choice of fuels changed with convenience and availability. Coal rapidly replaced wood, and oil and natural gas – where and when available – soon found places in the energy markets of industrialised countries. The changing pattern of fuel usage in the United Kingdom (where only coal has been indigenous until quite recently) over the last fifty years is shown in Figure 1.

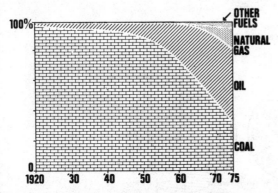

FIGURE 1.   % Contribution to primary energy: U.K.

*See especially p. 217.

World-wide the situation recently and projected forward to the year 2000 is shown in Figure 2, although there could be some minor changes as the new relative prices and availability of fuels affect the forecast pattern. There will be shifts in favour of coal in those areas with indigenous coal reserves, and therefore some reversal of coal to oil trends in the U.K. and in the U.S. There may also be some minor and local developments in the use of other fuels in some areas. But even with these changes in the supply picture, it will be apparent that the contribution of oil to our energy needs will continue to be dominant.

Figure 3 shows the growth in world consumption of oil over the last ten years. The percentage growth has been highest in Western Europe, Japan and Russia, and whereas Russia's oil is indigenous, the

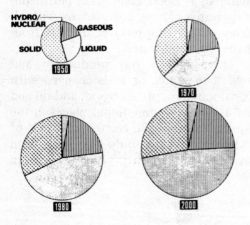

FIGURE 2.   World energy increase.

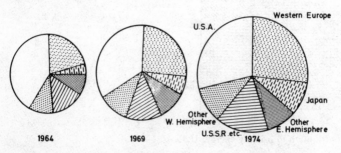

FIGURE 3.   World oil consumption.

other two rely mainly (but not entirely) on imports from the Middle East. Figures 4 and 5 show in diagrammatic form the main oil movements by sea, ten years ago and today, and perhaps explain, in very simple terms, the reasons behind O.P.E.C.'s attitude on supply quantities and prices.

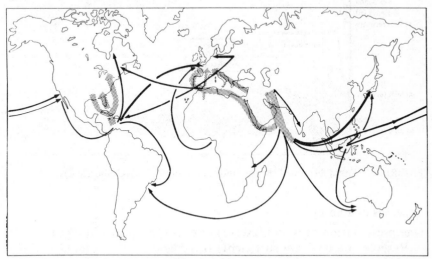

FIGURE 4.   Main oil movements by sea: 1964.

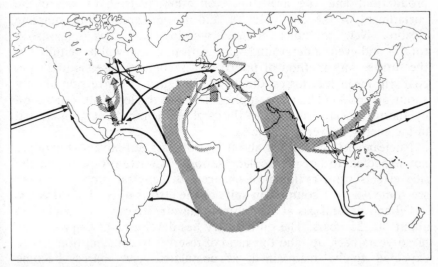

FIGURE 5.   Main oil movements by sea: 1974.

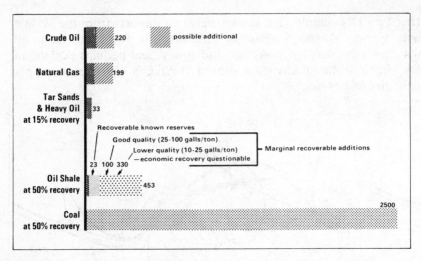

FIGURE 6.   World recoverable hydrocarbon reserves (10^9 tons oil equivalent)

Reserves of Energy

One presentation of world reserves of energy is shown in Figure 6.

Reserves of coal are sufficient to last about 300 years at current consumption rates, but the social and political overtones of coal production, and the availability of other fuels, have led to the curtailment of the coal industry, and in some areas to its complete closure. New methods of coal winning, and developments in total – and even underground–gasification of coal will be required in the future. Any method of preparing a secondary/gaseous fuel from coal will mean fuel losses, due to an efficiency of conversion of only about 50–60%. (The same applies of course to electricity generation by thermal means: about two-thirds of all the input energy is wasted in the energy conversion process.)

Nuclear fuels could last about 1,000 years but advances here are not expected to be spectacular. Disposal of waste products and the side effects from radiological change are technical problems which are some way off solution in spite of the efforts of the last 30 years.

Oil and natural gas at the moment have reserves which could last about 30–35 years. The oil industry has developed having about 25 or so years back-up, and this ratio of reserves to consumption can be expected to be maintained, as postulated new sources become available. However, as will be seen from Figure 7, the main areas

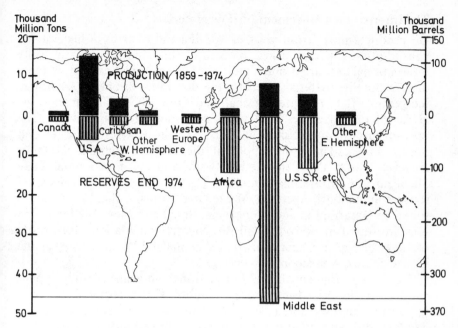

FIGURE 7.   Total discovered oil.

from which future supplies are likely to be forthcoming are Africa, the Middle East and the Soviet Union.

On a thermal basis, there is well over half as much natural gas available as there is oil, and, so far, consumption of natural gas has not been at this rate, as compared with that of oil. Like oil, natural gas is nearly always found well away from the high energy consuming economies originally based on coal. Until about 1950 natural gas was used only relatively close to its source. Over the last twenty years, large diameter high-pressure pipelines have conveyed it, in gaseous form, overland for many thousands of miles (and even – for shorter distances – under water).

In liquid form (methane may be liquefied at −163°C) natural gas can be carried in ocean-going tankers, like oil, but differences in temperature and bulk density of the cargo make the costs of using such tankers about eight times that for the equivalent fuel value of crude oil. In spite of these economic disadvantages however, natural gas is now an internationally transported energy source, and this method of moving it is becoming increasingly important.

The International Movement of Raw Materials

Oil products move from areas of low demand to areas of high energy consumption, necessitating a world oil industry with fully international resources and facilities. The minerals industry is more diverse but the materials used by the developed countries are not all indigenous. It too is international, and draws its supplies from some areas where, currently, local needs are much less than average. The ores of chromium are found in Cuba, Russia, Rhodesia, Turkey and South Africa. Those of copper in the Rocky Mountain areas of America, Chile, Peru, the Congo Basin, and an areas around Lake Michigan in Central Canada and the United States. Lead has its chief sources in Missouri, Australia, Mexico and British Columbia. Nickel is found in Ontario, Finland, Venezuela, Brazil and New Caledonia. Tin ores are found in Bolivia, Thailand, Nigeria and Alaska, whilst those of tungsten are in China, Bolivia, Tasmania and Burma as well as the United States. And so on.

The need for so much international movement of supplies emphasises the need for political stability. This is required not only to ensure uninterrupted supplies from sources currently being worked, but also to provide the economic stability to attract the investments required to seek out (and use) the future mineral sources indicated as being needed. This can only come from a mutual understanding, by the producing and consuming countries of each others' economic problems and aspirations. Excessive rights of sovereignty by one or the other could endanger this.

The natural resources of the world no longer "belong" to those States lucky enough initially to find coal in temperate climates. In these days of mutual international interdependence, the existence of a group, class or nation which feels deprived (and considers action to remedy this) is a threat to the livelihood of all.

Is there a Crisis?

I have studiously avoided the word "crisis". I have also refrained from the "Doomwatch" approach to resource needs which is popular in some quarters. I have however not dealt with environmental problems which could, by themselves, be the subject of another lecture − or series of lectures. It must be obvious however that further demands on natural resources mean more infringements of our natural environment − whatever that is − both in the winning and working of ores and the fabrication of the goods we wish to make from their derivatives. The combustion of increased amounts of fuels to provide our energy needs means more transport, more boilers, more furnaces, more power stations, more pylons and more discharge to the atmosphere of waste products and waste heat.

We must perhaps ask ourselves whether there is some point at which we try to evaluate our present and future demands for goods and services having regard to environmental and resource considerations. It would seem to me to be wrong to expect our "quality of life" to be enhanced if, in response to politicians' and economists' appeal for a 3% or more increase in Gross National Product, we achieved an "increased standard of living" at the expense of a countryside littered with the debris of a technology based on built-in obsolescence.

A realisation of the need for conservation will avoid all approaches to "crisis" conditions. Metal (and other material) recovery and re-cycling must be as assiduously applied as it was in the War – and with rising costs this may be economically as well as socially motivated. Increases in the costs of fuels of all types will reflect particularly on the costs of metals, since a large element in their costs is the cost of the energy required for their extraction and refining.

The end of "cheap energy" (an era which started when slaves were chained to oars and animals worked treadmills) will mean a basic re-appraisal of our priorities of those "qualities" we want in life. It should also encourage us to accept a view that the efficient use of fuel is the key to minimising the initial costs of our raw materials, while at the same time limiting their impact on the environment.

On the other hand, any working of grades of ores lower than hitherto practised, could lead to more environmental impingement since a higher proportion of waste material will need to be disposed of, and a proportionally higher quantity of energy required for their production.

The Way Forward

The initial utilisation of our resources should be more efficient, whether at the winning or the form-fabrication stage, and subsequently there should be serious regard to recycling, so that resources can be better conserved. Furthermore all such operations should occur with regard to the environment around us, which is basically of air and water, and animals and vegetation, both of which need these two commodities as much as we do.

So it's "back to the drawing board" for chemists as well as for engineering design draughtsmen. Let us have a new look at basic chemistry. Let's forget — just for a moment or two — the wonderful world of molecular architecture, and sort out a few simple oxidation and reduction reactions. Let's understand fuel technology and extraction metallurgy. Let us see these — admittedly elementary, and even on occasions rather primitive — sciences in a new light.

Let us therefore examine these subjects from first principles, and what better than to go back a few thousand years and look at the four elements? For just as — in my view — all the wisdom of the world is to be found in Ecclesiastes, so all the science we want for our present studies is contained in an understanding of AIR, EARTH, FIRE and WATER.

The significance of these to fuel technology and metallurgy is obvious. It was from the primitive hearth, where fuel and metal ores were accidentally intermingled and in some magical way produced fire, and heat to melt and cast the metal, that combustion and metallurgy were born. Left behind from the reaction was a different ash (or ore) from that originally used: the cycle of "ashes to ashes" was complete: the philosophy of transmutation was beginning to develop.

We take all our elements for granted.

AIR — almost universally and freely available and therefore abused and misused.

EARTH — Nature's treasure chest of minerals for us to plunder like pirates finding Spanish gold.

FIRE — the magical mystical thing which is the basis of all religious symbolism and is now (renamed Fuel and Energy) the essence of Power Politics — in both senses of the adjective.

WATER — the universal catalyst, the almost perfect medium for transportation (either on it or in it), the crystalline part of minerals; and now in many places barely adequate for irrigation, for hygiene and for life itself!

Four other papers are dealing with these subjects in more detail. I believe the views expressed by their authors will supplement those which I have tried to introduce and lead to a composite view which I am confident the chemist can accept.

Resource conservation and environmental protection go hand in hand: attention to both is the hall-mark of the man who claims to have a professional ethic and a social conscience.

Most of the Tables and Figures in this paper were prepared by the author, during the course of his employment with the British Petroleum Company Limited, from data gathered from a wide variety of sources. Figures 3, 4, 5, and 7 are reproduced from the *B.P. Statistical Review of the World Oil Industry*, and Figure 6 is reproduced from *World Energy Prospects*, also published by B.P. The author is grateful to the British Petroleum Company Limited for permission to reproduce this material.

Fresh Air

by J. E. Lovelock; Bowerchalke, Salisbury, Wilts.

ONCE upon a time the fresh-air smell of the briny sea was said to be that of ozone. The word "ozone" had a romantic connotation, no doubt aided by its value as a word almost specifically designed for the game of Scrabble. In those days of innocence, as Dr. Reay remarked last year, even the London pea-souper was regarded as a familiar, almost welcome, event. Not so today, for now there can be hardly anyone, chemists included, who does not associate the word ozone with that thin, insubstantial veil up there in the sky, alleged to be our sole shield and protection against the deadly ultraviolet rays of the sun. It is right and proper to be concerned about the conservation of the quality of the air we breathe but so insistent has been the campaign by some enviromentalists that few of us now use an aerosol-propelled product or contemplate a flight in Concorde without a sense of guilt, a fear that we may be contributing to the demolition of a vital part of the atmosphere.

The original Puritans did have some cause for their concern over the corruption of 17th century society, but their zeal tended to overrun their compassion and commonsense and led to excesses of repression more repugnant than the evils they sought to extirpate. Could this also be true of the present-day Puritans of the environmental movement? Is our fresh air truly in danger of degradation or is our concern for the environment manipulated for reasons unconnected with the conservation of the air? To answer these questions we need to know more about the nature of fresh air. We need to know more about the interaction of the atmosphere with the living and with the physical world. We need models or hypotheses which can be exposed to scientific tests.

It used to be believed that the world was created by a thoughtful and considerate god specifically for our benefit. This Judeo—

Christian view has tended to give way in recent times to the similar humanistic view of the world summarized by that phrase "the space ship earth"; where again everything is on the planet for our advantage but now we rather than God are in charge.

Religous and humanistic world models use faith rather than science as a guide. Whether they are right or wrong they are not very helpful in our search for knowledge. Enlightenment in science comes mostly from a natural selection among hypotheses in a ruthless environment of experimenal test. Fortunately there is an older and alternative world model to the religious and humanistic and one which is more open to tests. In this model the whole world was seen as a living entity in which our species was a part or a partner rather than a possessor. This view of the world is normal to many who live closer to living things than do we city dwellers. In deference to the earliest literature citation my colleage Lynn Margulis of Boston University or I could find, we have chosen to call a biophysical version of this model "Gaia" after the ancient Greek personification of the Earth Goddess.[1] Our neo-Gaian view of the world postulates a biosphere which is able to control the physical and chemical environment so that it is kept at an optimum for life on Earth. The introduction, or reintroduction, of a candidate hypothesis of the world as dynamic biophysical regulatory system can only be justified by a substantial amount of scientific evidence. Very briefly, the highlights of this evidence are as follows.

Firstly, the chemical compositions of the atmosphere, oceans, and crust of the earth are profoundly different from the expectations of steady-state abiological equilibria. Thus the presence of methane, nitrous oxide, and even nitrogen in our present oxidising atmosphere represents violation of the rules of chemistry to be measured in tens of orders of magnitude. Disequilibrium on this scale suggests that the atmosphere is more than merely a biological product but maybe a biological contrivance. Not living, but like the paper of a wasps' nest made to maintain a chosen environment.

Secondly, a large suite of planetary properties are, and apparently always have been, close to optimal for life. The surface temperature, the sea salinity, and the pH have not changed from their present levels throughout the history of life. In the last few hundreds of millions of years the oxygen concentration has similarly remained at the present safe level. This constancy of properties has been maintained in spite of probable large changes in solar output and

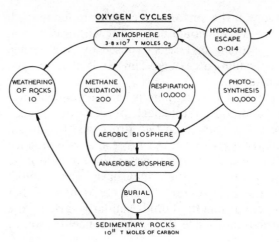

FIGURE 1

certainly in the face of large changes due to the emergence of oxygen itself as an atmospheric gas. Perhaps everything has always been for the best by chance; perhaps God has so kept it; self regulation seems to be a more reasonable alternative.

A few examples of what may be Gaian mechanisms follow. The first of these concerns oxygen and the possible role of methane for its regulation. Figure 1 illustrates the major biogeochemical cycles concerned in the regulation of atmospheric oxygen. The fluxes are in units of teramoles per year and are taken from the works of Walker[2] and of Holland[3]. Nearly all of the oxygen is produced by the green plants and algae, but is used up by the consumers within a year or so of its production. This process can never yield a net increment of oxygen. It used to be thought until quite recently that oxygen accumulated in the atmosphere as a consequence of the photolysis of water vapour at the outer reaches of the air. Here water molecules are split and the hydrogen atoms are light enough to escape the Earth's gravitational field. This process certainly can produce a net increment of oxygen but important though it may have been in the past it is a negligible source of oxygen now. There is little doubt that the important process which adds oxygen to the air is the one first proposed by Rubey[4], namely, the burial in sedimentary rocks of a small proportion of the carbon fixed by green plants and algae. Approximately 0.1% of the carbon fixed annually is thus buried leaving one oxygen molecule in the air for each carbon atom removed. Were it not for this process oxygen would be steadily withdrawn from the air by reaction with reducing materials exposed by weathering, earth movements, and volcanic outgassing. Thus it is that oxygen maintains a steady concentration.

You may well wonder how it is that there is an exact equivalence between carbon burial and the abiological process of oxygen removal, for in no obvious way can these two processess be linked. Indeed Walker has speculated that in warmer times as a consequence of the lower solubility of oxygen in warm water there would have been an increase in carbon burial and there may have been as much as 25% more oxygen in the atmosphere than there is now. Other changes in the global environment could similarly affect the proportion of carbon buried and hence the oxygen concentration of the atmosphere.

One of the items of evidence which led us to the Gaia hypothesis is the little known fact that the probability of fire is a steep function of oxygen concentration. At the present level a change of 1% in oxygen changes the probability of fire by 70%. In an atmosphere containing between 30 and 35% of oxygen, grass and forest fires would become overwhelming holocausts and lightning always provides a source of ignition. Before long all standing vegetation on land surfaces would disappear. The persistence of standing vegetation since the metazoa first appeared suggests that oxygen never did rise much above the present levels. Could there be any mechanism by which the disastrous consequences of oxygen accumulation might be prevented? Photosynthesis is inhibited by oxygen but the effect is not great enough to function as an efficient regulator. A more probable regulator is the production of methane in the anaerobic muds of the sea beds, marshes, wet lands, and river estuaries. Once carbonaecous matter has reached the deep anaerobic zones where methane is made by bacterial fermentation it is already committed either to make methane or to be buried, hence any mechanism which can alter this proportion will effectively regulate oxygen. At present the production of methane is vast, nearly 1000 megatons a year representing something like 4% of the photosynthetic energy. Nearly 20 times as much carbon is used to produce methane as is buried. Consider what might happen if methane were not made in anaerobic regions. Twenty times as much carbon would then be buried and the oxygen concentration would rise by 1% every 10^4 years, within 10^5 years life on the land surfaces would be impossible. This is of course an unproven speculation and the time scale for oxygen change is hardly our concern when talking of air conservation now. Where it is relevant is to draw attention to the probable importance of the anaerobic zones of the continental shelves, marshes, wetlands, etc. which are undeniably the seat of carbon burial and which may also be the places where regulatory compounds such as methane are made. There is experimental evidence to suggest that these same regions are important also in the cycling of other elements including sulphur and iodine and also as the source of atmospheric N_2O.

Within the context of an intelligent biosphere it is appropriate to ask what is the function of a gas such as methane. It is no more illogical than asking what is the function of glucose or of insulin in the blood. Table 1 lists some of the atmospheric gases and their properties and considers hypothetical functions for each of them in turn. The first column of the table lists the atmospheric abundances which go from 80% for nitrogen to 1 part in 10^8 for ammonia. It might be thought that the trace gases, methane nitrous oxide and ammonia all present at parts per million or less were of little importance. The second column which lists the fluxes of these gases through the air illustrates the unwisdom of such a conclusion. The least abundant gas, ammonia, is passed through the air in quantities as great as that of nitrogen itself. The third column lists the extent to

Table 1.

Gas	Abundance/parts per million	Flux/megatons per year	Disequilibrium $\log_{10}$ units	Hypothetical functions
Nitrogen	790,000	100 to 1000	-10	Pressure builder; inserting; sink for nitrate
Oxygen	210,000	100,000	$-$	Energy reference gas.
Methane	1.35	1000	-36	Oxygen regulation; ventilation of anaerobic zones.
Nitrous oxide	0.3	60 to 300	-13	Oxygen regulation; ozone regulation.
Ammonia	0.01	100 to 1000	-36	pH regulation; formerly temperature regulation.

which the atmospheric concentrations of the gases depart from the expectations of equilibrium chemistry. Even nitrogen departs by more than ten orders of magnitude. The other gases are so anomalous as to be beyond the capabilities of calculation. We think that an atmosphere which bears simultaneously oxygen, methane, nitrous oxide, and ammonia is so unusual as to be more than a biological product; it is probably a biological contrivance. The last column of the table lists the hypothetical function of the gases. If there were no life on the Earth, it is probable, as first observed by Lewis and Randall, that the nitrogen would be present as the nitrate ion dissolved in the sea. What advantages are there to the biosphere in keeping the element nitrogen in its gaseous form in the atmosphere? There are three possibilities: firstly, a stable climate may require a one-bar atmosphere and nitrogen is a convenient pressure-building gas. Secondly, as we have seen a pure oxygen atmosphere would be disastrous, thus nitrogen may serve as a diluent for oxygen. Thirdly, if all of the nitrogen were in the sea then the molarity of the sea would be increased by 0.2 units. This would raise the total ionic strength of sea water to a level inconsistent with almost all known forms of life. Any of these would seem important reasons for the biological processes which return nitrogen from the sea and the land to the air.

Methane may serve to regulate oxygen in the manner already discussed but it may well have another important function, that of ventilating the anaerobic sector of the biosphere. The continuous upward flow of methane through the anaerobic muds ensures that these regions are continuously swept clean of noxious and toxic substances. These include oxygen itself which is highly toxic to anaerobes, and also the volatile methyl derivatives of many toxic elements such as tetramethyl-lead, trimethylarsenic, dimethylmercury, dimethyltellurium, etc.

Nitrous oxide production also takes place in the anaerobic sector. It may serve to sequester oxygen in a nontoxic form; it may participate with methane in the regulation of atmospheric oxygen. Nitrous oxide also has the property of depleting stratospheric ozone through its decomposition in the stratosphere into other oxides of nitrogen which catalytically destroy ozone. Could it be, that there is an optimum ozone density and that too much is as undesirable as too little is said to be? If this is so then nitrous oxide would serve also with that other natural ozone depleter methyl chloride as a regulator of stratospheric ozone.

Ammonia is produced in almost exactly the quantity required to neutralise the natural formation of acids during the oxidation of nitrogen and sulphur compounds of the air. Were ammonia not made then the rain everywhere would fall at a pH close to 3. The whole world would then experience the present problems suffered by Scandinavia alone.

If our planet is indeed self regulating it is best to think of a mechanism for regulation analogous to that which we use to maintain our temperatures constant. The mammal thermostats not by reference to some fixed point as is done in engineering systems but by a more subtle process involving a consensus of desired temperature amongst sub-systems which constitute the whole animal. In such a system no fixed point of reference is needed. The physiology of this process for the human is well described by Riggs;[5] the search for possible regulatory mechanisms in the biosphere should be enlightened by this example.

Gaia is still a hypothesis. The facts and speculations just given are only part of our collection, but the whole only corroborates, not proves, the existence of Gaia. Let us continue to assume that she does exist and see if the hypothesis has any useful bearing on the problem of the atmosphere.

The first thought that always comes to mind in this connection is pollution and without denying its importance to our species, to the planet as a whole it looks less important than we tend to think. It is forgotten that pollution is the way of life of many natural species and was so long before chemical industry became large enough to notice. Substances such as tetramethyl-lead and dimethylmercury have been dumped into the sea by anaerobic microflora for hundreds or thousands of megayears. It is their way of disposing of the poisonous waste of their anaerobic world. Perhaps the greatest air pollution incident the earth has ever known was the emergence of oxygen. When this happened whole suites of species must have been destroyed and others driven underground never to return to the surface. Just imagine a marine system able to produce chlorine by photosynthesis on a global scale, and the magnitude of the oxygen poison incident is revealed.

Our present capacity to pollute on a planetary scale seems trivial by comparison. The system seems robust and capable of withstanding major perturbations. The doomsters' cliché "and will destroy all life on earth" when applied to some minor change such as the depletion of the ozone layer by a few percent is in the Gaian context, foolish exaggeration. On the other hand, a pollution which stimulates a minor adjustment by the system to maintain homeostasis could be gravely disturbing to us as species. Thus to Gaia a glacial epoch could be no more important than is a fever to us. The consequences of the growth of CO_2 and of dust aerosols in the atmosphere should be thought of in this context.

More serious than the blind chance damage from pollution is the purposeful biocidal activity of agriculture. Urban dwellers – and this includes most scientists – tend to forget that good old Farmer Giles regards all living creatures other than his crops and livestock as weeds, pests, or vermin, and there to be destroyed or at least restricted to the local Nature Reserve. It may be that we can escape the consequences of this activity on the land surfaces. Recent measurements of the total biospheric productivity suggest that there has been no adverse effect which could be attributed to the present level of agriculture. But if farming were to be extended to the continental shelves, marshes, or wet lands then we might be in peril. It would seem that these regions are the seat of our hypothetical regulatory systems. Here is buried the carbon which sustains oxygen and here are made the methane and nitrous oxide which may control it. In the sea also marine algae are a source of a wide range of trace gases and on a scale large compared with chemical industry. Thus methyl chloride, a natural product of these regions, is the principal chlorine compound of the atmosphere. If we are to be concerned about the presence of chlorocarbon pollution by Industry or about oxides of nitrogen from combustion then we should be equally concerned about the production of these same gases or their precursors from natural biological sources. Agriculture especially if extended to the continental shelves could drastically alter natural production rates. McElroy[6] and Crutzen[7] have already warned of the possible danger of an excess of nitrous oxide production as a consequence of some farming practices.

The consequences of our presence on the planet seem mostly to be a matter of scale; we now manipulate whole geographic regions to our short-term advantage. What happens when we are obliged to use the whole planetary surface to feed our greatly increased numbers? Not long ago it would have been said that we had then won our final victory over Nature. The Earth would have been truly ours, our space ship with the crops and livestock our life support system. Maybe future agricultural science will be sufficiently subtle to produce a stable system of this type. But if we are right about Gaia, whoever owns this planet must be able to drive it. On us would then fall the daunting if not impossible task of planetary engineering and the maintenance of that optimum environment for life which we now get for free.

References

[1] J. E. Lovelock and L. Margulis, *Tellus*, 1974, **26**, 2–9.
[2] J. C. G. Walker, *Amer. J. Sci.*, 1974, **274**, 193–214.
[3] H. D. Holland, In "The Origin and Evolution of Atmospheres and Oceans", Wiley, New York 1964, pp. 86–101.
[4] W. W. Rubey, *Geol. Soc. Amer. Bull.*, 1951, **62**, 1111–1147.
[5] D. S. Riggs, "Control Theory and Physiological Feedback Mechanisms", Williams and Wilkins, Baltimore, 1970.
[6] M. B. McElroy, Personal communication.
[7] P. J. Crutzen, *Ambio*, 1974, **3**, 201–210.

Mineral Recycling: a Down-to-Earth Approach

by A. K. Barbour; RTZ Services Ltd., Bristol

A strong feature of recent debates about the future of our modern way of life has been concern for resources and the need for their conservation in the light of the rapid growth of world population and the universal demand and expectation for higher living standards, at least as expressed in material terms.

Most concern has been expressed about future food supplies and much has recently been written about future energy supplies. Here I review some considerations about the future supply of non-ferrous metals, particularly zinc and lead, without which our technology-oriented society would be impossible. Conclusive "answers" are not possible about these major philosophical questions, but my endeavour will be to outline some current thinking, to provide some current figures and information, and to demonstrate once again how difficult it is to reconcile short-term thinking based on hard information with long-term prediction based on extrapolation. Compound interest calculations for even a few decades ahead give huge ranges for numbers based on apparently minor variances in the basic data.

It is important at the outset to recognise how short-term is the thinking of most industrial and governmental institutions. Most senior people in industry and government are responsible for managing short-term or immediate situations; some have to think in terms of the life of a new product or process which will probably be a few years only, rarely more than 10 or 15. We must recognise the difficulty that most people have in coming to grips with the "prophets of doom", who forecast disaster in periods variously in the range 20 to 200 years ahead. The time-scales are totally different. So we have to adjust to trying to determine our current actions on the basis of numbers which are necessarily highly unreliable. This is very difficult for scientifically-trained people to do — but we have to do it

Table 1: World consumption 1964–1973 ('000 Tonnes)

	1964	1965	1966	1967	1968	1969	1970	1971	1972	1973
Aluminium	6110	6670	7592	7756	8841	9699	10030	10732	11768	13601
Copper	5980	6171	6421	6158	6506	7165	7284	7350	7985	8786
Lead	3128	3173	3306	3280	3517	3839	3855	3979	4158	4421
Zinc	3964	4054	4221	4259	4668	4999	5056	5172	5709	6283

if we are to come to terms with the extreme environmentalists and conservationists and then help to determine sensible company and national policies.

We must also attempt to weigh two other major imponderables:

(i) What are the limits of future scientific and technological invention and innovation?

(ii) What are the future desires and aspirations of people world-wide, who are currently categorised as under-privileged?

The impact of modern technological society on resource consumption is illustrated by the fact that between 1950 and 1970, mankind consumed half of all the zinc produced in the world up to 1970 and between 1960 and 1980 it will probably consume as much zinc as was ever produced before 1960. Similarly, for lead, production during the decade 1970–1980 will exceed the total production during the whole of the last century.

Recent data (1964–1973) are given for aluminium, copper, lead and zinc in Table 1.

Zinc

Zinc is distributed widely and Table 2 illustrates world mine production over the last decade. It is noteworthy that Canadian out-

Table 2: Mine production of zinc; '000 metric tons of Zn content

	1964	1966	1968	1970	1972	1974
Eastern Europe/U.S.S.R.	710	812	942	1080	1170	1303
Western Europe	566	581	683	743	734	698
U.S.A.	522	519	480	485	434	449
Canada	621	875	1052	1136	1129	1122
Australia	350	375	422	487	507	454
Asia	255	304	340	372	400	418
Africa	275	259	256	261	246	256
Mexico & South America	506	538	576	664	751	785

Table 3: Zinc consumption '000 metric tons

	1964	1966	1968	1970	1972	1974
U.S.A.	1089	1285	1221	1074	1286	1174
Japan	364	380	523	623	708	679
West Germany	321	310	362	396	413	389
United Kingdom	292	273	281	278	279	269
France	204	197	202	220	264	306
Belgium/Luxembourg	133	112	122	137	145	195
Italy	108	125	155	178	203	202
Australia	113	94	105	122	128	133
Canada	94	96	115	107	136	141
Eastern Europe/U.S.S.R.	632	714	870	994	1106	1263

put has almost doubled and now represents 21% of total world production. Mine production grew at about 5% per annum during the 1960's while the growth in consumption of zinc metal was 5.6% per annum. A current expert prediction for free-world growth during the seventies is 3.7% per annum.

Slab zinc consumption is growing at an accelerating rate, estimates being:

1900–1940   1.5% per annum compound
1950–1960   4.5% per annum
1960–1970   5.6% per annum

but these rates are modest compared with those for many plastics and aluminium. The balance of factors discussed later is expected to result in a reduction to 3.5% to 4.0% per annum over the decade 1970–1980.

Statistics for the major consuming countries are given in Table 3.

The dynamic growth of zinc consumption in Japan is particularly striking, the 1973 peak at 815,000 tons being nearly 4½ times the

Table 4: Major end-uses for zinc 1964–1974 ('000 metric tons)

End-use	United States			Japan			United Kingdom			West Germany		
	1964	1969	1974	1964	1969	1974	1964	1969	1974	1964	1969	1974
Die-casting alloys	476	523	391	52	118	134	75	78	70	49	85	83
Galvanising	414	448	448	219	328	371	101	99	92	104	140	149
Brass	123	163	161	56	80	80	128	116	101	87	106	96
Rolled zinc	40	44	35	19	32	25	27	22	22	85	75	60
Zinc oxide	18	38	60	12	16	19	26	35	38	–	–	–

1960 value of 186,000 tons. In contrast, the U.K. position has been quite static; consumption being 272,000 tons in 1960, peaking at 305,000 tons in 1973, and back below the 1960 figure in 1974.

The major end-uses for zinc are shown in Table 4.

Lead

Lead is distributed widely and commerical deposits have been reported in about fifty countries. Major lead-producing countries are the U.S.A., the U.S.S.R., Australia, Canada, Mexico, Peru, and Yugoslavia. During the 1960's the annual growth rate of mine production was about 3% per annum while annual consumption grew at an average rate of about 3.8%. These are very modest rates compared with most materials and predictions for the future are for a lowering of growth rate, reflecting the significant application losses for lead in cables, petrol additives, and pigments discussed later in this paper.

Statistics for the major lead-producing areas of the world over the period 1964–1974 are summarised in Table 5.

Table 5: Mine production of lead ('000 metric tons of lead content)

	1964	1966	1968	1970	1972	1974
Australia	381	371	389	457	396	377
U.S.A.	260	297	326	519	562	602
Canada	185	273	309	353	335	296
Western Europe	341	422	464	474	459	405
Mexico	175	182	174	176	164	218
Peru	151	162	155	157	189	193
Japan	54	63	63	64	64	44
Africa	205	229	186	203	196	175
Eastern Europe/U.S.S.R.	553	604	635	685	753	823

Table 6: Refined lead consumption ('000 metric tons)

	1964	1966	1968	1970	1972	1974
Australia	61	65	66	62	63	72
U.S.A.	728	822	912	943	1016	1030
Canada	53	66	60	55	64	74
Western Europe	1184	1194	1272	1354	1367	1385
Africa	35	31	33	39	49	55
Japan	164	148	181	211	231	224
Eastern Europe/U.S.S.R.	630	681	739	807	905	998

Table 7: Lead – major end-uses ('000 metric tons)

Application	U.S.A.			Japan			United Kingdom			West Germany		
	1964	1969	1974	1964	1969	1974	1964	1969	1974	1964	1969	1974
Batteries	389	528	669	64	123	198	88	99	80	94	108	118
Tetraethyl-lead	203	246	227	–	–	–	35	40	56	–	–	–
Cable sheathing	51	49	35	67	27	21	123	67	45	83	86	52
Pigments/Chemicals	94	93	96	24	44	37	34	36	37	39	65	80
Solder, etc.	65	66	49	18	21	24	41	35	32	–	–	–
Sheet, pipe, foil collapsible tubes	63	58	34	45	39	28	82	63	50	58	65	54

World refined lead consumption has risen from approximately 3.13 million tons in 1964 to 4.42 million tons in 1973. Consumptions in the major consuming countries are summarised in Table 6.

The current U.S. Bureau of Mines forecast for world consumption in the year 2000 is in the range 6.78 to 9.45 million tons.

The major end-uses for lead are summarised in Table 7.

Future Demand Patterns

The prediction of future demand for materials is notoriously difficult, particularly in the case of lead where traditional applications are undergoing significant and fundamental changes. In general terms, world population growth and rise in living standards generates increasing markets for buildings (residential, industrial, commercial, educational, and hospitals), power, communications, and consumer durables (such as motor cars and domestic appliances). All of these markets demand increasing tonnages of engineering and decorative materials, but modern process and applications technology in both metals and plastics ensures that the increasing demand will not impact equally upon all materials.

This is particularly noticeable for non-ferrous metals. The growth in use of plastics in the last twenty years has resulted in a lower growth in demand for metals than would otherwise have occurred. The metals supply–demand picture would probably look very different had not the production of low-cost plastic materials [such as polyethylene, polypropylene, poly(vinyl chloride) and polystyrene] from petroleum sources been perfected during this period. The effect of this complex set of balances is that the use of metals is tending to be restricted to those applications which demand either superior physical properties (e.g., tensile strength, resistance to creep, thermal or electrical conductivity, relative indifference to elevated temperatures) or, where the end-product fabrication cycle, (including finishing and scrap recycling) offers better economics, or where component quality is regarded as more important that cost. In comparison with the use of plastics in decorative and non-stressed applications, engineering plastics have made relatively small inroads into the traditional metal fields, partly because of intrinisic property limitations but also because plastics such as ABS, polyacetals, ("Delrin", "Celcon") polycarbonates ("Lexan"), nylon and GRP are relatively expensive. A major question for speculation is the extent to which the next few decades will see cost reduction in real terms for engineering plastics and also, of course, the extent of evolution of entirely new plastics and composites possessing improved physical properties which will, in turn, permit enhanced field performance of fabricated components.

Zinc

The overall demand picture for zinc is much more stable than for lead. In galvanising, zinc has a major end-use which is unrivalled for the protection of steel structures from the costly ravages of corrosion. Modern society makes ever-increasing use of major steel structures requiring long-life corrosion-protection (e.g., high-rise buildings, power transmission pylons and supports) and, as the continuous strip galvanising process makes available a wide range of galvanised sheet and strip for automotive and consumer durable applications, the continuing increase in the amount of zinc required for galvanised products seems likely to continue.

Diecastings will continue to provide a major requirement for zinc but here severe competition exists between zinc and aluminium within the diecasting field, while further competition is felt from end-products fabricated in a variety of plastics, particularly in decorative and non-stressed uses. Nevertheless, the growing world demand for motor cars and domestic appliances is likely to maintain a substantial long-term use of zinc in diecastings which are unrivalled for the large-volume production of complex components where accurate replication of detail is required. Brass remains a steady market for zinc but it is likely to be substituted wherever practicable by other metals and plastics due mainly to the relatively high and variable price of its copper content. Rolled zinc is relatively a much more important market in Europe than in the United States. Its use in rainwater goods (gutterings, downpipes, etc.) has been eroded severely by plastics such as PVC but in Europe it retains a significant market as a roofing material and appreciable R & D continues in this area aimed at increasing its use in all categories of buildings. Demand for zinc oxide has recently been stimulated by its application as a coating for the papers of one of the widely used document-copying systems and there seems little prospect of its losing its traditional markets in rubber reinforcement, plastics, paints, and in pharmaceutical preparations. The relatively small usage of zinc dust in paints may be expected to grow with increasing appreciation of its value in anti-corrosive systems, but it is unlikely to become a major factor in consumption.

Lead

Significant changes have been taking place in end-uses for lead and this continuing picture makes particularly difficult any accurate predictions for the future. In "developed" countries, storage batteries are showing a continued strong growth in lead usage in line with growing car and truck populations, but most of the other major uses are showing little growth. In particular, the use of lead for sheathing power-transmission cables is declining as a result of substitution by plastics (and, in some cases, aluminium) while current and impending legislation on the use of lead additives to petrol will halt or reverse the growing consumption which would otherwise have occurred through the rising population of motor cars, especially those requiring high-octane fuel. Concern about possible health hazards arising from the misuse of lead-based paints and pigments will probably halt the growth of lead usage in this area. Statistical predictions are also complicated by the relatively high scrap recycling rate, due to the chemical inertness of the metal and its relative ease of handling (over 80% of the lead in automotive batteries is recovered) whereas metal used in petrol additives and paints is irrecoverable by current technology.

Looking further into the future, it is reasonable to speculate that environmental pressures in high-traffic areas will stimulate the demand for pollution-free commercial vehicles and cars. The present near-exclusive use of lead—acid batteries as energy sources for such vehicles may be challenged by other battery systems (e.g., zinc—air), by controlled external combustion systems based on the Rankine or Stirling cycle, or by combinations of such systems. At the present time, substitution of lead–acid batteries as secondary storage batteries in passenger cars seems to be less probable.

Reserves

It is the current fashion to estimate the time it will take to exhaust known reserves of minerals assuming that the recent rate of increase in demand continues, and making various assumptions about the possibility of further discoveries of minerals.

While such estimates are of considerable interest and draw attention to the evolutionary changes which may be expected in the utilisation of our natural resources, publications of "years to exhaustion" estimates are misleading. Reserves as published today are determined by today's prices for the metals and minerals and today's technology used for their extraction. In any case, industry has traditionally viewed a known reserve of 20 or 30 years as a reasonable figure beyond which it is difficult to justify the expense of further costly exploration.

Substantial reserves of both zinc and lead are established as shown in Table 8.

No detailed study has been made of the effects of higher prices at constant production costs, although in the U.S.A. it is estimated that a 25% increase in zinc price would increase the economically recoverable reserves by 30%.

The U.S. Geological Survey has recently published estimates which are considerably more comforting. For zinc, identified reserves of ore

Table 8: Metal content in millions of tons

	Zinc	Lead
U.S.A.	34	35
Canada	25	12
Eastern Europe	14	12
Western Europe	14	8
Asia	10	5
Australia	9	10
South America	8	5
Africa	6	4
Mexico	4	4
Total	124	95

Table 9: Mineral content of oceans and the earth's crust (million metric tons)

Metal	Known reserves	Total resource figures used in "The limits to Growth"	Total natural occurrence in oceans including the seabed	Total natural occurrence in the first mile of the earth's crust (under dry land)
Aluminium	4250	5850	15,500	138,244,000,000
Copper	364	1540	4650	119,000,000
Iron	109,000	500,000	12,400	84,630,000,000
Lead	94	455	465	27,400,000
Mercury	1.1	0.1	47	850,000
Nickel	90	334	3100	135,960,000
Tin	4.4	21.5	4650	67,760,000
Zinc	306	615	15,500	224,000,000

from which metal could be recovered economically with present technology are put at 235 million tons of metal content (world-wide). It goes on to record that identified deposits of ore which are at present uneconomic contain the equivalent of 1275 million tons of zinc and quote estimates that resources as yet undiscovered will eventually turn out to contain more than 5000 million tons of metal.

For both zinc and lead, future reserves may well include other potential sources at present untapped. Thus the Kupfershiefer formation which extends over a large part of Europe and which has been mined for copper, lead, and zinc in East Germany, may well contain more than 1000 million tons of zinc and only slightly smaller quantities of lead.

The total spread of resource options for metals is well illustrated by the data (Table 9) compiled by the Commodities Research Unit.

Recycling

It should now be clear that the resource question has to be analysed both from a tonnage and an economic viewpoint — in practical terms the two are inseparable. It is also probably true that ultimate reserves of any material in the earth's crust is finite in a practical sense.

Thus, increasing emphasis will undoubtedly be placed on the recycling of the metals on which we have expended large amounts of energy and effort to concentrate.

Substantial quantities of metals have for many years been recycled. Interpretation of the mass of detailed information available is not easy but I have endeavoured to present a picture in Table 10 for zinc, lead, copper, and aluminium over the past decade.

Table 10: Recycled as % of total consumption – U.K. ('000 metric tons)

	1964	1966	1968	1970	1972	1974
Zinc	23	24	24	25	24	24
Lead	57	57	65	67	64	61
Copper	35	39	42	41	35	38
Aluminium	33	33	33	33	34	28

To make meaningful deductions from tables of this kind is not easy. The good showing of lead is mainly due to its chemical inertness and the high percentage used in car batteries which are easy to collect and re-process. Copper has a relatively high recycle rate partly because of its chemical unreactivity and high value. Clearly, however, the recycle percentage is not increasing with time, in spite of the resource crisis about which we hear so much.

In trying to analyse the reasons for this, it is helpful to distinguish between "new" scrap (i.e., the waste material arising during fabrication) and "old" scrap which is re-processed after a period of use as a fabricated article or component. A high proportion of "new" scrap is generally re-processed because it arises at definite locations where collection is easy and economic and it is relatively un-contaminated. On the other hand, "old" scrap, paticularly in capital goods, takes a long time to return. Copper in medium-sized transformers may remain operational for 15 years, generators for up to 25 years while cables may be operational for 30–40 years. Similarly, the aluminium used in window frames, etc., in modern buildings will presumably remain out of circulation for the life of the building, say 40 or 50 years.

A proportion of new consumption is, for practical purposes, irretrievably lost and so the recycle percentage can never reach 100%. For example, the lead content of the tetra-alkyl-lead additives to petrol, the zinc loss in providing galvanic protection, zinc oxide in tyres, lead and zinc in paints and paper coatings.

Like some other mines, the "mine above the ground" of high purity material, awaiting only collection and delivery to the nearest smelter, is at least partly mythical. Recycling provides no quick and easy solution to our resource problems, but an increased level of recycling could at least be of significant assistance and would be of value in "balance of payment" terms. Why does progress, as exemplified by the figures seem so slow?

The answer is, I believe, mainly economic. Recovery from consumer durables, such as scrap motor cars, washing machines, refrigerators and the like is primarily a question of arranging for the delivery of such items to a series of large processing plants. If this major hurdle could be overcome, impressive technology has been developed, both in the U.K. and the U.S.A., for the separation of non-ferrous items from ferrous metals and from the plastics, glass, etc., components of motor cars, and then for the separation of the non-ferrous items themselves. It may well be that some scope exists in the initial design of items, so as to make them more amenable to separation in a recycling process; the humble aerosol can is sometimes cited as an example of this, but again economics are a big problem.

Improved processing technology could also play a significant part in better resource utilisation, but here again economics in the form of transporation costs and plant occupancy for relatively dilute materials are a major problem. Processing has to be done either within existing plants or close to them to be worthwhile against the processing of normal concentrate feeds. Thus, many zinc residual wastes contain 7–15% of metal but it is currently uneconomic to work plants to higher recoveries or, generally, to process existing materials, for example by fuming or leaching. Electrozinc plants accumulate large quantities of leady and irony residues; in geographically favourable situations, the former can be reworked but the iron residues are simply not worth recovery. Similar considerations apply to the iron-containing "red muds" which arise during bauxite processing. In the iron and steel industry, world-wide pressures to reduce dust emissions are being successful from the viewpoint of reducing atmospheric pollution but will generate dumps of dust containing small amounts of heavy metals which constitute a potential ground-water contamination problem. Much thought is currently being concentrated on the question of heavy-metal recovery from these dusts which could then be re-processed through the iron blast furnaces.

In apparent contradiction of the data presented in Table 10, my belief is that in the long-term normal economic forces will permit the recycle percentage to rise. I know of no economic system which will encourage a sudden and dramatic rise in recycling which is what the resource picture would seem to require. Thus, scope for economic innovation in this field continues to exist.

How can scrap be collected more efficiently and processed economically? Some initiatives are apparently encouraging. In the United States, Reynolds Metals, a major primary aluminium producer, re-processed 43,000 tons of scrap in 1975, double the 1974 level, as a result of a special scheme to encourage recycling of aluminium scrap.

One final word of environmental caution, or perhaps technical challenge, on the question of recycling. Many recycling operations generate very complex technical problems — often at least as difficult as the processing of primary feeds. The "scrap" processors and many secondary smelters are often relatively small-scale operations compared with primary smelters. Serious environmental problems in these industries have already been encountered and, to some extent, overcome. Well-known examples are the fume emission problems in copper-cable-stripping and the black smoke emissions arising from paint, grease, and oil contamination of scrap car components. Raising the recycling level may very well imply the use of feeds which are more complex and difficult to process. It may well be that such recycling will in future increasingly take place at primary smelters which have the technical facilities to deal with these complex environmental problems.

The statistical data in this paper are derived from publications by Metallgesellschaft AG, the World Bureau of Metal Statistics and the U.S. Bureau of Mines, to whom acknowledgement is made.

Fire, Flames and Energy

by G. R. Bainbridge; The Energy Centre, University of Newcastle upon Tyne

SCOTLAND'S domestic and industrial past could not have been such a comfortable and prosperous one without fire, flames, and energy. The peaceful application of them is now ensuring this country's future.

Water in this part of the world has always been of the highest quality and abundant, off the rocks and out of the peat. Scots water, blended with selected grains and herbs from the earth, then tenderly raised in temperature over Scots fire and flames gives a product of greatly added financial, and energy generating, value. So it will be, one may anticipate, when the oil and gas bonanza of today has run its short history; fire-water, whisky, will mean by and large wealth for Scotland.

But the fire that makes the steel, and the flames that cut it and weld it into the energy raising power station and factory boilers and the energy transporting ships; these must also be part of our record.

Fire

Some 2,000 million years ago the earth fragment was ejected from the sun, our sun, born in fire. The temperature of the molten earth mass, as it emerged from the flames which flash out from the sun's surface most prominently on occasions of eclipse by the moon, would be several thousand degrees. The present sun's surface temperature is in the region of 6,000°C, and the fusion reaction heated centre possibly in excess of 15 million degrees.

In terms of its temperature, the earth has been going down-grade ever since. Little that man has done to-date has had much effect in reversing that time-trend. Had the earth been less conveniently or fortuitously placed in its new found equilibrium orbit in relation to the sun, its average temperature could have been much higher or much lower by now. Both cases would have been less comfortable and would have given greater energy problems for man than there are. The earth's diameter, rock composition, or surface form could have been different, which again would have affected the temperatures, the atmospheric composition, the amount of surface water, and other physical and chemical properties; more likely to man's disadvantage than benefit.

A few hundred million years ago this planet became fit for primitive vegetation and life, and eventually man came to inhabit it. Already by the time of his advent man's energy destiny had been established, as the fossil hydrocarbons (gas, oil, and coal) have been maturing in store for over 300 million years. The fissile uranium and fertile thorium were already bound in the rocks, along with the fusile materials sources, lithium for tritium and water for deuterium. The sun had for many millennia been beaming 174×10^9 megawatts of heat to the earth, 32×10^6 megawatts or so was flowing from the inner depths of the earth to the surface, and 3×10^6 megawatts was being generated in the tides by earth—moon—sun interaction.

Fire, the process whereby chemical substances converted to the gaseous state combine to produce heat and flame, has an infinite history. Traces of it appear among the earliest human relics. But some peoples have managed to live without it. Even they probably had knowledge of it, if not the need or inclination to use fire, for they would see volcano, lightning, and sun-ignited grass fires. Man prefers to be over-warm rather than cold, being more comfortable when unclothed and subject to 90°F (32°C) than when in furs or woollens at 60°F (16°C) or below. Somewhat lower temperatures can be tolerated when the humidity is raised, but fireless people tended to take up residence between the latitudes 25°N and 25°S, hot, dry, and inactive rather than cold, wet, and working.

With improvements in the control of fire, the provision of warmth-retaining clothing, and the invention of improved protection from caves and more advanced architectural structures, man was enabled to migrate progressively to the higher latitudes, where he could lead a more vigorous and mentally active life. Without fire, clothing, and shelter in these more frigid climatic regions he would perish.

Fire has thus been highly beneficial as a meas to invention and human development. It has enabled new land areas to support larger populations, with cooked foods including meats procured by hunting with spears of fire-hardened and sharpened wood, and later with metal tipped and pointed weapons.

It is probable that an understanding of the force of steam preceded James Watt, though the application of steam only progressed rapidly afterwards. Hot baths are probably older than the Romans, and the remedial application of heat and the killing of bacteria by cauterisation may be as old as medicine.

Throughout time, however, fire has also caused innumerable set-backs for man, through accidents and deliberately hurtful applications of it. London's fire dates alone are recorded for 798, 982, 1666 (the "great" fire), 1834 (Houses of Parliament), 1866 (the Crystal Palace), 1915 (Zeppelin raids), and 1940–45 (World War II raids). Most of the major cities of the world have accumulated similar records. 1544 Leith, 1700 Edinburgh (the "great" fire), 1824 Edinburgh (High Street, Tron Kirk, and Parliament Square fires). The last-mentioned fire led to the modernisation of the Edinburgh fire engines and draft rules for the conduct of police, firemen, magistrates, and property owners in the event of fire.

But it is in domestic and industrial applications that the sophistication of fire raising has progressed unwaveringly. Fossil fuels have been burned in recent years ever more voraciously to raise steam, to smelt and to melt, to warm buildings, and to power vehicles.

Flames

In most fires and flames the temperatures are relatively low. In the luminous part of a candle flame and similar "diffusion" flames, where the fuel migrates from a central feed core to the mixing and ignition region surrounding it, the temperature does not reach 1500°C.

Coal gas in an optimum mix with air can reach 2000°C in the ignition envelope. Natural gas and air attain only 1900°C. Pre-heating of the air can raise the flame temperature; for each 100°C preheat of the air up to 50°C of extra flame temperature can be achieved, and an increased efficiency of burning.

Man's inventiveness has been applied to improve flame performance, e.g., for glass blowing and plumbing, with more rapid delivery of the fuel–air mix in blow-lamps. To weld and cut steel the oxy-acetylene flame gives both elevated temperature and heat flux.

In the hydrogen-blanketed arc-welding torch atomic hydrogen

combining to the molecular form releases heat to raise the temperature to 3800°C, besides keeping the weld clean of oxidising or contaminant gases. With fluorine and hydrogen the heat of reaction raises the flame temperature above that of hydrogen alone, to the region of 4000 to 5000°C.

Energy

Sources to alleviate the energy situation in the world are sufficient to supply all foreseeable needs. Conservation of energy will, however, have to be practised by most countries, to reduce oil imports and redress balance of payments positions. Development and application of nuclear power and perhaps solar, wind, or water energy alternatives will supplement what remains of the fossil fuels. These all tend, however, to be more capital-intensive at present than plants designed to use fossil fuels.

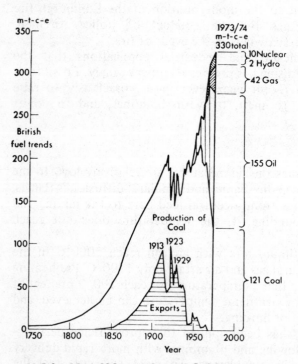

BRITISH COAL PRODUCTION AND EXPORTS

FIGURE 1   British coal production and exports.

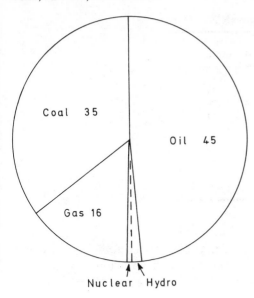

FIGURE 2   British energy, %.

In most countries windsails and waterwheels have given way to cheap and convenient fossil fuels. Britain has had coal in abundance, Fig. 1. Over 200 million tons p.a. was produced in the 1950s,[1] compared with about 120 million tons p.a. now. Deceptively cheaper oil has proved a temptation too great to resist. In a few countries a proportion of hydro-power has been introduced and in others some natural gas.

In the 1960s, nuclear power programmes began to be realised, in which Scotland was able to share. Britain, however, now relies for much of her energy supplies on imported oil,[2] Fig. 2. Europe imports over 60% and Japan 70% of energy requirements as oil. Even the U.S.A., which is rich in indigenous energy resources, imports about 15% of energy use, including 35% of its oil.

In the early 1970s, changes in the oil supply scene increased the need for oil-importing countries to protect their energy and economic futures. An Organisation of Petroleum Exporting Countries brought pressures to bear on the international oil companies. These OPEC countries are responsible for 90% of the international oil trade[3] (Table 1). They control 55% of proven world oil reserves.

Table 1: World oil production and reserves MTCE(MTO)

1973	Annual production		Reserves ×10³ (proven)	
Middle East	2100	(1140)	90	(50)
Africa +	540	(300)	17	(9.5)
Asia	270	(150)	4	(2.2)
Europe	36	(20)	4.5	(2.5)
U.S.A.	860	(480)	9	(5)
Canada *et al.* +	340	(188)	6.8	(3.8)
Venezuela	32	(18)	3.6	(2.0)
Russia *et al*	880	(490)	27	(15)
Total World	5000	(2800)	160	(90)

Living standards

There has been increasing concern that high priced fuels[4] may restrict improving living standards. The world has a voracious appetite for energy (Fig. 3). Without some surprising change of attitude the

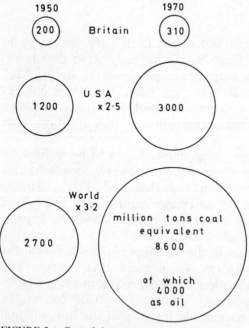

FIGURE 3   Growth in energy use.

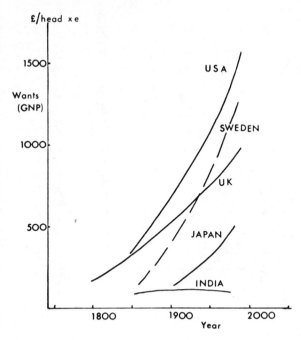

FIGURE 4   Growth of national product.

demand for more energy seems likely to continue as prices today are in real terms little different from those in 1950.

All countries have sought economic growth[5] in terms of Gross National Product per head, (the annual value of cars, buildings, refrigerators, and other goods and services produced, averaged over the population). For the advanced countries, such as the U.S.A. and Sweden, the GNP/head is large, Fig. 4, and it is still rising. The poor countries have a low, perhaps decreasing, GNP/head. Germany and France however achieve their GNP figure with less energy than Britain, Fig. 5. Sweden is a low energy user compared with Canada, and Japan compared with the U.S.S.R. Improvement in the energy usage of some advanced countries may therefore be possible without reduction in standard of living.

Education, advertising, and amendment of political and religious dogmas have relatively less effect on birth rate[5] than has standard of living, Fig. 6.

In the great majority of countries population is growing and

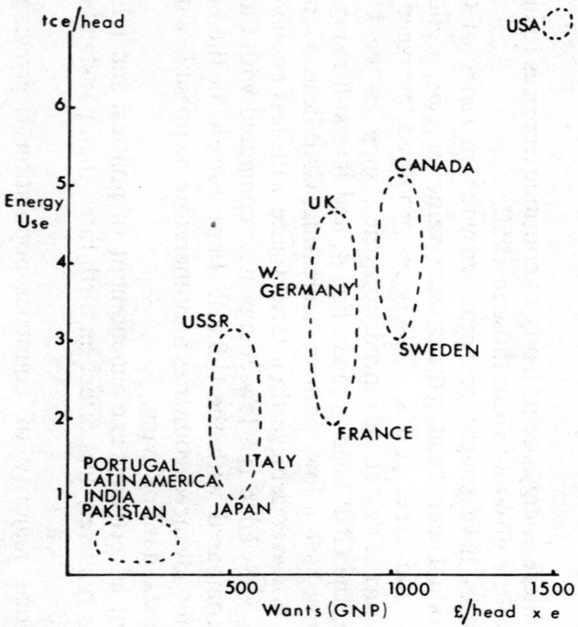

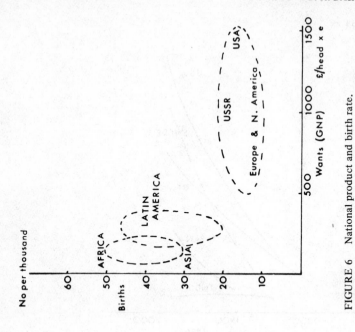

FIGURE 6   National product and birth rate.

FIGURE 5   National product and energy use.

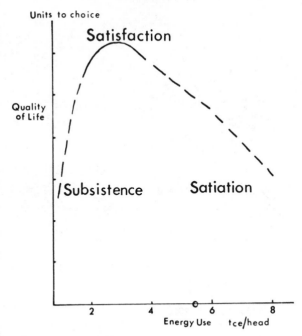

FIGURE 7   Quality of life and energy use.

standard of living is improving, so energy usage per head and in total is rising. Such ever increasing world energy use cannot be supplied with fossil fuels alone.[7]

People worried about eventually inadequate fossil fuel supplies seek ways of delaying the time of shortage. An interesting proposal[6] has been that the high-standard-of-living countries might progressively reduce their GNP/head and energy usage but thereby improve their quality of life; they would be represented as moving up the right hand slope of an inverted U curve, Fig. 7. Countries with low energy usage might then be able to move up the left hand slope of the inverted U, improving their quality of life also.

Energy needs and supply
With present world population of over 4,000 million people and a growth rate above 2% p.a., a total of over 7,000 million will be reached by the end of the century.[8] Therefore (Fig. 8) world demand for energy could be 16,000 million tce by the end of the

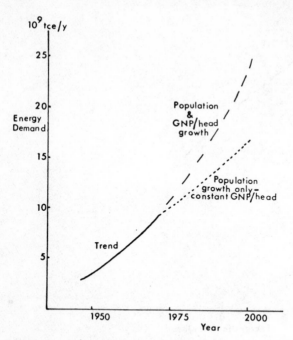

FIGURE 8   Energy demand growth.

century on the basis of population increase alone, or 25,000 million tce (over 3 tce/head per year) with rising standard of living.

Oil and coal use seem likely to increase in the face of demand and then decrease,[7] as they, among several mineral resources,[9] get depleted, Fig. 9. Many factors, e.g., alternative energy resources, scarcity prices, geographical distribution of resources, and limitations on extraction and transport will in fact cause adjustments. With increasingg usage, oil may be scarce within a few decades, and coal in a few centuries. World proven oil reserves at 160,000 million tce equate with little over 30 years of present extraction at around 5,000 million tce. Discovery of new resources of the magnitude of the North Sea or Alaska fields will be required almost annually in the years ahead to prolong the period of plentiful availability of oil. Allowance has to be made for a greater proportion of future energy being supplied as electricity and the slow moves to reduce wastage of heat rejected from the thermal cycle, amounting to two thirds of the total heat supplied. The alternatives of possibly supplying process

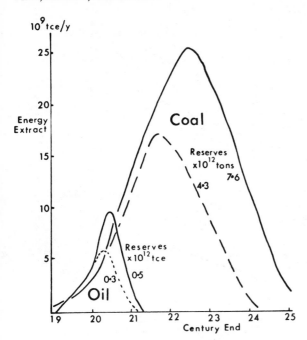

FIGURE 9   World fossil fuels depletion.

heat and urban heat as well as electricity from large power stations, or of using smaller total heat units tailored to the energy needs of individual factories, will because of the cost and difficulty of implementation, modify the trends of growing energy usage, only marginally during the next 25 years. There is the assumption that a substantial capacity of nuclear powered electricity will fill the gap. But the nuclear component for Britain, Fig. 10, and a few others among the leading industrial countries is providing only a few percent of total energy now, Table 2, and the competition between the energy supply industries for scarce development resources seems likely to intensify.

So in looking for sources of energy for the world and for Britain it is for increasing amounts above today's figures that one must be concerned. One cannot yet see the possibility of any leading country going alone and continuously on the path to constant or decreasing energy use while still maintaining or increasing production of those things necessary for the home and export markets. One can,

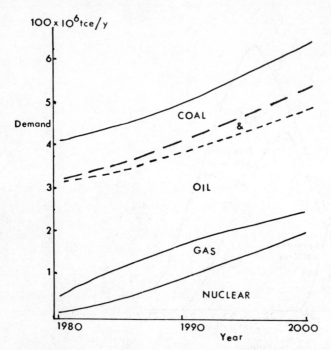

FIGURE 10   Future British energy demand.

however, see more clearly the wisdom of diversifying energy usage to reduce the risk and cost of dependence on imported fuels.

Table 3 summarises the world fossil fuel reserves upwards of 5,000,000 million tons of coal equivalent from which to supply demand of 25,000 million tce p.a. at the end of the century.

Dividing the first number by the second gives an upper limit for

Table 2: British energy use (MTCE)

	1973/4	1972/2
Coal	121	128
Oil	155	158
Natural gas	42	38
Nuclear	10	10
Hydro	2	2
Total	330	336

Table 3: World coal, oil, and gas reserves (prospective; 10^{12} TCE)

Coal	4.3–7.6
Oil*	0.32–0.56
Gas	0.2–0.45
Total	4.8–8.6

*Excluding sands and shales

the time to exhaustion only if extra reserves are not found and the rate of demand does not increase. There are many interposing difficulties. The potential users of fuels do not coincide geographically with the suppliers. Transport for oil by sea is established world-wide but, much as for coal, oil reserves are not always close to ports; this is so for the vast and much discussed tar sands of Canada and oil shales of the U.S.A. Extraction from them can be very disruptive to the environment and so may be limited in practice. Gas transport by sea is growing, but liquefied gas supply plants and the transport ships are comparatively costly, depressing the price that can be paid at the source for supply into a distant market. For coal, large-scale transportation would require expansion of bulk carrier fleets not yet contemplated, or plants for conversion of coal into oil or gas in the mining areas to raise the value and ease transport problems for the product.

Britain has over 10,000 million tons of coal equivalent for an end-of-century demand of 600 million tce p.a., Table 4.

One hears views that there may be 2 to 3 times the amount of oil shown,[11] and other views that less than half of that shown will be

Table 4: British coal, oil, and gas reserves (10^9 TCE)

Coal*	3.5 Classified working
Oil†	3.1 Licensed probable 10
Gas	2.0
Total	8.6

*Excluding sea. Plus 2.5 unclassed, 20 accessible
†4.6 Licensed possible

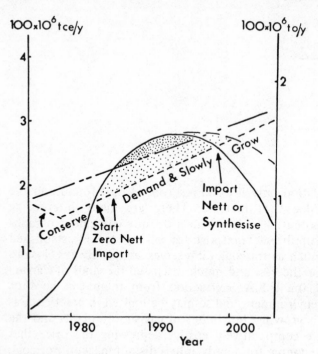

FIGURE 11   North Sea oil prospects.

extracted. Intensified exploration, particularly out under the North Sea, has already substantially increased the amount of workable coal.

The reserves of the fossil fuels extractable depend on many factors,[12] including product price, taxation, and technology. British oil discovered so far, if applied only to the extent required by Britain to avoid nett oil imports could be used up in a few decades, Fig. 11.

There are nevertheless interesting strategy options for it provided the other fuels – gas, coal, and nuclear – can be marshalled in support. British oil can be conserved or exported during a possible 10 to 20 year period of production in excess of needs.

British coal can also supply this country with a proportion of between a quarter and a half of her energy for the next 50 years. If the undersea reserves are successfully exploited there would be a very much longer period of assured coal supplies. There could be coal for export as well as oil and perhaps natural gas.

Nuclear power can provide an increasing proportion of the energy needed in the years ahead;[13] it is already giving over 10% of Britain's electricity, and a greater proportion in Scotland. Quite modest expectations of economic growth in the world are almost bound to be frustrated without nuclear power. This energy supplement depends on the extent of uranium and thorium supplies and the reactors in which they are used. Little has been reported on the amounts of these materials indigenous to Britain, though it is known that there are at least low-grade ores in the highlands and islands of Scotland. Supplies can, however, be purchased and stockpiled well ahead of need, so uranium and thorium, and in due course plutonium, can be treated as indigenous even if imported. The world quantities of fissile fuels at low cost are illustrated in Table 5.

Table 5: World uranium and thorium
reserves (million tons)

	$\leqslant$\$15/lb	$\leqslant$\$30/lb
Uranium*	0.7–1.5	1.3–3.3
Thorium	1.4	

*In sea water there is 4×10^9 tons of uranium. 1 M tons of uranium is equivalent to 26×10^9 TCE (thermal); in reactors (2.6×10^{12} TCE fast).

Three million tons of uranium are thought to be available[13] at a price below \$30/lb. Used in the world's thermal reactors that would last 30 to 40 years for electricity generation. The energy equates with about a fiftieth of the coal reserves. Thorium would add half as much energy again.

Breeder reactors can further supplement energy resources, making more efficient use of the ^{238}U in natural uranium by converting it into ^{239}Pu; also ^{232}Th to convert into ^{233}U. The energy worth of low-cost uranium reserves alone can thus be brought up to the same order as the coal reserves.

In these discussions account has not been taken of the many millions of tons of uranium and thorium salts in sea water. Though they are extractable, the cost would be high due to the large amounts of water which would have to be pumped in the process.

Any remaining problems or doubts about nuclear power stations and their supporting chemical plants must be resolved speedily if they are to form a basis for growth of energy production. In

Scotland it has been demonstrated at Hunterston A and B power stations that nuclear power can be a valuable asset.

Acceptably safe and economic commercial designs of breeder reactors suitable for industrial siting will be necessary in the 1980s in order to make the best use of fissile fuel reserves. In this field of endeavour the Dounreay power station is already a successful pioneer.

With fusion, nuclear fuel resources are expanded effectively beyond limit. Power stations using pulsed fusion plasmas are still several decades away in achieving economic viability. The objective of deuterium–tritium fusion temperatures sustained in the region of 100 million degrees for about one second now seem to be achievable, but when the physics is proved possible the achievement of economic viability remains a formidable task.

The fossil, fissile, and fusile resources (coal, uranium and thorium, deuterium and lithium) together appear adequate for man's needs far ahead in time. Allocation of some effort to other alternatives from the renewable sources nevertheless seems worthwhile,[14] both as a speculation and to provide a measure of insurance.

Energy income sources
Solar, geothermal, hydro, tidal, and wind energy have all been harnessed previously, though usually in small-capacity units. It is thought that it may also be possible to extract energy from waves and ocean temperature gradients. The large plants needed could not, however, be built without some loss of amenity. Acceptable capital costs and long-duration reliability in operation are not yet seen to be achievable.

Sun
It is possible with relatively simple flat-plate solar collectors to provide warmed water and enable some space-heating for homes and offices which is particularly useful when the buildings are well insulated, and thermal capacity sufficient for the carry-over of energy from day to night is arranged.

Although solar radiation incident on Britain alone is of the order of twice the total world energy usage it is only a third of what is received on the same area of South Mediterranean land. In this country, large-scale collection could not be economic but a few tens of square yards of collector surface can suffice to give supplementary home heat input.

Only about half of the solar radiation incident on the earth's atmosphere reaches the earth's surface to give about 22 watts per square foot available – more near the equator and less at high latitudes or in unfavourable weather or terrain. However, the whole surface receives about 20,000 times present world energy usage, so the effect of man's incremental input to the environment is quite small. Some of the solar radiation could be collected and converted directly into electricity rather than heat, with panels of silicon or cadmium cells. Regrettably at present the cost would be very high and the efficiency of conversion very low.

In good conditions over a surface area of 4 to 5 square miles of earth, one might generate 100 MW with a convertor plant. That is about half as much as a large modern power station and could save 2,500,000 tons of coal each year. The problems, even in favourable areas, are essentially those of maintaining the collectors clean and working while integrating the electricity yield before distribution.

A large-scale energy option being assessed in the U.S.A. is that for putting a few (say 25) square miles of solar cells some 20,000 miles outside of the earth's atmosphere in stationary orbit and beaming the 10,000 MW of energy down to earth.

Earth steam
Geothermal steam[2] has been used in volcanic regions in many countries to generate electricity. The operating world capacity in many plants to date, however, only adds up to the amount produced by the Wylfa nuclear power station – a bit over 1000 MW. There is world scope for about 50 times that amount to be developed over the next half century in selected geographical locations, but none in Britain.

Hot rocks
Deep drilling of the earth[15] and fissuring of the subterranean rock there in order to get increased steam-raising surface and reduce pumping power, is thought to have prospects. Heat, thought to come from radioactive decay at greater depths, might be usefully extracted at about 6 miles down, as temperature rise with depth is of the order of 40°C per mile. Within that distance under the continents there is available about 5000 times the heat content of the coal reserves, or 6 million times the present world annual usage. Selective use of rocks, using only the best, could possibly provide a large fraction of energy needs for many years to come.

Tides

Tidal power prospects[16] are regularly investigated for usable shallow seas and estuaries which amplify the regular rise and fall of sea levels due to moon/earth interactions. The La Rance Scheme in France is unique as a development from the tidal energy available world-wide. Tides of over 3 yards rise are desirable, compared with below 1 yard on average. Plans are being made to build a 2000 MW tidal plant, 5 times as big as La Rance, in the Bay of Fundy, Canada. Reassessent of the Bristol Channel has indicated a potential capacity almost twice that of Fundy and it could incorporate useful pumped storage capacity, freshwater storage, and two cross-channel motorways. It is quite attractive if it can be made environmentally acceptable.

Waves

Wave energy[17] has also been in the news recently, particularly with development work progressing at Edinburgh and the National Engineering laboratory, East Kilbride. There is about 140 Megawatts per mile available round British coasts. It could make a useful contribution to our needs; about twice that of the U.K. generating system is available provided we are prepared to forego the pleasure of waves on our shores. Had it been easy or low-cost, of course, it would have been done before. The building of large ships and oil rigs in the North Sea may now give engineering data to establish if wave energy extraction equipment can be made to withstand the elements.

Wind

For local industry wind[18] has been a motive force for machinery, particularly for cornmills and irrigation, for many hundreds of years. In remote locations it is used now, for example, to trickle-charge electric battery storage and to pump water from below ground to the surface.

Windmills to drive large (1 MW or so) electric generators are probably feasible. It is almost 30 years since a number of such schemes were considered to provide electricity in Scotland, but they could not compete with diesel generator sets and hydro power. The problems are in maintenance and control of 200 ft diameter blades at the tops of tall towers, and having them adjust to both violent gales and dead calms. As for several of the renewable energy sources, alternative supplies have to be available for those periods.

Location of the many thousands of units that would be needed for national distribution would not be easy, though perhaps a few tens of locations could be found for, say, 100 to 200 MW total at each. Windmills to supply the horticultural industry where many individual fossil fuel boilers provide heating energy seem a logical line for investigation.

Windvanes for local domestic energy supply of a few kilowatts must be produced at a low enough cost for wider use than has so far happened — rather like the growth in use of washing machines and motor lawnmowers it is not impossible to visualise. Some 80% of household energy is used as heat so the associated energy systems need not be fully electricity-generating.

Policy

Energy policy in Britain must be to produce more indigenous fossil fuels and near-indigenous nuclear energy in the future and to economise in energy usage. The coal industry is concentrating on its new task of producing about 15% more coal than previously[19] thus reversing the trend of the last decade.

The oil and gas trading role of British and international companies with North Sea interests is going to increase quickly now.[21] The first oil and gas is coming ashore. The technology of North Sea fuel exploitation is difficult, and the rate of development to a peak over the next 20 years or so could be slower than expected, as well as more costly.

To achieve the long-term growth in energy use of 2 to 3% p.a., which even the most conservative forecasters predict to be necessary for national well-being, (world growth in energy usage exceeds 5% p.a.) nuclear power has to play a major part. With 10% of Britain's electricity coming from nine (Magnox) nuclear power stations of capacity 5000 MW, and another six (AGR) stations of 6000 MW coming to power, interest in taking the next step has been regrettably slow. A Government declaration of interest was made[20] in 1974 to build up to 4000 MW of a new (SGHWR) design but the work and progress towards an actual order for four or even the first two of the 600 MW units seems too slow for the resolution of an urgent energy and financial crisis. Sodium breeder power stations must follow quickly.

Endeavour to produce plentiful and low-cost indigenous energy soon and firmly for the long term should be given priority. It has greater attraction than policy aimed at many and small, some of them transient, savings. It may include a proportion of plants to exploit renewable energy resources, which will be helpful if their first cost can be reduced to an acceptable level and if they can be kept operating reliably.

References

[1] National Coal Board Annual Reports & Statistics.
[2] "Energy Prospects to 1985", Organisation for Economic Co-operation & Development, 1974.
[3] "Exploring Energy Choices", Energy Policy Project of the Ford Foundation, 1974.
[4] J. Maddox, "Beyond the Energy Crisis", Hutchinson, 1975.
[5] J. Randers and D. H. Meadows, "The Carrying Capacity of our Global Environment", in H. E. Daly: "Toward a Steady State Environment", Freeman, 1973.
[6] M. W. Thring, "Energy and Humanity", in "Mankind and the Engineer", Vol. 2., Peter Peregrinus.
[7] M. K. Hubbert, "Energy Resources", in "Resources & Man", Freeman, 1969.
[8] D. H. Meadows et al., "The Limits to Growth", Universe Book, New York, 1972.
[9] P. Cloud, "Mineral Resources in Fact and Fancy", in "Environment, Resources, Pollution and Society", Sinauer Associates Inc., 1971.
[10] Department of Energy: "Production and Reserves of Oil and Gas in the United Kingdom", 1974.
[11] P. R. O'Dell and K. E. Rosing, "The North Sea Oil Province – A Simulation Model of Development", Energy Policy, 1974, 2, (No. 4), 316.
[12] G. Armstrong, "World Coal Resources and their Future Potential", Phil. Trans., 1974, A276, 439–452.
[13] T. N. Marsham and R. S. Pease, "Nuclear Power – The Future", Atom, February 1973, 196.
[14] Survey of Energy Resources, World Energy Conference, 1974.
[15] L. J. P. Muffler and D. E. White, "Geothermal Energy", The Science Teacher (USA), 1972, 39, 40.
[16] M. K. Hubbert, "Tidal Power", in "Resources and Man", Freeman, 1969.
[17] S. H. Salter, "Wave Power", Nature, 1974, 249, 720.
[18] W. E. Heronemus, "Wind Power, A New Term Partial Solution to the Energy Crisis", EASCON of Institute of Electrical & Electronic Engineers, 1973.
[19] Coal Industry Examination Final Report, 1974.
[20] Report to Parliament by the Secretary of State for Energy: "Nuclear Reactor Systems for Electricity Generation', Atom, July 1974, 198.
[21] Department of Energy: "Development of the Oil and Gas Resources of the United Kingdom", 1975.

The Thirst for Water*

by R. S. Silver; Department of Mechanical Engineering, University of Glasgow ·

Water, the Forgotten Industry

THE production of a ton of steel requires over 40,000 gallons of water; of a ton of aluminium 300,000 gallons of water. Producing a ton of petrol in a refinery from crude oil needs 20,000 gallons of water; of a ton of artificial fibres from a chemical plant about 200,000 gallons of water. One gallon of beer produced uses about 350 gallons of water in course of its production. Taking these and other similar statistics for other industries together, we find that, over all the industrial activities of the modern world, one ton of an industrial product represents an average use of the order of 200 tons of water. In short, in terms of tonnage produced the water supply industry of an industrial country constitutes about 99.5% of industrial activity, while all the rest constitutes only about 0.5%. That fact implies some very important economic fundamentals which have been too long ignored. The first is that industrial expansion or development is impossible without water in large quantities. The second is that unless the water can be obtained at a very much lower cost per unit than all the other materials involved in an industrial product, industrial production will be impractically expensive. Thus for example until recent years the price of water supplied in the U.K. was generally less than 1p per ton, corresponding to only £2 per ton contribution to the cost of an average industrial product. But now the cost of water in the U.K. is rising because of rising costs of reservoirs and distribution schemes, and because the most convenient

*The paper is based on part of the author's contribution to "Environment and Man" Volume 5 (edited by J. Lenihan and W.W. Fletcher) to be published by Blackie, Glasgow and London, 1977. The publisher's permission to use parts of the contribution relevant to this Symposium is gratefully acknowledged by the Author and by the Symposium Organisers.

237

catchment areas were all fully exploited in the early period of industrial expansion. It was the fact that Europe had copious supplies of easily accessible water as well as of coal, which made the Industrial Revolution possible. Without water no such expansion could have taken place, despite the coal and despite the inventions on which the Industrial Revolution was based.

This aspect of economic history has not been fully realised by economic historians, who like most of us, have tended to take water for granted. But it is brought sharply into focus in the present day by the curious circumstances that so much of the world's oil fuel resource is found in the arid zones of the Middle East. The severe water deficiency there limits crucially the possibility of industrial-isation — or would have done so were it not for the development of desalination. The essential feature in the development of countries such as Kuwait and Saudi Arabia has consisted in using a proportion of their oil resources to produce fresh water by desalination of sea water or brackish water. The supplies of water thus gained provide the basis not only for domestic supplies but for the industrialisation in which these countries are now participating.

To summarise this point we may say that in water-blessed countries such as the U.K. the water industry, which in tonnage output dwarfs all other industries, has tended to be forgotten, while in water-deprived countries, it has been recognised as the basic industry which has to be developed prior to any other.

Water and Energy

While the Western world has on the whole under-rated the importance of its water, everyone knows that the whole rate of development from the industrial revolution has been made possible only by the invention of the heat engine, to make things move by the burning of fuel instead of by human, animal, wind, or water, power. The dependence of all our industrial civilisation on fuel energy is now well appreciated. One of the main ways in which we use fuel energy is in the generation of electrical power which is essential for all modern industry and for modern domestic standards of living. Thus in the modern world, as industrialisation and living standards develop, electricity consumption increases. We have already seen that water use increases also, and it is extremely interesting to consider the ratio of water use to electricity use.

Evidently if we had assessed the ratio water use/electricity use in

1850, it would have been infinite, since electricity use was zero. In the period round about 1930, in both U.S.A. and U.K., the ratio was about 100 gallons of water consumption per kilowatt-hour of electricity consumption. In the next 30 years although water consumption was increased, electricity use rose far more rapidly and by 1960 the figure in the U.K. and U.S.A. was down to about 10 gallons per kilowatt-hour. This raises an interesting question – how low can this ratio become and still give an acceptable social standard? The problem has not been studied in great detail but experience in the Middle East countries suggests that a minimum of 2 gallons per kilowatt-hour is necessary. If there is less water available than that in relation to electricity use in the community, conditions seem to be unacceptable. The U.N. Resources office has adopted a figure of 5 gallons per kilowatt-hour as an advised norm for planning purposes, i.e., if you expect a developing community to be using 500 MW electrical capacity, i.e., 500,000 kilowatt-hours per hour, you must have a water supply of the order of 2,500,000 gallons per hour, i.e., 60 million gallons per day.

Against this norm of 5 gallons per kilowatt hour advised for planning in developing countries it is somewhat alarming to examine the most recent available U.K. figures. Year-Book data give for the U.K. (excluding Northern Ireland) in 1972, the amounts 2.06×10^{11} kilowatt-hour and 1.38×10^{12} gallons – a ratio of 6.7 gallons per kilowatt-hour. This fall from 10 g/kWh to 6.7 g/kWh in 12 years indicates quite clearly that our industrial expansion is pressing on diminishing water resources. If this rate of fall continues the U.K. will be down to the advised norm for planning in developing countries by 1978. It is a prospect which must call in question all the political and economic hopes of increasing growth rate to maintain the U.K. position as a leading industrial nation. Even if energy became more abundantly available at less cost the water supply situation might be found to be a limitation.

It therefore becomes relevant to consider whether the U.K. will have to follow the example of the Middle East and introduce desalination to supplement its water supplies. The situation is less straightforward, for we do have substantial rainfall and there are obvious alternatives to desalination. These alternatives taken together all imply a revolution in water management, and various aspects of this are now under study. These include new types of reservoirs extensive development of systems by which contaminated water can be made suitable for re-use, perhaps several times, exploitation of underground water, and of underground storage systems, etc., etc. All such schemes are technically feasible, and no doubt many of them will be implemented. But one certain result is that water supply and water as a product is going to cost far more, even without allowing for inflation, than has ever been known heretofore in the U.K. An equally certain result is that these changes in water supply procedure will impinge on many environmental aspects of life, on agriculture, on drainage, on canal and river transport, and even on local climate, as well as on many amenity and social aspects. For these reasons the actual social cost will be exceedingly hard to assess, beyond the flat statement that it will be much higher than the apparent cost. And when it is all done, it is still subject to rainfall variation, It is therefore quite likely that desalination, which gives freedom from rainfall vagaries, minimum environmental reaction, and does not interfere with other water functions, may become attractive in certain parts of the U.K. Until recently it would have been said that acceptability or otherwise depended only on its comparative cost. Now however when everyone is conscious of an energy crisis for the U.K., the acceptability of desalination will depend not only on its comparative cost, but on whether, even if its cost is favourable, it is thought to be a wise expenditure of energy.

This section has dealt with the general relations between energy and water use in an industrialised country, and the possible need for desalination is shown to arise from these considerations. We now must turn to consider what desalination itself demands in energy.

Energy Requirements of Desalination

All possible processes of desalination require the consumption of energy. The energy may be consumed in either of two ways, viz., as heat, or as work. While the latter form can, in principle, be obtained from wind or water power, the practical situation of desalination being used to provide water independent of climatic conditions and in sufficient quantity means that the work-consuming processes must be supplied with power generated from thermal power stations. Hence the energy quantity requirements of all desalination processes can be compared on the basis of their ultimate thermal energy needs. In this comparison it must be recalled that, for thermodynamic reasons, any thermal power station can only convert a portion of the thermal energy supply into work. Even in the best of modern practice, for each energy unit going in thermally, only 0.4 unit is produced as work, with 0.6 unit being rejected at a temperature lower than that of supply. A representative average of current practice may be taken as the division of each thermal energy unit supplied into 1/3 unit of work output with 2/3 remaining as lower-temperature heat output. Hence to assess the ultimate thermal energy requirements of any work-consuming process, we shall multiply its work energy consumption by 3.

In making these assessments there are two figures which should be borne in mind. The first is that the thermodynamic potential energy difference between sea water and fresh water is 3.53 kWh per 1000 gallons, giving a minimum theoretical thermal energy requirement of 10.6 kWh per 1000 gallons i.e., no possible process can ever be found which will use less thermal energy for desalination than this figure. The second important figure to bear in mind is what is actually achieved at present in proved reliable desalination processes for large-scale water supply. The only proven reliable process established at the present time for supplying fresh water from sea water in quantities sufficient for population and industrial development is the multistage flash process of distillation (henceforth referred to as M.S.F.). This process is one of the class which consumes its energy directly as heat, and the average requirement now established in practice is 315 kWh per 1000 gallons. Thus the best we can do reliably at present uses about 30 times the theoretical minimum. To the layman this may seem a very poor performance. Actually in terms of practical engineering it is very good. For technical reasons which dominate practice, many conversion processes are much further away from the thermodynamic energy minimum.

Against the background of these two figures, the minimum theoretical value and the representative figure of present day reliable performance, we can now look at the possibilities of alternative processes. First we can make some assessment of the best we are likely to achieve in distillation as a result of research and development. It seems unlikely that M.S.F. or any other viable distillation process will reach below 180 kWh per 1000 gallons.

Two other possible processes are by freezing and by reverse osmosis. The lowest expected *power* energy consumptions for these processes are respectively 35 kWh and 16 kWh per 1000 gallons. The corresponding *thermal* energy requirements for these power productions are 105 kWh and 48 kWh respectively. Thus although neither of

242

Table 1: Energy requirements of desalination processes kWh/1000 gallons

	Distillation	Freezing	Reverse Osmosis
Existing reliable established performance	315	–	–
Probable best attainable	180	105	48

these processes has yet been proved viable nor reliable for desalination, we can picture the following general comparison of thermal energy requirements in kWh per 1000 gallons. (Table 1).

These figures show a very great energy advantage for reverse osmosis and also an apparently substantial advantage for freezing. However, before accepting these as conclusive we have to consider the practical situation of power production and distillation more closely. We have already noted that in power production, only part of thermal energy supplied is converted to power while the remainder is rejected thermally at lower temperature. Now a point of crucial significance is that the rejection at lower temperature is available for use in distillation, so that the thermal energy requirements of the distillation process can be met by energy which would otherwise be rejected. This point is of very great importance and must be considered in some detail.

In a power station of normal design the rejection temperature is of order $33°C$. This temperature is too low to be of use in desalination. We must raise the rejection temperature to about $120°C$. This requires operating with higher back pressure. The result means that the power generating efficiency is reduced to about 75% of its previous value. Hence a station which on normal design produces $\frac{1}{3}$ power from 1 thermal unit, rejecting $\frac{2}{3}$ units thermal at $33°C$, will produce $\frac{1}{4}$ unit power when modified, rejecting 0.75 unit thermal at $120°C$. *The whole of this rejection at $120°C$ can be used for thermal distillation.* The loss in power to obtain this is $\frac{1}{3} - \frac{1}{4} = \frac{1}{12}$. The amount of water obtainable by distillation from the thermal rejection now made available is, using the basis of 315 kWh required to produce 1000 gallons, $(1000/315) \times 0.75 = 2.4$ gallons. This is produced in association with $\frac{1}{4}$ unit of power, so that the combination station can satisfy a water/power use ratio of 9.6 gals/kWh. This is well above the recommended planning norm of 5 gals/kWh, and indeed above the use ratio in the U.K. Evidently this

Table 2: Extra energy with distillation

Water/power Use ratio gallons/kWh.	2	4	5	6	8	9.6
Extra energy consumption %	6.9	13.9	17	20.8	27.7	33.3
Percentagé of modification	20.8	41.6	52	62.5	83.3	100

facility is gained by the sacrifice of $^1/_{12}$ unit of power per $^1/_3$ unit of power which the station would have produced on normal design. Thus to meet the same power requirements as before the energy consumption must be increased in the ratio $^4/_3$. The attainment entirely by desalination of a water supply sufficient to satisfy a use ratio of 9.6 gals/kWh therefore requires a 33% increase in energy consumption for a given power demand.

Lower use ratios can be satisfied without so much increase in energy consumption, since they can be met by only partial modification of the power station conditions. Suppose for example that we leave 50% of the power production at the original conditions while the other 50% is obtained, in association with water, at the modified conditions, we shall provide for a use ratio of 4.8 gals/kWh with an extra energy consumption of 16.7%. Table 2 gives the approximate extra energy consumption required for communities with varying water/power use ratios, where all water supply is provided by distillation.

When we consider the freezing and reverse osmosis processes from the same point of view the important fact is that these processes both require energy input in the form of power. Hence freezing, for example, requires 35 kWh of power input per 1000 gallons of water produced. If the use ratio is 5 gallons per kWh, this will represent an addition of 35 kWh to a power load of 200 kWh, i.e., an extra 17.5%. For a lower use ratio, the extra power required will be less, while it will be greater for a higher use ratio. Thus Tables 3 and 4 can be produced for freezing and reverse osmosis, for comparison with Table 2 for distillation.

Table 3: Extra energy with freezing

Water power use ratio gallons/kWh	2	4	5	6	8	10
Extra energy consumption %	7	14	17.5	21	28	35

Table 4: Extra energy with reverse osmosis

Water power use ratio gallons/kWh	2	4	5	6	8	10
Extra energy consumption %	3.2	6.4	8	9.6	12.8	16

Several important deductions can be drawn from these Tables. First it must be borne in mind that while the distillation figures are attainable already in established practice, the freezing and reverse osmosis figures represent the probable best if ever these processes became practicable for water supply. They are not viable at present. The distillation figures can be improved by research and development. It is evident that the freezing process offers no advantages in energy consumption.

These figures denote the extra energy consumption as percentages of energy used for electricity generation. To consider the overall situation, they require to be reduced to a percentage of the total national energy consumption. This can be estimated approximately on the grounds that fuel for electricity generation will be somewhere in the region of 20% to 25% of total national fuel use. On that basis we may divide the figures by about 4.3.

The result is that we could supply all the water requirements for a use ratio of 5 gals/kWh totally by existing M.S.F. desalination for an increase in national energy consumption of 4%.

In a non-arid country such as our own, it would be absurd to try to meet all our water requirements by desalination. One might expect that we could operate successfully with a 25% contribution from desalination, which would cost us a 1% increase in overall energy consumption. The essential point of this paper is that if we do not accept the need to do something of that order, our industrial and social expansion will grind to a halt.

These figures also show quite dramatically the importance of desalination research and development directed to the possible reduction in energy consumption of distillation and to attaining a practical reverse osmosis process. Perhaps even more important, they show up emphatically the value of our rainfall in providing the water resources which we do enjoy. Future pressure on these resources will undoubtedly drive the use ratio down. If it is to be prevented from falling below 5 gals/kWh, we shall certainly have to resort to some proportion of supply by desalination. Even for the fuel-rich but

Table 5: Comparison for a use ratio of 5 gals/kWh

	M.S.F. Distillation (existing proved technology)	Freezing (probable best)	Reverse osmosis (probable best)
Percentage extra energy consumption for power	17	17.5	8
Approximate percentage extra on total fuel consumption	4	4	2
Contribution to water requirements by a 1% extra on total fuel consumption	25%	25%	50%

water-deficient countries of the Middle East the foregoing analysis indicates clearly the energy sacrifice associated with necessary water development. Water control policy will be valuable in their resource conservation.

Conclusion

I have not discussed the money cost of desalination as distinct from the energy use because it is a matter so much affected by individual site location, interest rates, and fiscal policy. The main point to bear in mind is that mentioned at the beginning of the paper. Water must be provided as cheaply as possible otherwise industrial costs will soar beyond control. Capital investment to make increasing use of natural water supply will mean a continuous rise in water costs and a point will be reached where desalination is cheaper for many areas.

To sum up, the industrial growth rate to which we have been accustomed, and which the politicians continually assume as the answer to their economic and employment problems, cannot possibly continue without increased water use. Conventional water resources are limited and increasing pressure on them will cause irreparable damage to many environmental amenities. Desalination offers an alternative which can help to maintain both amenity and industrial growth − but only if we have access to sufficient energy. Happy the land that has both energy and fresh water!